CROW IS MY BOSS

THE CIVILIZATION OF THE AMERICAN INDIAN SERIES

Kenny Thomas Sr. Photograph by Craig Mishler.

CROW IS MY BOSS

Taatsą́ą' Shaa K' exal<u>th</u>et
The Oral Life History of a
Tanacross Athabaskan Elder

Kenny Thomas Sr.
Edited by Craig Mishler

Translations by Irene Arnold
Transcriptions by Gary Holton

UNIVERSITY OF OKLAHOMA PRESS : NORMAN

Also by Craig Mishler

The Crooked Stovepipe: Athapaskan Indian Fiddling and Square Dancing in North-east Alaska and Northwest Canada (Champaign-Urbana, 1993)

(ed.) *Neerihiinjìk: We Traveled from Place to Place: The Cewich'in Stories of Johnny and Sarah Frank* (Fairbanks, 1995/2001)

(with William E. Simeone) *Han, People of the River: Han Hwech'in: An Ethnography and Ethnohistory* (Fairbanks, 2004)

Black Ducks and Salmon Bellies: An Ethnography of Old Harbor and Ouzinkie, Alaska (Kodiak, 2004)

Crow Is My Boss: The Oral Life History of a Tanacross Athabaskan Elder
is volume 250 in The Civilization of the American Indian Series.

Publication of this book is made possible through the generosity of Edith Kinney Gaylord.

Library of Congress Cataloging-in-Publication Data

Thomas, Kenny, 1922–
    Crow is my boss : the oral life history of a Tanacross Athabaskan elder / Kenny Thomas Sr. ; edited by Craig Mishler ; translations by Irene Arnold ; transcriptions by Gary Holton.
        p.   cm. — (The civilization of the American Indian series ; v. 250)
    English and Tanacross.
    Includes bibliographical references and index.
    ISBN 0-8061-3659-6
    1. Thomas, Kenny, 1922– 2. Athapascan Indians—Alaska—Tanacross—Biography. 3. Athapascan Indians—Alaska—Tanacross—History. 4. Athapascan Indians—Alaska—Tanacross—Social life and customs. 5. Tanacross language. 6. Tanacross (Alaska)—History. 7. Tanacross (Alaska)—Social life and customs. I. Mishler, Craig. II. Title. III. Series.

E99.A86T44 2005
979.8'6—dc22
[B]
                                                                              2004055323

The paper in this book meets the guidelines for permanence and durability of the Committee on Production Guidelines for Book Longevity of the Council on Library Resources, Inc. ∞

1 2 3 4 5 6 7 8 9 10

Contents

Illustrations

The Tanacross Writing System

GARY HOLTON, ALASKA NATIVE LANGUAGE CENTER

The orthography used to represent the Tanacross language in this book employs several symbols not found in English writing. The most prominent of these is the so-called barred-*l* or Indian-*l*, written *ł*. This represents a sound similar to an English *l*, but with considerable friction, or noise. The apostrophe is used to indicate a glottal stop (the sound found for example between the two syllables of the English exclamation uh-oh). When it follows certain consonants (*tth'*, *t'*, *ts'*, *tl'*, *ch'*, *k'*), the apostrophe indicates a glottalized consonant, produced with a slight explosion of air. The underscore is used to indicate a sound that begins noisier and becomes less noisy. Thus, an *s̲* begins sounding like *s* and ends sounding like *z*. The vowels may be marked with symbols to indicate nasalization and tone. Nasalized vowels—those pronounced with air coming through the nose as well as through the mouth—are marked with a small hook underneath the vowel, as in *ą*. Tone (meaningful pitch distinctions in words) is marked by a symbol above the vowel. Thus, é, ê, and ě correspond to high, falling, and rising tone vowels, respectively. Low tone vowels are not marked. Tone distinctions can be seen in words such as the following: *nen* "you," *nén'* "land," *jêg* "berries," and *ts'ěd'* "blanket." A full list of Tanacross consonants is given in the table below.

		labial	dental	alveolar	lateral	palatal-alveolar	palatal	velar	glottal
Stops/ Affricates	unaspirated	b	ddh	d	dl	dz	j	g	'
	aspirated		tth	t	tl	ts	ch	k	
	glottalized		tth'	t'	tl'	ts'	ch'	k'	
Fricatives	voiced		dh		l	z		gh	
	semi-voiced		<u>th</u>		<u>ł</u>	<u>s</u>	<u>sh</u>	<u>x</u>	
	voiceless		th		ł	s	sh	x	h
Nasals	voiced	m			n				
	voiceless				nh				
	stopped	mb			nd				
Approx	voiced	w					y		
	voiceless						yh		

CROW IS MY BOSS

Introduction

CRAIG MISHLER

In the last decade, American Indian oral autobiography has come into its own. Dozens of elders who have led rich and interesting lives are now coming forward to tell their stories. They clearly see that books are a useful way of preserving their traditional knowledge and their values for future generations. Kenneth Thomas Sr. of Tanacross, Alaska, is one of these elders.

Tanacross is a northern Athabaskan village located on the banks of the Tanana River just a mile off the Alaska Highway, about fourteen miles northwest of Tok, in Alaska's Interior. It is a northern boreal forest community of about 150 people. Originally called Tanana Crossing because the river there was shallow enough for horses to ford, the village was situated on an Indian trail that developed into the Valdez-Eagle military trail and telegraph line during the gold rush era. By 1912, the village consisted of an Episcopal mission and a couple of trading posts. In the early 1920s, the Episcopal missionary Frederick Drane proclaimed that "Tanana Crossing and the adjacent country always seemed to me the prettiest part of Alaska. There was the majestic Alaskan Range of the Rockies coming down to the river; there were the beautiful hill-girdled lakes; there was abundance of wild game, moose, caribou, and mountain sheep, and in summer plenty of fish in the lakes."[1]

Most of the residents of Tanacross began to move there from Mansfield, Kechumstuk, Salcha, and Sam Creek after a school was opened

3

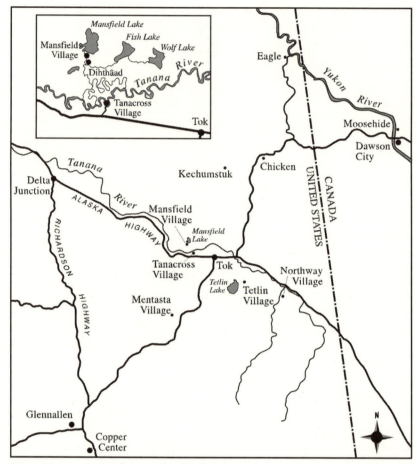

Upper Tanana regional map. Carol Belenski.

in 1932. A private airfield was built on the south bank in the late 1930s and was upgraded by the U.S. military during World War II. The village was relocated across the river to its present site on the south bank during the early 1970s. After the settlement of Alaska Native land claims by the federal government in 1971, Tanacross established a village corporation called Tanacross, Incorporated, which was entitled to select ninety-two thousand acres of land.

I first met Kenny at the Tanacross Village Council office in July 1988, right after I was hired to conduct subsistence research and oral history for Tanacross Impact Services, a subsidiary of the Tanacross Corporation. The purpose of this research was to document the social and economic impacts of a proposed early warning Over-the-Horizon Backscatter Radar antenna system designed by the U.S. Air Force. The air force had decided to locate its radar towers on Indian lands in Gulkana, Tetlin, and Tok. The Tok facility was to be built on lands owned by the Tanacross Corporation. Ironically, the system was never built due to the end of the Cold War and the collapse of the Soviet Union as a nuclear threat.

I was particularly concerned in my reserach with the possible impacts of the radar towers on birds, animals, and cultural resources on these lands and the attendant loss of subsistence hunting and fishing opportunities for the villagers. It was my duty to interview elders and document their knowledge of these resources and of existing subsistence uses on tribal lands in the Tok and Tanacross area. I closely coordinated my activities with Jerry Isaac, president of the Tanacross Tribal Council; with Bob Brean, president of the Tanacross Corporation; and with Bob Betts, Bill Shepard, George Sherrod, and several other archaeologists who were doing field surveys on the lands. Alice Brean, Bob Brean's mother, was hired to be my translator and accompanied me on many of my interviews. I also got to know Kenny's wife Ellen, who was working as a village health aide in the clinic attached to the council office.

When I arrived in the village, I decided one of the most important things I could do was to record Tanacross place names and stories about those places, not only in the project area, which extended for a ten-mile radius from the proposed Backscatter site, but for the entire homeland of the Tanacross people. I set up my office in a room behind the Tanacross post office, where I had a large drawing board for displaying maps. One at a time, I brought in elders to help me locate and identify traditional names for rivers, lakes, creeks, hills, and mountains. Kenny was one of those elders, and it quickly became obvious that his knowledge was prodigious. I taped interviews with him on at least four occasions in August and September 1988. With his assistance, and that of other knowledgeable elders such as Silas Solomon, Julius Paul, and Oscar Isaac, I compiled a set of maps and annotated Native place names that is now stored in the tribal office to be used for land-planning and resource management. It was one of the best summers of my life.

As I quickly found out, Kenny is not only an articulate storyteller but also the village song and dance leader. He loves to dance and play the harmonica. One of the things I like best about Kenny is that his life encompasses much of old Alaska. At one time or another he has tried his hand at nearly everything connected with the outdoors. He talks here at length about his days working on Tanana River boats, about mushing dogs, trapping and prospecting, firefighting, and road building. He talks too about World War II, when he served in the Aleutian Islands and Okinawa and earned a Purple Heart. And for the first time ever, he tells how his wartime combat experience led to years of mental anguish and guilt. He talks openly and honestly about his recovery from the dark days and years of alcohol addiction after the war, and he has gone on to counsel others about the dangers of drug and alcohol abuse. This honesty has made him a stronger person and an example to others. His mind is as sharp and clear today at the age of eighty-two as it was when he was twenty-one.

I also took to Kenny's sense of humor, for he was always teasing me about something. "We don't want any cowboys coming around here," he would often say. "We're Indians, and if we see you coming around with a cowboy hat and cowboy boots, we're liable to shoot you on sight." I teased him back, noting that one of his Indian friends from Copper Center who was campaigning for the Alaska state legislature, arrived in the village wearing cowboy boots. "You better shoot him," I said. Recently I have discovered that Kenny himself would love to have a cowboy hat—for the style, I think—but he knows he could never live it down socially.

On August 1, 1988, Kenny took me up to Mansfield Village in his flat-bottomed riverboat. Far older than Tanacross, Mansfield Village is a sacred place now used seasonally by Tanacross residents because it was the home of many of their ancestors. In my field notes I wrote:

A delightful afternoon, going up in Kenny's riverboat, winding around bend after bend of Fish Creek. Saw a big bull moose cross in front of us going up, and another one, very majestic, coming back out. Mansfield is a very pleasant and picturesque village with a grand view of the Alaska Range to the west and a partial view of Lake Mansfield to the north. There are lots of graves on both ends of the village, which sits on a saddle between two hills.

On the west end were two newly painted grave fences, decorated on the outside with a series of red, blue, and yellow kerchiefs. . . . Kenny is a great teaser, introducing me to everybody as the game warden.

And so began our friendship. On the afternoon of September 29, I went back to Mansfield in a helicopter chartered by the archaeology crew. Kenny Sr. and his son Kenny Jr. went along as guides. This allowed me to take some aerial photos of the old village. In my field notes I wrote:

From Mansfield we hiked over the trail to Dihthâad, about a fifteen minute walk. Dihthâad is located in a beautiful setting—a splendid view of the mountains, which are now frosted in white and magically transformed by swatches of sunlight and swirling cloud. I teased Kenny Sr. about the sardine can I found in one of the house pits: "Now I know what your ancestors ate for lunch."

"Hell no," he said. "Some white man left it there."

"No way," I replied, "that's just like those popsicles and pies you've got in your home freezer!"

In October 1988, I was invited to attend my first traditional potlatch, held in Northway, upriver from Tanacross. Kenny made a potlatch to honor the memory of his older brother, Silas. Lengthy speeches were made by the late Walter Northway and by Andrew Isaac. A large number of Minto and Copper River singers were also present. I estimated 250–75 people attended in the evening.

My employment on the Backscatter project ended that winter, but in 1991 I went back to Tanacross to attend the tenth annual Denakkanaaga elders and youth conference, and off and on over the years I kept bumping into Kenny at the Athabascan Old-Time Fiddlers Festival in Fairbanks, held every November. Kenny and Ellen are always there, dancing away, and sometimes I would also meet and talk with their daughter Diane and her husband, Ray Titus. In November 1995, I happened to have dinner at the festival with the Thomases, and I had just finished editing a book of Gwich'in oral history, autobiography, and traditional stories, *Neerihiinjìk—We Traveled from Place to Place: The Gwich'in Stories of Johnny and Sarah Frank*, published by the Alaska

Native Language Center. I had a copy with me that I showed to them, and Diane immediately said that she wanted someone to work with her father and do something like that for her children. When Kenny also expressed a strong interest, I decided it would be a very worthwhile project, one to plan on.

After my retirement from the Alaska Department of Fish and Game in early 1999, I suddenly had some time to devote to it. On July 8, 1999, following Kenny's invitation, I drove to Tanacross from my home in Anchorage, a distance of some three hundred miles, to attend the annual culture camp in Mansfield Village. Again, more teasing: "I want you to meet Craig Mishler, but be careful. He's a troublemaker. Don't introduce him to your girlfriend or he'll try to steal her away." For three days I camped out in a tent and had an opportunity to see Kenny and his extended family in action, teaching arts and crafts and songs, dances, and games to Tanacross and other Indian youth. All of this culminated in what Kenny calls a "training potlatch," where participants give away handmade gifts they have made at the camp. They are taught to know their clans and to give these gifts to persons of the opposite moiety.

On December 7, 1999, I drove up to Tanacross again to begin interviewing Kenny in earnest. When I walked in the door, I found him freezer-wrapping moose meat from earlier in the fall. We talked informally about recording his life history and his stories, and he began to rehearse the topics he wanted to talk about. We also talked about applying for a grant of some kind to assist us, but then we decided not to worry about funding. We both felt it was important to press forward, and that we would both work voluntarily.

We began work the following morning, December 8, using a Sony TRV-900 camcorder mounted on a tripod with an external lapel microphone. The swing-out LCD panel on this camcorder allowed me the freedom to be both camera operator and interviewer. For more than twenty-five years I had been using a cassette recorder and microphone to record northern Dene elders, but this was my first attempt with a camcorder. My reasoning was that the videotapes would do much to preserve the stories as performance, allowing future generations the chance to see Kenny's facial expressions and body language. Kenny accepted this technology very graciously.

We continued to work together for three straight days until December 10. Then we met again off and on for the next three years, whenever I had a chance to spend time with him. All our recording sessions, a total of fifteen hours, were held in his house at the kitchen table or in the living room, but we also did one session in Kenny's hotel room at the Westmark Hotel in Fairbanks, when the Athabaskan fiddlers were playing. Ellen was usually present, cooking or sewing, and Kenny would occasionally consult with her about something. Sometimes other family members would come by to sit and listen. Sometimes we would be interrupted by the telephone ringing or the oil-fired water heater banging. When they became annoying, we disconnected the phone and turned off the water heater. The big fifty-five-gallon barrel woodstove got so hot one morning I broke into a sweat. So much for ambience! When we finished we had thirteen hours of primary material. After each session I mailed copies of all the videos to Kenny and his family. This was both for them to watch and to provide security backup copies of the original tapes.

Our ongoing work was interrupted twice by breakdowns in Kenny's health. In early July 2000, Kenny suffered a severe heart attack. His daughter Diane drove him to Fairbanks Memorial Hospital, and from there he was quickly transferred to the Alaska Native Service Hospital in Anchorage. He soon underwent a balloon angioplasty, which seemed to help, but a few months later he had to return to Anchorage for a carotid artery bypass, a risky procedure. But Kenny is a tough guy, and with good doctors and lots of family support he recovered quickly. Following his surgery I drove him back home to Tanacross. Just a year later he went in to Fairbanks for cataract surgery.

While he was waiting for surgery on his eyes, I invited Kenny and Ellen to visit the archives at the Rasmuson Library at the University of Alaska. There we found a photo of his mother, Sarah, and his father, Peter, whose likeness he had not seen since their death some seventy years earlier (see Chapter 1). A few days earlier I was in the archives looking through the John Hajdukovich Collection and came across a receipt given to Kenny by John on January 8, 1941. It was a list of supplies that included forty pounds of cornmeal, ten pounds of sugar, one pound of coffee, one package of matches, and one box of macaroni, for a total of $10.50. I could not resist ribbing him: "You must really be crazy for cornbread, Kenny, going out and buying a big forty-pound sack like that! Holy smokes, I'm going to call you the Cornbread Man. And all along I thought you were living off the country."

"No, no, no," he said with a chuckle. "It was for the dogs. I cooked it and fed it to the dogs."

In August 2001, Kenny's children threw a big potlatch at the village community hall, celebrating his return to good health, and I was invited to attend with my family. In October 2001, Kenny rode all the way from Tanacross to Anchorage on a bus to sing some drum songs for my Phillips Barry Lecture at the annual meeting of the American Folklore Society. All of these things have brought us closer together and added to the urgency of completing this book.

As he makes clear in Chapter 10, Kenny's motivation for making this autobiography was to give something of himself to his children, grandchildren, great-grandchildren, and other members of the community. Kenny has nurtured a large, loving family and has maintained the sacred traditions of his ancestors for their sake. The proof of his success is the active participation of village youth in traditional singing and dancing, and the ongoing strength of the potlatch. Still, there is something in his story for all of us about how to live and love. In a symbolic way, this book is a great potlatch gift.

UPPER TANANA REGIONAL LITERATURE

Readers interested in knowing more about the cultural history of the upper Tanana region may wish to consult a small but growing number of books. One of the first to appear was a benchmark anthropological study called *The Upper Tanana Indians* by Robert A. McKennan.[2] Based on McKennan's fieldwork in Nabesna, Tetlin, and Lower Nabesna (Northway) during the winter of 1929–1930, the completed ethnography was interrupted by the outbreak of World War II and plagued by funding problems that delayed its publication for another thirty years. However, in 1962 McKennan visited Tanacross to interview elders and recorded a number of them on audiotape. These tapes are now housed with many of McKennan's papers at the University of Alaska Fairbanks Rasmuson Library.

Tanacross land claims were a topic of considerable interest to Walter Goldschmidt, who visited Tetlin, Tanacross, and Northway right after World War II and compiled a valuable report that helped justify village corporation land selections under the Alaska Native Claims Settlement

Act (ANCSA) in the early 1970s.[3] Unavailable for many years, this report has recently been revised and retyped by Meg Hayes and is now available in Alaskan libraries Another valuable land-use document, based on public meeting oral testimony in the mid-1980s, is the Alaska Native Review Commission Report for Tanacross.[4]

A monograph of great interest for this culture area is Marie-Françoise Guédon's *People of Tetlin, Why Are You Singing?*[5] This ethnography is focused on kinship, social organization, and the potlatch ceremonial. Although she did not spend time in Tanacross, Guédon documented the clans of the Tanacross people as well as those they have married into. Tetlin people frequently potlatch Tanacross people, and Tanacross people reciprocate.

Emphasizing the way Upper Tanana people harvest, process, and distribute wild foods, Libby Halpin's study of Tetlin subsistence patterns has contributed significantly to the scholarship.[6] A notable ethnography of the Tanacross potlatch ceremonial, *Rifles, Blankets, and Beads,* has been published by my colleague and collaborator Bill Simeone, who lived for several years in Tanacross as an Episcopal church lay worker. And Curt Madison's video footage of a lower Tanana potlatch provides an important visual and aural record of this great social and religious institution.[6]

Students of the upper Tanana will be interested in the exploration journals kept by Lt. Henry Allen, E. Hazard Wells, and Alfred Brooks, who independently descended the Tanana River between 1885 and 1898 and made contact with the Natives. Two retrospective histories of the region written by C. Michael Brown and by Geoff Bleakley help synthesize both the Native and non-Native experience since the gold rush. Additional background on Tanacross village history may be found on the community's own web page.[7]

Oral autobiographies of other Tanana River elders should also be mentioned here, notably those by Howard Luke, Andrew Isaac, and Walter Northway. Finally, it is reassuring that the residents of Tanacross have published a few books of their own. Alice Brean's *Athabaskan Stories,* for example, presents English versions of stories she grew up listening to in the Tanacross language, and Gaither Paul's *Stories for My Grandchildren* appears in a bilingual format.[8] Native language texts for Tanacross are in short supply, despite a respectable number of fluent speakers. One project currently underway to remedy this shortage is a Tanacross learner's dictionary, being prepared by two contributors to this book, Gary Holton and Irene Arnold.[9]

FORMATTING AND EDITING

To process Kenny's Mini-DV videotapes into text, I dubbed the audio portion of the videos onto cassette tape. These audio cassette tapes then became the medium used for transcribing. In my role as editor, I decided it was important not to standardize Kenny's English. English is his second language, but he is fluent in it. At the same time, his dialect is distinctive and representative of the linguistically diverse ethnic community where he lives.

The chapter texts consist largely of interactive dialogues between Kenny and myself, resulting in what some writers have called "narrative ethnography." Too often folklorists and ethnographers try to remain detached and invisible in a story, or to hide in the shadows. Although it would be an easy matter to edit myself out of the book, it is essential that readers grasp the ongoing sense of collaboration and conversation that characterizes and shapes these texts. More and more we realize that culture is to a large extent negotiated and created through social interaction.[10]

Indeed there is an interrogative component here that opens the doorway to learning. Andra Cole and Gary Knowles have said: "The questions we ask, the observations we make, the emotions we feel, the impressions we form, and the hunches we follow all reflect some part of who we are as person and researcher." And as Julie Cruikshank has written, "listeners become part of the stories"; indeed, "no telling can be separated from the setting, the audience, and the life stage of the narrator."[11]

Because "voice" is so important in the production of authentic texts and in the creation of Native identity, I have resisted the temptation to tamper with that voice. In recent years the introduction of Native voices both in Native language texts and in nonstandard English texts has changed not only the way ethnographies and biographies are created, but also the way they are critically regarded.[12] Occasionally I have inserted words in brackets [ ] where clarification is needed, but the need for clarification is pretty rare. The only two rhetorical devices of Kenny's that I have largely omitted are false starts (that is, incomplete sentences) and the oft-used phrase "you know," which works well enough orally but becomes shopworn on the printed page.

There are some occasions too, where I have deleted my responses to Kenny because they were phatic and not substantive. For these reasons, the stories presented here are not pure verbatim transcripts. Kenny always takes the lead, and usually he provides an extended monologue, but after these monologues he always responds to my questions, my comments, or my laughter in ways that clarify and reshape the text. It is his way of confirming that I am interested and attentive. To guide the reader, all of my questions and responses to Kenny are displayed in a sans-serif italicized font. Serif-italics are used to highlight vocal emphasis within Kenny's English.

With this interactive dialogue, readers benefit from rarely heard commentary on the stories, as well as the stories themselves. This is especially true for the traditional texts in Chapter 9. The conversation between the interviewer and the storyteller is part of the context, part of the setting that frames and reframes the narratives.

Another element that shapes these texts is the discursive nature of our conversations. Kenny would often revisit his favorite topics, such as the Mansfield culture camp, or the potlatch tradition, during different recording sessions on several different tapes. Sometimes I would encourage him to revisit topics for the purpose of elaboration and clarification. So most of the tapes ended up being a patchwork quilt of different subjects. To focus these topics into chapters, it was essential that I cut and paste related material together. I never change Kenny's words, but in the interest of wholeness, I oftentimes interweave paragraphs or clusters of paragraphs from several different tape transcripts. I put them out of order in order to put them into order, to create patterns of extended thought, and to make his arguments more persuasive. This deliberate rearranging also prevents the texts from being literal transcripts.

The title, *Crow Is My Boss,* which translates in Tanacross as *Taatsǫǫ' Shaa K'exalthet,* comes from a statement Kenny volunteered to me one day off the record, and it was so vivid I quickly wrote it down in my field notes. Later on when we were looking for a concise title for the book, I suggested this to Kenny, and he liked it immediately. The significance of the title is that Kenny's daily life is largely focused on his

Tanacross Clans
(from Jerry Isaac)

First Moiety

A. Naltsiin (Crow)
B. Ałts'ii dendeey (Marten)
C. Niisaas (Wolf)

Second Moiety

D. Ch'aadh (Seagull) / Tandîidz altsiil
E. Dik'aagyu (Silver Fox)
F. Tsesyu (Red Ocher)
G. Checheelyu (Fish Tail)
H. Wudzisyu (Caribou)*

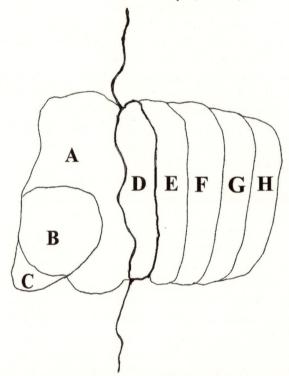

* There are no longer any members of this clan living in Tanacross, but it remains historically important

clan affiliation, his kinship duties and obligations. He belongs to Ałts'įį dendeey, a subdivision of Naltsiin, the Crow moiety.

Moiety is a term used to describe a social organization consisting of two major descent groups. Within each moiety there are several distinct subgroups called clans or sibs. Each clan is associated with a certain animal. Tanacross children belong to the same moiety and clan as their mother, but they are supposed to marry someone of the opposite moiety.

In the contiguous United States, the Crow (*Corvus brachyrhynchos or Corvus caurinus*) and the Raven (*Corvus corax*) are distinct species, but in interior Alaska where there is only one primary species (*Taatsą́ą́* or Raven), many Natives still use the vernacular and refer to Raven as Crow. This may well have been the result of slang introduced by early prospectors and trappers in the region, from whom the Tanacross people first acquired English. Whatever the case, the Ałts'įį dendeey people have always been known to be great song and dance leaders, and they have always been known to make many potlatches. Each clan is associated with certain qualities.

Like all Tanacross people, Kenny takes his clan affiliation from his mother's side, and this matrilineal clan loyalty and solidarity invokes a worldview that permeates the book. It is a worldview based on a complex system of exchange and hierarchy with other clans. In turn, this formal exchange and hierarchy are what infuse the potlatch tradition with power.

ACKNOWLEDGMENTS

Many people contributed to this project. My daughter, Susanna Mishler, did most of the transcriptions, with some assistance from Kenny's daughter, Debbie Thomas. Irene Arnold, who grew up in the village and now teaches the Tanacross language at the University of Alaska Fairbanks, worked diligently with me on several occasions to translate two of the tapes on which Kenny spoke his Native Tanacross language. Mildred Jonathon, Kenny's oldest daughter, also assisted with translation and annotation. Kenny's wife, Ellen Thomas, deserves many thanks for listening in on the recording sessions and offering her insights at every turn. She provided me with many hot meals and snacks on the days we were recording. I appreciate all her kind, quiet hospitality.

Craig Mishler and Kenny Thomas Sr. on Kenny's front porch in Tanacross, April 2001. Photograph by Michael Thomas.

Between sessions, I often conferred with Kenny's daughter Diane Titus, who stayed closely involved by suggesting topics she wanted her father to talk about.

Gary Holton, a linguist who joined the faculty of the Alaska Native Language Center at the University of Alaska Fairbanks in the late 1990s, has capably transcribed one of Kenny's stories, "The Crippled Boy Who Saved Mansfield." He supplied an overview of the Tanacross orthography and proofread the manuscript for spelling. I thank Jerry Isaac for encouraging me to work on this project and for explaining the Tanacross clan and moiety system. I thank Bill Simeone for generously loaning his precious photos and sharing his extensive census data. I appreciate the assistance of the staff at the Alaska and Polar Regions Department of the University of Alaska Rasmuson Library in locating historic photos of Kenny's family. Kenny's daughters Debbie Thomas, Betty Denny, and Diane Titus all read early drafts of the manuscript and offered excellent suggestions. To all of these people, I am deeply grateful, and of course, any errors that survive rest in my lap.

CHAPTER 1

Dihthâad Oxtẹn—Mansfield Man

My Family and Childhood

Using formal oratory, Kenny Thomas introduces himself and estab-lishes his identity through his lineage, his clan, and his Indian name. Kenny's childhood was marred by the tragic loss of his parents and sev-eral of his siblings. But instead of leaving him helpless and dependent on others, these experiences toughened him to hardship and made him more resilient and independent. He became a man almost overnight. Although the language, culture, and society he grew up in have changed almost beyond recognition, it is very clear that the place where he comes from is still essential to his status and position in the community today.

MANSFIELD MAN

I was born and raised in Mansfield, and my Dad comes from Mans-field, Alaska. And he is really Mansfield man, my Dad is; his clan is Dik'aagyu. And my Mom comes from Batzulnetas and Copper River, and her clan is Ałts'įį dendeey and that is my clan.

And, my wife, Ellen is the same thing. Her Mama comes from Mans-field, and her Dad comes from Chena, so we are both half-and-half.

My grandfathers Paul, Sam, and all of my uncles are the ones who named me. My old Indian name is Wu eł nahts'aa xughin xeed.[1] As children when we were living in Mansfield, all of us had Indian names. My Mom's name is Xeh Xulnah.

The Thomas Family, ca. 1920. Left to right: Kenny's mother, Sarah; unidentified sister; brother, Silas; and father, Peter. Taken two years before Kenny was born. Frederick Drane Collection, ACC 91-046-563. Rasmuson Library, University of Alaska Fairbanks.

I don't know too much about my Mama's family. I understand what my Mama always say is, she come to this country and she met my Dad here and married my Dad right here. And ever since then she never go back. And at the time, the epidemic flu was in the country and cleaned out everybody down that way.[2] There was Suslota, Manzanita, Nabesna, Chisana, all them people, nothing left today.

Anyway, I'm going to explain myself, where I'm coming from. Like I'm here in Tanacross. This is where I live most of my life, but my Mama come from Manzanita [Batzulnetas], that's in Copper River. My Mama was Ałts'įį dendeey, so half of me is Ałts'įį dendeey. And my Daddy come from Mansfield. And my Daddy's clan is Dik'aagyu, same clan as my wife. Dik'aagyu is my Dad. So, I'm a half of Mansfield, half of Batzulnetas in Copper River area.

And to me, right now, the way I look at it, there's nobody left in Mansfield area. Right now [that's] the way it is—there's no more Mansfield people. Like I say, my Dad is from Mansfield and he's Dik'aagyu. And I'm part of Mansfield, half Mansfield. Mansfield, they call it Meṣiin Tsiits'iig.

I'm what's left of Mansfield, plus my wife, and her sister. I mean Ellen and her sister, Martha. Their Mama come from Mansfield, and their Dad come from Salcha. So [they're] half of Salcha, and they're half of Mansfield. Only three of us that I know of that belong to Mansfield, the Mansfield people. You would call us Mansfield people. That's what's left of Mansfield people.

Right now I just want to let you know who I am and why am I saying this. A lot of people say, "Who is that guy that is talking?" This way I explain to the people who I am, where I'm coming from. And in our own way, our Native way, that's what we got to know before we'll talk. Let people know who we are. And that's what I'm doing.

Mansfield was one of the biggest places in Alaska. I would say when I was a kid, I swear there were two thousand people that used to live in Mansfield, and I can just see the picture in my head right now. There were tents all over Mansfield. And then some of them lived in Dihthâad and some of them lived in Fish Creek, and there was no such thing as Tanacross at that time.[3]

Tanacross was established somewhere around 1912 or something like that. Long ago, right here in Tanacross on the other side of the river, the telegraph line come through. There was Native trail from Valdez all the way from here to Valdez. There was a Native trail, and there was a Native trail all the way to Eagle before the telegraph line and that is what the telegraph people were using when they established that telegraph line. So what happen was they come through with the telegraph line, and every so many mile there was a station— relay station, I suppose. And one of them is at Tanacross. It was called Tanana Crossing a long time ago, way before my days. And later on in years, around 1940 or something, then they cut it down to Tanacross.

So anyway at the time when I was a kid, I remember everyone was in Mansfield; there was nobody left in Tanacross at the time. There was a telegraph station and a horse barn. The only thing they used at the time to maintain the telegraph line was the horses. And that's all there was, horses. And they come across the Tanana right here at the river. That's where they [were] crossing. That's why they call it Tanana Crossing, [because at this point the river was shallow and could be forded on horseback].

And later on, somewhere around 1912, something like that, the boats start coming from Big Delta. There was an old steamboat running and quite a few different boats that come through. I was really small at the time, it was in 19—, gosh I couldn't tell you what year that first boat came through, but there was a stampede in Chisana at the time, so all the prospectors or people looking for a job [were] going to Chisana. And right now today, that old steamer *Chisana* [steamboat] is sitting in the Tanana River, up the other side of Northway. That's where it sunk.

I guess most of the people from there would walk into Chisana.[4]

But later after that there were still a lot of other boats. I know the last boat that I remember—old Flannigan used to have an old steamboat. He used to haul freight for the store; it was really too big of a boat for the river. And later on, way before, after that, my wife's Dad and David Paul, who was a lay reader in Episcopal Church, helped to bring stuff for the missionary, Episcopal Church, just starting. They used that pull boat to haul the freight from Delta, pull boat by hand. Him and David Paul, my wife's Dad, Joe Joseph.

Ellen: You know what year the school start?

No, I really don't know what year. Anyway, they say it was way before me, when the church started. Joe Joseph was very young and David Paul was very young too. Joe wasn't even married at the time, to my wife's Mom. So he must have been pretty young and husky, that's the only way that they could bring that boat all the way from Delta to here by hand. There was no power of any kind, [except] manpower.

The old church bell over there [in the old Tanacross village] was brought by David Paul and Ellen's Dad, Joe Joseph. I remember way back that they say they brought some church people from Delta, by pull boat. Once in a great while there was a steamboat that come through, up to Northway and back to Delta, that is twice in the summer, I would say. And he have a lot of stuff on the boat that you can buy. He buys fur, he buys snowshoes, and stuff like that, I remember. Anyway the church was started way before me. I remember when I was a kid, I would say [19]28 or '29, I was really a young boy.

What year were you born?

I was born in 1922, and we used to go to church down here [at Tanacross] from Mansfield. Everybody is up at Mansfield. Nobody lives

The Thomas Family, ca. 1932. Left to right: Lucy, Peter, Lula, Sarah, Kenny (with striped cap and overalls), and Calvin. Photograph by E. A. McIntosh, courtesy of Bill Simeone.

here, no village, no nothing. And oh my Mom and a lot of old people go to church from Mansfield. We start early in the morning, so we get down here by eleven o'clock. We all come down, just whole bunch of us. Us young people we just run ahead of them and come to Tanacross early, and all the old people will walk down to the church and go to church at eleven o'clock.

And sometimes they make tea out with a campfire, and then they go back [to Mansfield] for the evening, same day. Us we go to church again at seven o'clock, you know, and then we run all the way back to Mansfield. That's seven miles. And there was nobody in Tanacross. The only thing that was there at the time was the mission, but they [the missionaries] were in a tent, when they first got there. That's what my Dad was saying, but Native people helped them out. They went upriver and cut logs and they raft it down, and they bring a whole bunch of logs, and they built a mission house [for] free and they built the church [for] free, and a lot of things they did, like later on, ever since the church keep going. Every Sunday we go to church, even in the wintertime we go to service, and it went on for a long time, and I am pretty sure it was before my time.

Today I know where my Mom and Dad are, because they did a lot of good things for people, and they are really Christian people. And I remember when my Dad hardly ever speaks English, but he understands a lot of things. Like, he always talks about the Ten Commandments. My Dad always say, "You look at this; you look at that. Don't take anything that's not yours. That is what this thing [the Bible] says. That is what God tells you to do, to obey this. If you obey this and live in this world, I don't worry about you," he say. You know the killing and all that stuff today, you know, that is really getting into Native people. That never was there, long time ago. We don't know what that is up until now, and people are shooting themselves and oh gosh, what a day. What a change, I would say.

Even today at my age at night when everything is quiet, I think I hear my mother and all of them praying. They prayed every evening. I can still hear their prayers. They prayed with thanksgiving to God every night. They didn't forget to pray with thanksgiving. A long time ago since preachers came to this country. My father and all of them began to learning the English words and praying the way the white man prays. The preachers across the river who first came in read the Ten Commandments to us. Even then, my father and them used to tell us that the Ten Commandments are so true. They told me, "If you follow the Ten Commandments, I won't worry about you when I leave this world." It's like if you take it out once in a while and look at it and read it, it will remind you how to be a good person. That's what my father and them told us.

Well, I must be pretty young when the school started. The missionaries were there, old Macintosh—oh no, no! I'll take that back. When I was really young, there was a Miss Graves, Celia [Graves] and them was there for the church, and later [an] old guy from Minto. He was married to some white woman. And they used to live there after that for the church. And he lived there for quite a few years, and I just forget when the school started. Anyways it was in my days, must be somewhere around the thirties, '29, '28, or '30, something like that. Anyway they had a little place there on the side of the building, and they built a little addition to that mission house, and they built a school for Native people.

So the school started, and long time ago there was no school, and my people didn't know how to speak English or anything else, and the school comes in. So what we used to do is, we used to go way out in the country, like every summer we move out in the country to dry meat, to dry the fish and whatnot, to pick our berries, anything for the winter time. But after the school comes in to the country, why we can't do that anymore. We come in to Tanacross, a lot of people move into Tanacross. They settle in Tanacross; people have to go upriver and get logs and then bring it in and build whole bunch of homes here, for the school. For us to learn in the school.

So when I was really young, we all went to school there, to BIA [Bureau of Indian Affairs] school. It was small, but it was something for us. Then I got to learn a little bit, and I was just forced to quit school when I was [in the] seventh grade; seventh grade was as far as I went in school, and I had to quit, forced to quit because of my [younger] brother. My brother and sister was very, very small. Anyway my older sister is under ten years old. And there was epidemic flu that went around when I was a kid.

Oh, I'm telling you. I seen people die every day, every day. I remember at the time, Jimmy Walter, Charlie James, Arthur Wright [as well as Moses Thomas and David Paul] were the only people that's not sick. They were the only people that bury the [dead] people. Sometimes I see that they just wrap them in the blanket, and wrap them in there and just put them down and bury them like that. There was no way you could build a coffin and stuff like that. And that's how they buried the people.

Was this flu at Mansfield or at Tanacross?

Tanacross. Most of the people died in Tanacross. Anyway, it's ridiculous how many people that died. And that's the first time that I remember that epidemic flu come into the country. And later on it come back again. That's at Mansfield. No, no, no—that was in Tanacross again. And gee whiz it took a lot of people again.

I remember when I was a kid. Tell the truth about, this was a great thing for me. That I was one of the healthiest kids in the country. Not only me, all of us. My Dad was healthy; my Mom was healthy, my brother. Everybody in the village that I know never was sick. We were really healthy people. Nobody sick. We don't even know what [Western] medicine is. We don't know what a doctor is. We never even thought of seeing a hospital or anything. We don't know what medicine is. And we got no use for it, because we're all healthy people, really healthy.

But right now yet, really today, I've thought about myself. That really today I'm in a different world. I wanted to live like white people. Look at all the good stuff that I've got here. I've got cream, all this good salt, napkins, towels, lights, tables, and stuff like that. When I was a kid really I never seen anything like this. We don't have all this junk.

"Atk'aas." Today I guess they call it "exercise." Me, when I was kid, the way I was trained. "Atk'aas" means they'll throw you out in the deep snow. You got to run out there and grab a little piece of stick and bring that to the fire before you come back to the camp. That's the way I was brought up. They put me in the water. Snow was on the ground, and they put me in mountain water. I take a bath in mountain water many time. They teach us, they train us how to be tough. You got to be tough in this world [speaks in Tanacross].

We don't care how far it is. Every day is a fifty-mile day, we walk in snowshoes. That's everyday thing for us [speaks in Tanacross]. Maybe something we eat. We have to be out there every day to get something. That's the way it is. That's how we get things to eat. In this world we were hardened to withstand the way of life back then. We did not know "hard times."

NOW AND THEN

There's a difference between material things of today and those of when I was growing up. *Today I really see the difference.* When I was really young kid, there was really nothing in this country like it is today. After I was born, and I began to notice my surroundings. What you see in my house today is very different from what I was born into. There's just no comparison between now and then. *Today you call it chair, table.* I did not see, even see, any tables in any houses when I was small. Dad was the first one in Mansfield who had a table in his house. That's what they told me. And nobody had any chairs. That's how different it was when I was small. When I was small there was nothing. When I was really small, I remember us hunting small game, as well as the older people hunting big animals. That's the only way we survived. Having enough food was all we were worried about.

I don't know how to explain it to you, but I wish I could have a picture here to show you where I'm coming from. I come from time when we were making a living off the country. I was with my Dad and Mom. I would live with them for quite a long time, and if we don't do anything, we don't get anything to eat. People never work; they don't know what "work" is. We don't know what "job" is.

Only thing we learn how to do things is how to make living off of this country. We got to learn how to hunt, we got to learn how to catch them birds, we got to learn how to fish, we got to learn how to catch rabbits and stuff like that. We got to learn *all* that, how you can get it; how you can get porcupine, how you can stuff like different things, like different birds. You got to learn how to do that. Every *day* we have to do something. If you don't do anything you're not going to get anything to eat.

I come from time when there was no bread, there was no candy, there was *nothing*! You are very, very lucky to get biscuit. That's where I'm coming from. I come from time when there was just a few people that have biscuit and rice and macaroni, or something like that. That's the only thing. No canned food, no pop, no steak, no beef—it's not there.

I tell you the very truth, that I never seen the bacon and eggs when I was a kid. In fact I don't even know what the hell bread is. We don't have that stuff. We don't have no sugar, rice, tea. We don't have that. I remember when I was really small, when we used to move around in the country.

Nowadays, there's TV and life is easy. Back when I was growing up, it wasn't like that. No electricity. No house like this. People were making a living off the country. Them was the days we didn't know where in the hell our next meal coming from. Everything we ate we had to go out and get. Whatever we had was not acquired easily. It was a very hard life.

I tell story to the school a lot of time, and them kids look at me like, "Kenny Thomas, it can't be all that bad."

(Laughs.)

I can see in your eyes that you might think in your mind that, "Kenny, it can't be all that bad." But, that's the way it *was*. Lot of times I wish I had picture over here to show you how it was when I was a kid, but I don't have anything. I mean I always wanted to be honest with people when I talk about something like this. In the culture camp, I think I did told you that I don't want to talk about something I never seen. I want to be honest to the kids I'm teaching. I don't want to talk about something that I don't know anything about. And that's the way I am. I don't want to make stories about something I don't know about. And I want to be true about this. But lot of times you can tell [with] these young high school kids. You can tell [that they're thinking], "Kenny, it can't be all that bad." But that's the way it was.

I see changes in my days. I see a lot of changes in my days. Like back in thirties, people they don't work. They don't even know what "work" is. We don't have time to work. We're making living off the country. We don't have time to work.

Anyway we been in Mansfield most of my life, off and on, when I was young. Anywhere from when I was born till about twelve years old. Riverboat. I started to work on the boat when I was twelve years old. I was forced to go to work. My Dad and Mom died two days in between [within two days of one another]. It seems like they died from a flu epidemic.

WORKING MAN

My Mama died first and two days after that my Dad died [around 1934]. That left me with my oldest sister who was only ten years old, and my brother is only three or four years old.[5] Anyway, I have to take care of them, so I went to work on a boat at five dollars a day. In 1932 [perhaps 1934], that was good money. I was deckhand on the boat for my brother, Silas.

Is this a steamboat?

No, no. It's a powerboat with a 120-horse[power] Redwing motor. And there was four or five boats that run [up and down the Tanana River] at that time. My brother is operating one of them and he hire me as a deckhand. Anyway, I got to be really good.

[They] left me with my little sister [Lula] and my really youngest brother, about three or four years old. In them days you don't get welfare or food stamps or anything like that. You don't get help from

John Hajdukovich's motor launch. Hajdukovich is wearing overalls with hands on his hips. At Big Delta, 1930. From Robert McKennan Collection, Box 37, ACC 88-098-995, Rasmuson Library, University of Alaska Fairbanks.

nowhere, so there it's up to me to make a living for my sister and my brother.

So what I did is, my oldest brother [Silas] was working on a river-boat, freighting boat. He haul freight from Big Delta to Healy River, then to Tanacross, then to Tetlin, and then to Northway. All summer they hauling freight. So I went and asked him, see if I can get a job as a deckhand. I know I could do the best I can, so I told my brother, I sat down with him and I talk to him, and he talk to me, "Could you handle some of the stuff? You know, when we're loading, we have to pick up at least one hundred pounds is the heaviest sack. You think you can handle that?"

"Aw, yeah."

(Laughs.)

To make everything easy for me, I thought, "If he can do it, I can." I was a boy at twelve years old, big enough guy. So I went to work with my brother. He hire me as a deckhand. Five dollars a day. That's 1934.

Gee whiz, that's good money for that year. And I notice some of the people used to work for fifty cents an hour or twenty-five cents an hour. I remember my Dad and a lot of other people used to sell a cord of wood for four dollars. Then it went up to six dollars, then up to eight dollars is the highest it ever went for the steam[boats] on the Yukon. And the schoolteachers and the churches, they sell a little wood to them. That's about all the jobs there is in the country.

And who is the captain of this boat? Is this John Hajdukovich?

No, John Hajdukovich owns the boat, and what we do is we run it for John, we haul freight. John had a trading post at Healy Lake. He also had one in Tanacross, Tetlin, and Northway. And what John does is he buy fur, he sells the groceries, so we have to haul lot of groceries to Northway, Tetlin, Tanacross, and Healy Lake. Besides that, we haul school freight and missionary freight.[6]

Later on, in 1938 or 1939, PAA [Pan American Airways] come into the country and have a station here so we have to haul *their* freight. We run a boat that carries anywhere from fifteen to seventeen tons. When the water is good and high we haul seventeen tons. If the water is shallow we usually go anywhere from ten to fifteen tons. Sometimes, the water get *really* low, then we going to have to go with a half a load. We run the boat until October, until the ice hits the river, the ice starts running in the river. Then we have to pull the boat out.

Anyway, later on, after I got to be a deckhand, got really good at it, I got to read water pretty good with my brother, and he really trust me, really good.

Which brother is this?

My brother Silas Thomas.

Oh, Silas.

Yeah, my oldest brother. Anyway, I got to be really good and I ran the boat for him while he asleep. I sleep for a while, he sleep for a while, just go on and on all the time. When the river is good he go to sleep close to me where I could touch him in case I need him. Anyway, I got really good at it. Him and I work together in one boat for at least two years, and after I got really good I started running *another* boat by myself with another guy with me. So me and my brother we had *two* boats running.

How many guys did you have on the boat? Two or three?

Three. One time in the fall time we had to have three, but summertime we only had two. But really high water.

So, what's your job if you're three? What do you do?

We have to relay sometime. You see you can't get through this channel here, you have to take the stuff over here, land over here, and then we reload it. That's why we take three. But in the summertime when we don't have to do that, we only need two, one deckhand and one captain. We take turn, too, as captain.

Gee. Did you have a name for these boats?

No, really we don't have no name. One of them have ninety-horse [power] Grey motor and one of them have eight-horse Redwing motor. That's our power—gas motor [gasoline engine]. You have to take care of them things like a baby. If you don't, why they won't run for you.

You guys break down very often?

No, hardly. Very, very seldom.

(Laughs.)

When we do break down we have to take it to [Big] Delta. We have to ferry back to Delta. Then we have to get a mechanic out of Fairbanks and get them to run again. It's very seldom we do that. Delta, that's the closest to the road [Richardson Highway] I'd ever been.

Rika's Roadhouse there [at Big Delta]?

Rika's Roadhouse.[7] Just right above that we have a couple big warehouse where all our freight is. They bring the freight in from Valdez. And Old John [Hajdukovich] is always there. He never was on a boat, never.

(Laughs.)

If he's not there [at the warehouse] he's up in Goodpaster somewhere. Old John is a really going guy. He doing some prospecting up in that area, and today it's the richest gold mine there is in the world up there.[8] And that old man knows that gold is there. But at that time, they didn't have two-man equipment to do what he wanted to do.

I heard he had a sawmill there.

Oh, I don't know about that. Someone said he had a sawmill there in that [Goodpaster River] creek but really I didn't see that. I was up in that creek. Me and my brother, we haul hydraulic pipe up there.

Up the Goodpaster?

Up the Goodpaster. All the way up to Central, *way* up.[9]

Gee.

We haul pipe. They use the water for stripping. We haul many, many feet of pipe up there.

This was hydraulic mining, with a big hose?

Yes, yes.

"Big Giants," they call them?

Yeah. It's pipe about yay big [gestures], pretty big size. We just pile it up in there. We had a boat that have a roof on. The whole boat is like boat that would be down here that we put all our stuff in. Then he had a roof on it with posts. We had to take all that roof off, just from the motor on back, we just cut that thing right across to pile that pipe in there.

Steel pipe?

Yeah. That's the only way we can get the pipe in there high enough. We have to have a payload to get up there. When we started up, oh boy, we had a lot of fun. We had to have a man who know how to do the dynamite thing. I'm not much of that; I never did too much of that, but I help a *lot* on the dynamite. We have to dynamite the drift [wood] pile. Drift pile is so bad in that area, in that Goodpaster River. We have to blast our way up most of the way. So we were going good after we hit another drift pile, then we have to open it [the channel] up again. We get way up to where we wanted to go, then we have to unload. We made four trips, four trips up there for John.

John, he had another bunch working for him up in the Goodpaster area. Then we run the boat for him, and he have people working for him running the stores, like Teddy Lowell is one of them and his brother Milo [Hajdukovich] is one of them that run the store for him. I remember Teddy Lowell and his wife run the store here and in Northway.

Didn't they have one at Healy Lake, too?

Yeah. Then later on . . .

His wife's name is Babe, I think.

Oh yeah, Babe. Yeah, we all call her "Mrs. Lowell."

(Laughs.)

Anyway, Old Jimmy Joe, one of the Native guys —when I land the boat we always take the freight up to the store, and the old man is always write. And I *watch* him all the time. I went to school, myself. I went to seventh grade, that's as far as I went. And I study the old man. The old man never was in a school a day in his life. One day, I wanted to find out how does he know how to write. "How do you learn how to write? And how do you learn how to read your name?"

"Well, first I write on them cans. Or on a sack."

Them days, a ten-pound sack of sugar, all that thing was written on there. Ten pounds of rice, and baking powder and lard and stuff like that. So he start writing them and he's teaching himself how to write. And that's how he got to be a storekeeper. He's running the store for Herman Kessler. And one day I asked him, "Jimmy, how do you learn how to write?"

"Oh, I teach myself." Sometime I talk to Jackson Giltin. He talks broken English but you can understand just what he's talking about.

Anyway, why the old man, I study him quite a while and I ask him how does he learn how to do all this. Them days, you have to learn to write down what you sell. They use that as inventory so that's what he does. He sell ten pound of sugar, he have to write it down. He sell the baking powder, he have to write it down. Pound of tea, he have to write it down. So there you go; that's how he teach himself how to write.

He run the store for Herman Kessler in Tetlin. And Teddy Lowell is the youngest guy. Milo and John, they used to run the store in Northway. And before that, there was store here, too, when I was really young kid. I wasn't even working at the time. I never *thought* about working. Old Flannigan was here. He had a big boat, a big sternwheeler. He hauled some stuff to here, just here [speaks in Tanacross]. And he had trading post here, too.

What was his first name, Flannigan? Do you recall?

Gee, I don't remember. Glenn Flannigan, I think. Anyway, he run the store here for quite a while. After that, John had store on the other side [of the river] right below the village and Flannigan had the store on *this* side of the village.

Oh, there was competition?

I think so, at the time.

Two stores?

Two stores. Before times, I was a really young boy and Tom Denny, he was married to one of the Native girls here in Tanacross. Him and his brother used to run their *own* store up there [in new Tanacross] where their house is now. Anyway, when the competition got here, why everybody bankrupt. They each under[cut] prices, and there's just no way they can get their stuff in. They have to pay somebody [to haul the freight]. When you're in competition with somebody they're on their own on the boat. They're not going to haul *your* freight if you're running against them and selling stuff against them.

(Laughs.)

So that's the way it was so they had to quit. I remember time they had the little school scale about yay big [gestures], and it weighs up to ten pounds only. Sometimes the one was with a little hook on it that you haul it up like this [gestures]. Five, six, seven, eight, up to ten pound. That's the only kind of scale they ever had. Way before the scale, I remember, [we bought goods] by the cup.

(Laughs.)

By the cup. You know them cup? I don't really remember what the price was on the cups.

You paid by the cup, huh?

Yeah. In ten-pound bag, maybe. I don't know, I think they paid by the *cup*, tell you the truth about it. I see them, when my Dad and them go to the store, they take a cup and put it in sack. This is long, long, long time ago.

Denny's getting better and better. And John [Hajdukovich] had store in Healy Lake, he had store here, he had one in Tetlin, and he had one in Northway. And that's in '35 or '36 that we run all that freight for them. In 1939 [or] '40, somewhere in there, they *combine* together. They went partners together, him and Herman Kessler. So Herman was running the store here too, and Northway, and here and there. His competition was John to start with and somehow they combine. So we was working for John and Herman Kessler both, at the time, at the end of it. Before that, John's the only one that we work for. John had three boats.

How did you like John? Did he treat you good?

John was one of the best men in the country.

It sounds like he trusts you with his boat.

Oh, gosh yes. We have to be pretty good. We have to read water *very* good, because anywhere below Robinson . . .
  [Phone rings. Interview interrupted.]

Yeah, we were talking about freighting, and I think where we left off you were talking about John and Herman Kessler.

Okay, John I remember he had a lot of things going. He had a hunting party going, a bunch of people from here that join hunting party with him. John, I remember he had twenty-seven horses and he get people from Lower 48 to come up and . . .

He had some millionaires that he guided, didn't he?

Yeah, that's right. Anyway, he take them out hunting every year. And John was [territorial] game commissioner at the time. He had to be because, them days, you don't want [hunters] to leave the meat up and take the horns. He have to see all the meat that comes back in. Anyway I never been out on a hunting party with him. I was really young at the time when it happened, but my brother and them did, Moses, and Andrew [Isaac], Charlie [James], Silas [Solomon], and whole bunch of them went with him, [like] John Healy and Paddy Healy.

They help pack?

They were guides. Native people were the best guides in Alaska, at the time. John didn't know hardly anything about the game. He's just another guy like you that don't know where he's at.

(Laughs.)

A lot of people like to brag. They've been up here six months and they know *everything*.

Yeah.

They start writing this book. They start writing a book on how Alaska is after living here six months. A lot of those books that I don't associate with at all.

Anyway, John is a wonderful man. He's good to everybody that I know of. John never was bad. What I want to say about John is he got a big store there in Healy River. Some year Teddy Lowell would run that, and some years that old Hammer—he used to live right in Healy there—he run the store most of the time. And John told me one year— this is 1928, I was only six years old at the time—that a big potlatch was going to go on at Healy River.[10]

And old man Healy, John Healy's Dad [and] Paddy Healy, Paul Healy, their Dad—them boys are all out trapping together and they're all bringing the stuff in. They got a bunch of fur and stuff like that and they always sell that to John.

And then one year, they want to have a potlatch. Old man Healy, he want to have a potlatch. So he talked to John. He told John that he want some stuff, and John said, "Well . . ." [John] don't know if he should trust this old man or what. But the more he thought about it, he took a chance, anyway. He took a chance and he gave that old man two thousand dollars' worth of stuff. Two thousand is a lot of money in them days. You don't see very many people have two thousand at the time.

This was Paddy Healy?

Oh no, no, no. Old man Healy is the one who's going to make the potlatch. John Healy, Paddy Healy, Paul Healy, and them is helping their Dad with the potlatch, somewhere around 1928.

Anyway, John [Hajdukovich] said he'd give this old man two thousand dollars' worth of stuff. Old John always tells stories at night. He said, "Kenny, I don't know what to do. I thought about it all winter long. I lost many hours of sleep over that two thousand. I don't know how the old man [Healy] going to pay me. I was really excited when we got our boat in the river from [Big] Delta," he said.

After we fix up the boat, paint it, and all that, we push it back in the river and we're ready to go upriver with the freight. He put on some stuff for Healy Lake. "I got to be on that thing," he said. "The first boat that goes to Healy."

"We got to run the boat all the way to the village," he say. "We got to go across the lake and up a creek for a while, and then across the lake to the village." So that's where they went across, and this old man went in the cache and brings all the fur out. He said, "Kenny, he paid me the two thousand and then I have to give more money for the fur, after he paid me." That's why I always say, "Don't underestimate *anybody*." Don't *never* do that. "I made a big mistake myself by not trusting the old man," he [John] said. "Don't underestimate another person that work just like you. You have to be careful," he always say.

Them days that old John [Hajdukovich] was an old white man, but he always gives me something good like that. He always talk to me about how I should be good, how I should be honest. He was really honest to everybody, and that's the way I try to be today. I always think about them times. The old man was different from me—he's a different color, anyway—but why is he saying that to me? He want me to be a good boy, that's why he say that. That's coming back to me *today*. I understand why the old man say that to me, *today*. He want me to be good to the people, he want me to trust the people, he want me to be honest. That's why the old man tell me that. And my old grandpa and my Dad and all of them people were saying the same thing [as] he [John] was saying.

Anyway, why, that's the biggest potlatch in Healy Lake, that's 1928. People come from Copper River came all the way there. John, that old man, he send a boat all the way up here, they come to Tetlin, they load people there, they come here, they put them on the boat and bring them to Healy Lake with the boat, one-way down.

You were just a young kid that time, huh?

I'm only six years old at the time. Anyway, after the potlatch, everybody had to walk back. Two days' walk to Mansfield. There's no Tanacross then, just Mansfield.

Anyway, why that's the story about old John [Hajdukovich], that he gave all that stuff to the old man, and the old man paid him in the spring. "What a day," he said. "What a relief."

When you worked for John, though, did he pay you?

Yes, he paid me five dollars a day . . .

In cash?

No, we trade it for food.

Food, huh? Rice and sugar and flour?

Yeah, that's in thirties. We're talking about maybe even before that. Even in thirties, the people are making a living off the country, *still* making a living off the country. We *still* go out in the summertime to get our dry meat and dry fish.

How about Abraham Luke, did he work for John?

A little while, off and on. Not very long.

And Frank Luke?

Frank Luke, he work for Kessler, once in a while. Right here, the first people that we are. Then at the end of the line, at the end of the summer when somebody quit, we pick up Abraham or Frank Luke or somebody. Not too long, just at the end of the year. Abraham Luke must have tell you that he work year-round, but he never did but just a few days, a few months. Them days, some of the people want to go out and hunt while the moose is good, so they quit, then we have to pick them up. How we pick up Healy Lake people and Abraham Luke. I remember he was living in Sam Creek at the time, with a bunch of kids. Frank Luke, he was up at George Lake by himself with the family. We pick them up every once in a while, and I remember we'd land there for Frank Luke all the time. And I remember he had to go back and pick up his personal gear. We waited for him. He was really a good guy, old Frank; he was good pilot. He knows the water. Anyway, the big change was the airfield. From there on, everybody is looking for job.

Wages, huh?

Wages. We getting away from trapping.

That [Tanacross] airstrip was built in the 1930s, somewhere in 1930s by hand. The Native people built that for the airplane that comes once a month with the mail. So all the Native people got together and they built it by hand. Cut all the trees down, burn everything. When we were kids, gee whiz it was a lot of fun for us! We just picking up all the wood and put into the fire. We help, when we were kids, I remember! And I remember my Dad and them had a pick and shovel with a wheelbarrow, trying to straighten out the ground, and that is what they use. We don't even know what Cat or Caterpillar or anything like that [is], nothing with power. Then later on, when the PAA comes to the country, Pan-American Airways have a station over here.[11]

CHAPTER 2

Trapping and Prospecting Days

*When he was not working for John Hajdukovich and Herman Kessler
freighting on riverboats, Kenny spent the winters of his youth out on the
trapline or prospecting for gold, traveling by snowshoes and dog teams,
or backpacking and dog packing into remote areas. His backcountry
mentors were a fellow Indian, David Tega, and an old Irishman, Pat
O'Connor. Kenny talks at some length here about the hardscrabble mining community of Chicken, located on the Taylor Highway and the setting of a famous Alaskan autobiography,* Tisha: The Story of a Young
Teacher in the Alaska Wilderness, *by Ann Purdy.*

TRAPPING DAYS: TAKE ONE

I'll talk a little bit about my trapline. Years ago when I started trapping
it was about [19]36, I think. It was '35 or '36 when I first started trapping. I had a choice to go to Kechumstuk country. After I work on a
boat, and I ran a boat for many years for John Hajdukovich and Herman Kessler on the [Tanana] River. After the season was over, I didn't
have anything to do.

And John always say, "Kenny, you ever was interested in trapping?"

Well, I told John I didn't have the equipment. My Dad died really
fast and didn't show me where the traps was, didn't tell me where the
snares was. I just have to start new.

I told John, "I'll try to go out this winter."

And he say, "I'll give you anything you want to go out."

And John gives me a hundred snares and he gives me a hundred traps, different sizes. And I had enough money for the food and stuff like that. I told Annie Denny's husband [Tom Denny] to build me a sled. A little sled like that, for Kenny Thomas only. Just my sleeping bag, traps, dog feed. What I did do is I relay from Tanacross to Big Hill. I relay all the food there and then from there I go to Long Cabin; I got another cabin over there. So I relay some of the stuff there. While I'm doing [that] I'm trapping back and forth. And from Long Cabin I go over through Dick's Ranch—Mitchell Ranch. There's a cabin there. I'm bringing my stuff and equipment there. While I'm going I have the line sitting out.

Then I finally reach Kechumstuk, is my base camp. Kechumstuk is about seventy-five miles from here [in Tanacross]. And when I reach there I look around. I look around, I look around, I snowshoe every day. I want to go up that creek, I want to go over there, I want to go up this creek. Just trying to find out where is the best spot, where more lynx track [are], or where more fur [is] in the country.

I was a really young man and I'm very strong and I can snowshoe fifty miles a day them days. And this is the thing that I do to make my living. So fifty miles a day on snowshoe is nothing; that's everyday thing for me. I hunt moose, I track the moose, I run down the moose, and I just bring 'em right to the camp and shoot 'em. That's how strong I was at the time.

Anyway, after I got to Kechumstuk I find a good spot. I went up Kechumstuk Creek. I went *way* up towards Joseph Village and I found good country for lynx there. Then I set my line out. That's two days' run from there. Then I come back. I went down Telegraph Creek. That Telegraph Creek is where the old [U.S. Army] telegraph go through from Eagle to Valdez. And I follow that and I went up—oh maybe— twenty miles, and I trap in that area too.

The first year I got out in that area, I got quite a bit of food, quite a bit of the grocery. At that time I was pretty young and mostly made my living off the country. And that helps for the groceries. And I didn't bother to come back home. I'm out there trying, really trying. First year I think I got about twenty-seven lynx or something like that, first year. Still looking for the right spot. And I remember trapping the marten the first year.

After I settled down I got to meet some people in Chicken [an early mining community, now located on the Taylor Highway]. Some old-timers, old mining people. I met a guy that had a little bit of store. He had a store of kind of heavy stuff like cornmeal, rice, sugar, tea, flour, lard, and stuff like that. And I met the guy and that's where I been getting my stuff. I sat down with him one night and he says, "Kenny, you see any marten tracks up that area?"

I said, "A lot of them."

"Go trapping. I'll buy it from you."

But the season's closed. We respect that season's closed in them days. Oh, heck. Nobody around anyway within one hundred miles, at greatest. So I just went ahead and trapped the darn things. Gee, they're easy to catch. Once you got a place where they stay you can catch 'em all. So, I got about forty-six marten in that first year. And forty-five dollars I think is what he give me, average.

Did he pay cash?

Cash money. He gives me the cash, and I buy the grocery with the cash. Right straight through, forty-five dollars. After he bought that thing from me he say, "You didn't know anything about the marten, I didn't know anything about it." Well, okay. Don't say anything about it. And it's like that every year from there on. Every year I just go ahead and trap the marten even though it's closed. The guy's buying it. So that helped a lot.

The first year I got there I most likely was looking, looking, looking every day to see a different spot, see where the cats were. That year I got twenty-seven lynx. And the old man that used to trap up there, his name is David Tega. He wasn't there at Kechumstuk when I got there. He was in Chicken. He was married to Silas Solomon's sister. Silas Solomon is my first cousin. Evidently, she is my cousin, too. Then what happened is they stayed in Kechumstuk all summer, then they moved for Chicken for the school for their kids, their children. They moved to Chicken and he's trapping from there coming *this* way. I'm staying right there in Kechumstuk, myself.

I never bothered to go back, even for Christmas.[1] So right around Christmastime, old Silas come in. That's David's wife's brother. He come in, so there's three of us. I think it was following year. First year it was David and me. And following year, Silas come in trapping with us, too. Gee whiz, I thought, I gotta make up the traps, and I got to pay for the snares, and all that good stuff. I only had three dogs. Dogs were hard to go by at the time. I had three dogs that were part MacKenzie husky—three big dogs.

They were pack dogs or sled dogs?

They were sled dogs. Either way, they can pack. Big dogs. So they'd take me where I wanted to go. They're three good big strong dogs. They'll knock you down if they ever hit you.

Do you remember their names?

Pike is one. Marty is another one. And Buffalo.

(Laughs.)

Yeah, old Buffalo is the one that takes the lead all the time. He's a smart son-of-a-gun dog. Across the flats, I swear it's a good four miles wide, and there was nothing in the country for four miles. You don't see *nothing*. Just trail. Every once and a while you see a stick just as a trail mark. And when it's blowing and you get this blowing like hell, then you don't know where the hell the trail is. That's when your dog is good, pretty smart. They just follow the trail. Just let 'em go, don't try to talk to 'em. They'll take you to the cabin.

Anyway, it went on and that winter, I tell you the truth, all the traps are paid for and to start again on the second year, I went and got some more. I was using steel lock snares is what I was using. David kept telling me, "You could get picture cord, make your own snares." And he showed me. He got rolls and rolls of that damn picture cord. That's for lynx.

For hanging pictures?

Yeah, yeah. That's why they call it picture cord. I got them and at night I'd make snares. What I'd do is I'd make two loop around. I'd go one loop around, then go another loop around. Two loops I made. So what that does is when anything gets caught, it just lock. It wouldn't slide back. You know those lock snares that we have, those steel snares? It locks. The tighter you get around the neck, it locks. And it wouldn't come back [loose]. Anyway, why, I'm making my own snares and that really help. Really help. All you got to do is buy a spool, a big spool. I make a lot of my own damn snares.

Man, I got started very, very good. Next year I got fifty-six lynx. And at this time, that old Johnny Funk is coming through there. He's an old trapper going up the Mosquito Flat. He come up through Kechumstuk, too. He don't even trap on the road or trail or anything like that until he gets way up in Mosquito Flats. He's got a place *way* up back there. And he just come through and use our trail. He's a really nice guy. He was in the country there for a while, and old Ben Arbrough come through every once in a great while, he's a trapper up in that area, too. In Mosquito Flat area. I never been up in that area because in them days you don't go in a different guy's trapline or try to come near it because we all know where the hell we're at. And lot of times I sit down and tell 'em where I'm at. They don't come close to it. They respect that.

Did you see David Tega?

I seen David maybe once a week. Or once every two weeks. He stayed with a family in Chicken, for the school. I always asked questions, every night, every night. I don't know why lynx are going through my snares, the first year. I made it a little too big around and the lynx just shhhhoooo right through the snare. Knocking down the snares. David always gives me like this how big it's going to be, like right here [gestures].

The loop?

Yeah, that's how big a loop is supposed to be. And I learned everything while I'm going. I told him I went down toward Joseph Village, up Kechumstuk Creek. I told him where I'm at, and I seen a *lot* of marten. I found old cabin where I put a pole back up where the roof broke in. I fixed the roof. I set a tent there and I fixed the roof. I put lot of spruce and moss and stuff like that up on top. It was about all I could do at that time. Cabin was really nice; it had a good stove in it and everything. I use that as my trapline cabin.

Anyway there's a lot of caribou up in that area, too. Woodland caribou. I shot three that year and later on when I was picking up my trapline I caught two more. But it's good country for lynx.

Anyway, I said, "Gee, lot of marten up there, David," I said.

He said, "You got to find where they at, where they live."

"What do you mean?" Where they stay is a little draw, creek like.

"You find where they at, where they go back and forth," he say. "Watch the track." I seen places where they go back and forth, back and forth. This is my first experience.

I set the trap. I knew how to set trap for marten and mink and weasel before I left there. I was with my Dad many time [on his trapline]. I didn't get the picture of how big that snare should be. I wasn't paying much attention to that. But I was with my Dad many times on his trapline. Them days, I was young, I didn't give a darn. I didn't try to learn, but I got a damn good idea. He walked way in the hell out there and then he come all the way back and then he set snares and traps in his track. Whenever the fur gets in there he goes out there and follow the track. And them kind of things that I got a good idea of that.

At that time I found a place where this thing goes back and forth, this marten. As I go I'm setting traps up that creek. I think I was packing about ten traps. And I got little fish that we catch in Kechumstuk Creek in the fall. I made good bait. When I was home at night I made bait behind the stove, where it's nice and warm. I went about halfway up and gee whiz, I'm missing something and I don't know what in the heck it was. Ahhh, all of a sudden David told me, "Build a smoke. Some kind. Build a smoke."

I see dry spruce limb. I got a whole bunch of 'em together and I put matches [to it]. It don't have to be on the ground; [you can] put it up in the tree and put the fire to it. And what that does is the marten get the scent of that. Then they go look around for it. They go back and forth for it. They travel to find out what the hell it is. And you can smell that smoke. And they does smell that smoke and they go back and forth, and they want to know where it's coming from.

They're not used to that smoke in the wintertime.

Yeah. No. They don't even know what the smoke is. So I remember that, and that's what I did. That's what I did in two places, that first time [trapping]. And I went home and on the way back, I already got one marten in my set. Gee whiz, I was all excited, and the next day I went back and got three.

Is the smoke still going?

No, no, no. Just the first day is all you do that. The first day when you find them. That'll make 'em move, make 'em go.

Yeah.

Anyway, why that's my good experience, right there. I learned something. From there I pick up whatever David tells me. And I listen to David for many, many years. He always yelling. Then I have to sit down and think about myself. And I have two little ones; my brother [Calvin] is only that big [gestures] and my sister [Lula] is only that big [gestures]. They're *my* responsibility to take care of these two young ones. So I thought to myself, David told me, "There's nobody going to do this for you. You going to have to do it for yourself. You got lot of responsibility for a little boy like you." I was about fourteen when he told me that. You remember when you need something, you got nobody to go to for help.

That night I thought about myself. I thought about Kenny. And he's [David] right. My brother's about oh a hundred miles away from here. If I need a cup full of sugar or something like that, who do I go to? If I need some money, who do I go to? I thought about all that good stuff. And it went on pretty darn good, and I just take it day by day from there. I try and get all I can from old David.

He go out on the line with you?

He had his own line. I got my own line. We're doing that for living. He got to make his living, too. You don't forget that. Besides that, he spend time with me to teach me lot of things at night, when we're together at night, like this. What I'm saying is, I'm trying to listen to what he's saying. Lot of things he said that I took. And I tried that. What he told me was, "When you find a place where they go back and forth, that marten?" Okay, the thing that I took was that fire. Well, I forgot it after that. I got all excited to see all those good tracks, forgot it. About halfway up I thought about it. Gee whiz, this is what he told me to do. And I did it right away. And on the way back I caught one marten. I want to catch more so I put [lit] another fire [laughs].

That's the way it goes. If you listen to the elders today, you'll get a hell of a lot farther. If you're trying to do things on your own you'll never get anywhere. What can you use? The people that talk to us, the elders that talk to us, they already have the experience that they're going by. Us, we don't have anything; we're like young people.

Anyway, that's where my trapline started from—here, Tanacross. And when I do go out, I stay out there. To make a living. It's the only way to go. I don't have time to come all the way back here and all the way back up there. It's seventy-five miles and breaking trail. It takes five days to get there with three dogs. I can do a hell of a lot more with them dogs, but I got to take care of them dogs just like kids too. I feed 'em all the time, and I give 'em the best bed they have. You gotta do that. Otherwise they won't work for you. You got to treat 'em good. I don't want to put too much mileage on them. Gee, them big dogs, in foot-and-a-half snow or something like that, they go right along.

You break trail for them?

No, no, no, no. Sometime I don't. Sometime when it's really bad, I have to break trail. That's the reason why I don't want to come back to here for holidays. Them days, people gather here for holidays. And I told my sister and them that I shouldn't come back, wasn't going to come back because it's too far. All that extra work for nothing and then all winter we never use that trail, and it's going to blow in with a lot of snow and it take a lot of work to come back. So I didn't bother to come back in.

Who was looking after your brother and sister at that time?

Oh, I got an old man. Do you know his name, Ellen?

Ellen: Uh-huh. Elgin.

Elgin. She remembers that. Whatever I said she remembers. She was small and she knows I was trapping. Anyway, why that's the way it went. I made good money in the wintertime, enough to live on.

I made good money on the boat, where I was getting five dollars a day. Five bucks a day. At the time that's good money. Five dollars a day, and I got to run that boat in the summertime. Me and my brother [Silas] running the boat. And he had a whole bunch of family up there to take care of in Northway. And he lives in Northway. He's not very much of a help to me but I got everything squared away, I didn't need any help.

Only thing is, this gentleman there [Elgin] told me he could babysit my brother and my sister. My sister at that time she was washing the clothes by hand on a washboard and stuff like that.

What would you get for lynx at that time?

Well, the last time that I was up there I got sixty-one lynx. The last season I trapped. That was '41, I think it was. George [George Leisel, an old trapper from Chicken] would tell the fur buyer that I was up there. This fur buyer was looking around for me. Finally in Kechumstuk he followed the creek all the way up to me and was circling around a long time. And I was hauling wood that day. I come back and I switch my sled to another one and then I went down to circle that big Flint Rock Hill, they call it?[2] Right under there is a big, long lake. That where he landed [his airplane on skis]—about five miles away [from my camp].

So he came to you for a change. (Laughs.)

Yeah. My God, I laid out all the fur. He took everything. I got about ten wolf and about seven coyote. That's the only things he didn't buy. But anywhere from fox to mink, he just bought the whole shebang. Paid cash for every damn bit of it. For sixty-one lynx and he gave me $62.50, average. No more, no less. Gee, at that time, that's good money. That's the highest I ever seen lynx ever got. Usually $30, $40. But $62.50! Man, I just went ahead.

What did you do with all that cash?

Well, them days, not much of anything. Just hang on to it. Like I said, my experience was to make a living. I had that in my head all the time: to make a good living.

My first year I do the same thing. Gee whiz, I got a lot of money. My Mom and Dad said they was going to make a party for my sister.[3] My

Dad's last year of life. And I bought all this grocery from Fairbanks and got it landed [by airplane] in Kechumstuk. Crazy! I thought about it today. That's the craziest thing anybody could do.

Anyway, my brother was with my Dad. I went up Kechumstuk and trapped. David was living in Kechumstuk at the time. So we trapped together. We don't have one line [together]. He go *that* way and I go *this* way. And that's the way we trapped. We know each other when we come back to camp. We have a base camp at Gold Creek, and we have a base camp at Kechumstuk, a base camp at Dick's Ranch, and Long Cabin. There's four different places to trap from. But the main base camp would be Kechumstuk. We trap out of there.

Anyway why the first year that I trap I sold all the fur. And the craziest thing that ever happened. I always say, "What the hell Kenny! Why do you have to do this?" At the time, Herman Kessler had a store here, trading post. Heck, I could have just went down and bought a hundred pounds of sugar, hundred pounds of flour, case of lard, and all that thing. Instead of that I bought this shit out of Fairbanks. With that same plane.

With an airplane?

With an airplane. They land it in Kechumstuk and from there I have to freight it all the way to Dick's Ranch, and [from] Dick's Ranch had to freight it all the way to Long Cabin, from Long Cabin to Big Hill, and oh God!

Lot of work, huh?

Really. Sometime I do damnedest thing that I think about it. How dumb can you get when you're young?

(Laughs.)

TRAPPING DAYS: TAKE TWO

I would like to hear a little bit more about your trapping life.

I was working for John and Herman Kessler on the boat, and I had to take care of my brothers and sisters. I left the home where my Dad and mother died. I left it. I don't want it no more. So I went and used a tent, one of the biggest tent I can find at the time. It was twelve by fourteen [feet]. I put another canvas inside of it. Then I had a Yukon, big stove— not Yukon stove, it was bigger than a Yukon stove. I guess you could call it a Yukon stove but it was a big one. I just set a tent and I took my brother and sister in there.

All summer I work, for ten years I would say, working for that freight. In fall time I quit working for Herman or John. Then I start trapping. I learn how to trap [because] I usually go with my Dad when I was kid. How you trap a lynx, how you trap a marten. At the time, marten was closed. Gee whiz, you can't even *touch* them. The marten was really closed season. So we catch coyote, fox, mink, lynx, wolf, wolverine. But you can't trap marten, but I knew how I could trap a marten.

I run my line from here. I make up my mind that I'm going to get a dog team and do what I can in the wintertime, too. So I set out a line all the way from here to Chicken Creek. I went back to the old man [John Hajdukovich] and said, "This is what I want to do, John."

"Well, that's a great thing you could do, Kenny," he said. "I want you to do that," he said.

"You can help that way, you can help with the food and stuff like that."

"What I can do, Kenny, I'll give you all the traps you'll need, all the snares you'll need. You can work that off or whatever you want to do. You going pay me with the fur. That's what we'll do."

So I just took that chance. I got 250 traps.

Gee, that's a lot.

Lot of traps.

These are spring traps?

Yes. Anywhere from number 4, number 3, number 2. That's as small as I got, is number 2. And I got a bunch of them snares for lynx, wolf. I got a whole bunch of traps, like I say, from John [Hajdukovich]. John is really good to me, for me to get on my feet, and he helped me a lot with it—what I wanted to do. He gives me the food to start with. I

Right to left: John Hajdukovich, Peter Albert, others unidentified, ca. early 1940s. Photograph courtesy of the Delta Historical Society.

think I make at least . . . well, two thousand, let's say. Two thousand bucks for the whole summer long. Maybe more, maybe less, but that's five dollars a day, every day.

Did you have days off?

No. No days off. No, no, no.

Seven days a week?

Seven days a week [and] about seventeen to eighteen hours a day in June. June, you have light all night. We have to keep on going. Just five dollars a day, board and room. You sleep anywhere on that boat [laughs]—that's the room.

Anyway, I work a lot for John. Whatever I work, my sister and brothers I have to keep them going with the food, too. I buy all the food for them and I have to hire somebody to take care of my brothers and sisters while I'm trapping, too. Have to get this gentleman [care-giver] what he needs. Clothes, tobacco, or whatever he needs, I buy that for him. Plus I give him a little money every once and a while.

This is after your parents passed away?

Yes, yes. We were in the tent, and he did a damn good job taking care of my brothers and sisters for me. Part of it, I think my wife remember that. Anyway, I start trapping and I've been trapping before that time, but I didn't have that long a line. But this line that I'm talking about is all the way to Chicken.

And you had cabins along the way?

I had cabins every fifteen mile. I set out trapping from there, too, some-times when it's really good. But most of that line is right on the trail.

So, could you remember the cabins? Do you know where they were?

Oh, yes. Sure, I know where they were. You got to have a good memory, you know. I know just exactly where I set them.

The fur is just like gambling. Sometimes a good year, sometimes a bad year. Some years are really good. Some years you just can barely get by. Anyway, I ran on that old trail. Long time ago, they were telegraph trail. Before telegraph trail it was Native trail that goes all the way to Eagle. The telegraph people, they follow that Native trail. That's where they string their wires for the telegraph line. That's how the buildings got there every fifteen miles, but most of the time it's our own house.

Ones that you built?

Yeah. The half-brother's, like Old Dick's ranch. There's an old ranch there and the people give it up and died off, so I use that, and Kechumstuk, my sister got a cabin there that I use. Not really my sister, but my cousin. Below that, like Mail Cabin, like Gold Creek, that was built by some old-timers. We hardly use Mail Cabin, but there's a cabin there. Sometimes we just run from Chicken all the way to Kechumstuk, without stopping anywhere.

That first year I laid out not half the trap that I got. John didn't give me no 250 traps at one time. Every year I get more, more, more. And I *say* I had 250 trap at the time I got really good and started. I had a lot of snares, *lot* of snares. Every spring I'd bring them back in and hang it up so I could use it again next year; that's the way it went. I got going pretty darn good and I was making money right along because of the work that I had. I also had something to eat because I know that I got more money coming from John yet from the work I did for him in the summer.

At the time we order a lot of stuff. My sister's and my brother's clothes we order from Sears-Roebuck or a place like that. We had a good time. My oldest brother, he's married at Northway. He got his own family to take care of.

Is that Calvin?

No, that's Silas. Calvin was only little boy, just little bitty guy maybe two or three years old when my mother and father died. My sister [Lula] is about eight years old.

Ellen: He had [other] sisters before, but they died, like Lena and Gracie.

Oh, that's years and years ago. I had a big family. There were about twelve of us, but, like I say, epidemic flu got to everybody.

A lot of them you've never seen, even, huh?

Yes, that's very true. Anyway, in the spring I trap muskrat and I hunt muskrat, and I get maybe a hundred muskrat at night sometimes.

Where did you hunt muskrat?

Up Tetlin. If I don't go Tetlin, I go to Northway.

I see.

It's between Northway and Tetlin, somewhere in there. Like Dog Lake.

Tanacross boys and men, ca. 1930s. Left to right, top row: Follett Isaac, Henry Luke, Big Albert, Joe Joseph, Charlie James. Bottom row: Silas Thomas (also known as Silas Peter, Kenny's older brother), Matthew Paul, and Peter Charlie. Frederick Drane Collection, ACC 91-046-811. Rasmuson Library, University of Alaska Fairbanks.

You have a partner up there or you stay with somebody?

No, myself and the dog. Sometime I take the dog and a pack and I walk from here all the way to Tetlin [about thirty-two miles].

Really?

Yeah, all the way to Northway [about fifty-five miles].

(Laughs.)

By the time I was kid. You remember that, Ellen? Yeah, I was just kid. A lot of the old-timers you talk to will tell you that I used to walk all the way to Northway. Yeah. In the spring. Around May. I sleep anywhere, right under the trees somewhere.

(Laughs.) Just a little pack on your back is all?

Yes, I got a dog pack, too. I maybe take a couple dogs. I carry enough food and things that I need. I don't need very much, I was just a kid having a lot of fun.

Then what do you do with your muskrat? Did you pack those out?

Yes, I used to skin them out and I started to tell you that a lot of times I had to throw them away sometimes, the carcass. Sometimes when I settled in one place, then I dry it. What I'd do is, I'd cut it flat out like, the muskrat carcass, and I'd hang it so it would dry. That's how my Dad used to teach me to do with muskrat. So, what I'd do is I'd cut it to where it's flat like this [gestures] and then I'd hang it and put a little fire underneath to smoke it. At the end we'd just squash it together and put it in a sack. It would keep for quite a long time. I would bring that back too, sometimes, on the way home. They're good eating, dried muskrat. Oh, we do lots of things for a living, at the time when I was a kid.

I get lot of muskrat, and I bring home some ducks. I'd dry some muskrat and ducks and bring them home. Sell all my fur to Herman Kessler or John Hajdukovich. Then, at the same time while I'm up there, sometime I leave the boat in Northway, most of the time in Tetlin, where we put our boat up.

Leave it there for the winter?

Yeah, for the winter. I'd take an old cork, you know them cork that we use, to cork [caulk] it in the crack? I take them all out, and I put a new cork in it. Then I put a black tar on it, put it in there with tar, and I paste it on there, in the crack.

Waterproof it?

Yeah. So it wouldn't leak. Then after that I'd have to paint the boat, the whole thing in and out. Have to wash it and clean it and everything. I got to be very expert on it and I had done that for years and years and years. I'd throw it in the boat and sometime it leaks and [I'd] bail it and bail it.

Whatever happened to those boats, I wonder?

Gee whiz, I don't know. I went in the army. I was going to tell you about the time when I did all that trapping. I made good money on trapping. But I went long ways. I would say a good 120 miles, way back.

Yeah. Tell me, if you start here [in Tanacross], where would you spend the first night?

I go to Mansfield. We have a cabin there. The next day I go to Big Hill; my Dad had a cabin there before he died. He used that as a trapping cabin. So I used that after he died. Then my half-brother, he had another cabin another fifteen mile—that's the Long Cabin. And then from there I go to Dick's Ranch, and there was a whole bunch of cabins, stables, and all that stuff there and I use one of the cabins.

That's on the Mosquito Fork [of the Fortymile River]?

Mosquito Fork, yeah. Right on the Mosquito Fork. And then from there another fifteen miles is Kechumstuk. And then from there another fifteen miles is Gold Creek. Then fifteen miles into Chicken. That's what we call it, maybe more, maybe less. But every fifteen miles . . .

Was there a cabin at Gold Creek, too?

Yes. There's a cabin at Gold Creek. There's a cabin at Mail Cabin and we never did use that. That's between Gold Creek and Chicken. Anyway, why, when I get to Chicken . . . this was in the thirties, and a lot of prospectors were there. All white people and no Native people at all; all old-timers and old prospectors and gosh I meet whole bunch of them. They *really nice* people, compared to today. White people were just like *really* our own [Native] people. They're *really* nice.

I tell you what. When I get there, and before I come down the trail again, the people give me couple loaf of bread or something to last me on the trail. Somebody gives me ten pound of rice or something. I don't know why, they just want to do that. Somebody say, "Here, take the ten pound of beans and use that on the trail." Slab of bacon. That's just the way they are. That's just how good-hearted them people were. And every night I'd be eating in different place.

They let you stay with them, too?

Yes. They want you to stay with them. They want you to eat with them. They just lonely. They got lots of money; they're digging all that gold. They got plenty to live on.

Do you remember any of them?

Yeah, I know old Jack Horn, old Frank Purdy, old Brooks, and Pat O'Connor.

They're probably happy to have the company, huh? (Laughs.)

Oh, Ben Orville, yeah. Johnny Funk, Joe Hansen. Oh, gosh, they're glad to see you and have company.

Long time before that, before me, my Dad and them been around that country. Them white people don't know how to hunt. They don't have meat. They have a hard time to get meat, they long ways from home. You can't get no meat, you come up in this country and you don't know how to hunt you're not going to get anything, and that's the way it was for them. So what my Dad and them do, they go out and get game and then they sell it to the people. There was no law at the time.

You could do that, huh?

You could do that. Sometime they exchange [game] for [processed] food. Some people, they have lots of money, they buy it. And some of them, they just trade for food and stuff like that. And they like that.

I tell you at the time when I was a young boy, Native people are *really* helping white people a *lot*. A *lot* that I know of. It's hard, very hard, to get anything. It's not like today, you go to Tok and buy all the food you want. Them days where I'm coming from, it's hard to get anything. You very lucky to get few cups of rice. and that's where I'm coming from. That's got to come all the way from Delta on a boat. If that boat don't run, what the heck you going to do?

After while, like 1940, '41. In '41 the war [World War II] brokes out, and I was at home, and I learned how to drive a Cat and to gold mine.

You worked in a gold mine?

Yeah, I used to work two years in gold mine.

At Chicken?

In the summertime, yeah. Just the summer. Good money, so I just took it: a dollar an hour. That's good money.

(Laughs.) At least you thought it was good at the time.

Oh, God, yes, for us. Sometime I make twenty dollars in one day, twenty hours. Long days in June. Ten, fifteen, twelve hours. Anyway, I got to learn how to drive this old gas Cat. This one old guy had the gas Cat. And I operate that a lot. And I strip with that quite a lot. I like it. Gee, I got to learn how to do that. So, that's my experience from working with the white people. They teach me that, besides trapping. I tell you something that all the trap that I bought, all the snares that I bought—my wife [Ellen Thomas] knows all that—and my dogs, my sled, extra sled, and I got one of the best operations there is in the country that anybody could have. The army got me in 1942. [In] '41 I was freighting that stuff from Slana to here.

With dogs?

No! With Cat. I got to learn how to drive that Cat and that's how I got on *this* Cat '41. I was freighting all this stuff and not only me, a lot of other people. Howard Bayless and . . .

You come right up the river, then?

No, no. From Slana, coming over the land. We were freighting with Go Devil, whole bunch of freight on Go Devil, we just put it on sled.

What's a "Go Devil"?

It's one of the big sled with big logs. Big logs you make sled there, and then you pile all your stuff on it.

Oh, I never seen that.

Oh, gosh, you got a lot to learn, then.

(Laughs.)

Anyway, why we pile all that material on there and then we start hauling it this way. We hauling it from Slana coming over that [Mentasta] Pass all the way through to here. We follow that old [Eagle] trail in the wintertime.

I see.

We bring all that material for six houses.

Lumber?

Yeah, enough for six cabins, I think. They building six cabins. Them days, the army is in their tents, them big tents. But we were bringing enough stuff for six cabins and then some more, I think, more than that.

This was the old village here?

No, no, no. Over *here* [at new Tanacross]. Over here on the field.

Oh, where they started the airfield. I see.

We hauled all that blacktop, black stuff, that . . .

Asphalt?

Asphalt. We hauled all that so they could have the field right away. That's June of '41. All that time I work until I got greeting card from the army.

(Laughs.)

I had to go. I went into Ladd Field and I left everything: my dogs, my sled, my cabins, everything.[4] At the meantime, my sister died, just at that time. It was TB. Me and Calvin were the only ones left. So what I did is I got in the army and I got an allotment, an allotment? . . . What do you call it?

A Native allotment?

No, allowance or something for my brother from my pay.

Oh, okay.

I told them I left my brother here and I wanted to give him what little I can give him, like part of my pay. I think they taking eighteen off of my pay, or something like that. The rest of [it] the government chip in. So he gets maybe seventy-five to eighty dollars, one hundred dollars— or something like that—pension while I was in the army. I got someone who took care of him while I was in the army. And I never got back until '46. I got in early '42, February of '42, so that's three months after the war broke out when I went in. And when I got back I lost everything on that trail. The people from Lower 48 comes up here, and they got into that trail, took all our traps . . .

Your trapping line got jumped?

Yeah, everything. I had extra guns, and extra stuff, gas lamps, and stuff like that all were taken. There was *nothing*. When I got back there was *nothing*.

You had to start all over, huh?

No, I didn't. It would take too much money to start again. The time when I got started was fairly good price on the traps and the snares. But back in '46, gee whiz, [prices] went wooooo, went up high. I cannot start again like that. I can't make it. The fur price is so bad. So, what I did is I keep on working. Work, work, work, work. The hell with traps, I just got away from it, just got away from it altogether. And that's the last time that I trapped was in 1941. I was trapping already until I got that job; they want me to run that Cat and bring the stuff over. I still had my trapline out. I tell you the truth, I still got some of the traps out when the army called me in '42. I didn't have time to pick up all of them.

PROSPECTING DAYS

My wife knows about what I did. Anyway, why I think what I did really is I go to Chicken every once in a while. I go to this white people all the time before I met old Pat O'Connor. I met him here in Tanacross when he was going by from Valdez. He was walking in the summertime. He was going through here to Fortymile country. And he settled in Chicken, where he prospected a lot. I knew Pat before he got to Chicken. That's the only one I really know in that area. And I goes to see him every once in a while and he always invite me to supper.

Different people there. That creek was just full of white people, Chicken Creek. I got to know quite a few of them. Every time I come back down there to visit they all want me to eat with them. Somebody always invite me for something. And I don't have too much time and I can't leave the traps alone. I'm ready to go in the evening after a couple days, maybe. Somebody will give me couple loaf of bread, and somebody over there will give me another couple loaf. One time I end up with twelve loaf of bread. You know, some of those old people, those old-timer? *Every* time I come in, someone give me pot of beans, big slab of bacon. "You need this." That's how good them people were at the time. The creek is full of good people.

Anyhow, why that's where I met old Pat O'Connor. Pat and I talked about it, and I asked him how he's doing on his prospecting. He said, well, he's not doing too good, and "There's too many people here," he say. "I want to get away," he say. I told him I know the creek and I always wanted to prospect. And we talk about it, talk about it, talk about it. While I was trapping that one year he came up to me. [The creek was] about seven or eight miles from where I was at. And I really wanted to prospect. He said, "Do you know that creek before?"

I said, "Yes. I spotted some color in that area before, in that creek in the summertime, in the fall time. We were hunting moose and I found some colors in that creek."

Just panning?

Yeah, just panning. We went very deep down. You gotta be way the heck down there. You gotta sink a hole *way* in the hell down there to prospect. You gotta dig down. So what we did is we sunk, I think, fourteen holes in that creek. There is money in that area, but we don't know *where* it coming from. The ore is there somewhere. It coming from the side of the hill there. Only thing right now you think of it, how does the gold get down in the creek? And the bank is just like this [gestures]. It must have fall into the creek somehow from somewhere up there. The ore has got to be up there on the side of the hill some-where. We went too far up one time. Two holes that we didn't hardly get anything. We were using this windlass. They call "windlass" thing? I would just rolling the buckets up like this and Pat would be way [down] in the corner.

Shoveling?

Yeah, shoveling. We take turns. I realize he was older than me. I was really young. At the time he was shoveling, I would run into the tent, put wood on the stove. That's too much for him. And that's what I do. While we're doing it I'm melting snow. We used the snow water to pan the gravel at night, to separate the gold. What we dig out from that hole we number every bucket and see how deep we are each time. And we measure how deep it is and where do we find the color? Where do we find *more* color? He was pretty smart at it. I didn't have too much experience in it. He was down in the hole and I was up there running back and forth between the tent. We had an old Yukon stove, with a big washtub on it was all full of snow in it. And then I remem-ber we had four five-gallon cans. We'd put all that water in that can all day long. And that night we'd pan.

Did you have a kerosene lamp?

We had [white] gas lamp. At that time he showed me how to use that wool blanket. Wool blanket will pick up fine gold. And he would show me that, and I learn as I go.

So you pour from the pan on the blanket?

Yeah, after you take everything out. You take all the big rocks out and put it on the side. We have to get rid of all that [tailings] that night before we go to bed. Clean it up. Take that big rock out and ready for the next day. That creek there we sunk fourteen holes, way in the hell up.

We didn't do too good. I remember at the end we split $750 each. At that time, gold wasn't worth a damn. I'm pretty sure it was pretty damn low, low as it ever went. We didn't do hardly any good at all. And I thought to myself, "Gee whiz, I could do better by trapping." So in the summertime from there on I really got caught in between. I have to run that boat up between here and Delta, and I didn't have any choice in the summertime to go out to prospect. I learn quite a bit from old Pat already and I could do it myself.

Did you say before that it was just one season you did this?

Just one season.

What year was that, then? Before the war?

That was in [19]30-something, '36, '37, something like that. He's older than me. Gee whiz, he comes in and he can hardly pan, I noticed. Me, I was pretty active. I was young. I do lot of work for Pat. I took him as my Dad.

Huh! [hears faint geese calls flying overhead] The geese is going home!

(Laughs.)

Anyway, I learned quite a bit from him, and I wanted to go out to some places ever since, but I was real tied up with that boat. A lot of responsibility. Later on, many years that I took care, more responsibility. More and more. Next thing I know, I'm running the boat *by myself*. I got to keep track of the stuff, where we can unload, where we're goin' to take it to. Lot of people in this village here, lot of people lives in Tetlin, lot of people lives in Northway, lot of people lives in Healy River [Healy Lake]. You gotta take care of all of them. So I was really tied up, and I was making good money by doing that.

Next thing I know I got up somewhere right around—[19]38, '39, something like that, I went up to a dollar an hour. Dollar an hour. So I was making more than five dollars a day. Time is changing. Time is changing. 1939–40 is the last time I ran the boat, '41 is when that road [the Alaska Highway] was coming through. So that's the last time I did that.

You work on the road, too?

No, no. I didn't work on the road. I was just a captain, most of the time. I walked a Cat from Slana to here, long time ago. There was no roads or nothing. So that's how I made part of my living, trapping.

Pat O'Connor is an Irishman, is he?

He was Irish. "I'll have some of that Irish tea," he always say. That green tea. He was a good friend of mine, really good. Pat and I, we didn't have a hamburger every day, we didn't have ham and eggs every day, but we ate what we can survive on. When you're out in the country making a living, you don't know what bacon and eggs is. Once in a great while we have a little pancake, or we have a little sourdough which we save all winter long. And that's about the only thing for breakfast, like rolled oats—lot of that. Even sometime for a change we use cornmeal in the morning. There's no such thing as bacon and eggs or ham and eggs. We don't even know what the heck that is. He ate whatever I ate. I make him a big moose stew. He like that. There's no choice, no choice. We survive on what we had. He's pretty good at it. And I notice nobody was ever sick. He never said he had a headache or anything like that.

Was he an old bachelor or did he have family?

No, he was a bachelor. He was a really nice man. One fall he came up. "I just want to stay a couple months," he say.

"Well, go ahead." And I was in Kechumstuk pretty early one fall, and I went all the way to Chicken, walking. He came back with me and he want to stay up there for a couple months, he say.

"I want to kill a moose," he say. And that's what he did. I shot a moose for him, and I show him how to make dry meat. That's all it takes. He hang it and smoke it.

I drew him a little picture of how a trap would catch all the fish coming back down Kechumstuk Creek. So we make trap like this. And we put lumber in just like that [gestures]. We had maybe about a foot wide where that thing goes through. What it does is the fish goes right through that little opening. And we have a big chicken-wire box behind it. Every fish that comes down that creek will go in there. Gee, lot of fish. Fall time—October, still that fish is coming down. We put it on the ice.

What kind of fish?

Little grayling. Oh, we put away lot of fish that year. I did a lot of prospecting in my days after that, here and there. But I didn't spend too much of my time on prospecting because I have to make a living too. After we lost our sister—she died—me and Calvin, my little brother, are the only ones. He's growing up to be a good boy. He goes to school all the time and pretty soon is big enough to cut wood. Gee whiz, he's a lot of help to me. He got to be a big boy. He was six foot four or six foot five.

Anyway, from there I got in the army and I got an allotment [allowance] for him that they take care of him every month, the army does. They send him a check. I don't know how much he was getting.

CHAPTER 3

Medicine People, Ghosts, and Stick Indians

Legends about medicine men and medicine women occupy a large place in Alaskan oral tradition. While Kenny insists that these people are all gone today, replaced by Western medical doctors, his youthful eyewitness experience of medicine people in his own family testifies to their power and pivotal place in northern Dene spirituality. At the same time, Kenny's own very real experience with ghosts, shared by many other residents of Tanacross, suggests that the community's general acceptance of Christianity is deeply infused with a variety of other traditional beliefs. Contrary to Western expectations, however, Tanacross ghosts appear before a person dies rather than afterward and are viewed as harbingers of death. Stories about the Stick Indians add yet another dimension to the community's folklore and oral history. Rather than being a single identifiable tribal group, the Stick Indians appear to consist of various bands of raiding warriors from outside the Upper Tanana region who tried to kidnap women and children.

DESHEN DENDEEY: THE MEDICINE PEOPLE

When I was a little boy I seen medicine people. My Dad and my grandpa were medicine men. They had the power. And from what I seen from medicine people, very few of them had it. Not all the people, just a few of them. Maybe five or six in the whole bunch of us. And I see that they made people well, and I believe there was a power that they were doing that with.

Because one time when I was a kid, my grandpa and them, they had a little boy named Alfred. We were at Long Cabin, Long Cabin country. In them days, when we make camp, they make water place [water hole]. They dig in the ground deep enough where the clear water will come in. Them days, permafrost was pretty shallow. And we get all the clear water in there and it's deep enough. So anyway, why I guess this little boy, what he was trying to do was get a drink of water. And he had to go down and get drink of water like this [head-first on his stomach] and he can't come back up it because it was deep. Pretty deep there. He had his hand out like this [gestures] and he held himself up quite a while and he was hollering, but it's quite a ways away from the camp where the water hole is.

Anyway, pretty soon his hand give up, and he just let go and just drowned in that little water hole. Anyway, they found him later on, and then I remember my Mom and my Dad and my grandma and all them, they bring the boy back and then they try to get all the water out of his stomach and whatever. They tip him over and I'm trying to see all I can, but I was really small, and all I know is that the boy is dead. Them days we don't know about the pulse and all these other things. My Mom and them were checking for breathing. Anyway we know that this kid was dead.

My Dad was there; my grandpa was there. And they made that medicine; they start singing. We were in a little tent, like. I know I was close to my Dad, and I know I was sitting close to my Mom. My Dad and my grandpa were dancing. Not [really] dancing, [but] like singing and they walk around. They walk around with the sun like this [gestures to show clockwise direction]. The sun goes down this way and it goes like that, *with* the sun. Pretty soon they walk around like that, singing, walk around. Later on, one of them say, "Put blanket over us." They lay that little boy right down. My Dad's over here and my grandpa's over here, and the boy is laying between [them].

We're trying to be quiet. Whenever they put that blanket on them, my Dad or somebody say, "Put blanket over us." With this little kid laying here and my Dad over there and my grandpa over here. When they put that blanket over [all three of] them, then my grandma and my Mom and them say, "Be quiet, be quiet, be quiet" [whispers]. So we all have to be quiet to let them do their thing. They don't want to be disturbed. That's why we had to be quiet. And dogs can't bark. Everything have to be really quiet so they can do their thing under the blanket. I would say forty-five minutes at least that they were in there, maybe more. Could be more because this was a long time ago. Anywhere between forty-five minutes to an hour they were in there, under that blanket.

Then, pretty soon that blanket just went like this [hand waving gesture to show trembling]. Just like you see a piece of cloth hanging on the wall will go like this when the wind hits it. That's the way it is, the blanket went just like this. It make noise.

Did it shake?

I was so damn scared. And I didn't know what the hell was going on. I was sitting close to my Mom, I know I remember that, and that thing [the blanket] was shhhhhhhhh. Just shaking like this. Pretty soon they took it off. My grandpa was ahead, and then my Dad behind my grandpa, and then that little boy he's holding [onto] my Dad, just dancing around [laughs].

In the tent?

In the tent. Around. They were dancing around. Then they sing again. They let him sit this time. It's just like he's Alfred. He's *there* and he can wink his eyes, and he's not *dead*. What the *heck?* I seen that. And then they sing again, and then they touch him like this with a feather and stuff like that. What they call Long Walking Cane. It's got a different deal on it. In our language they call it, Chuseh'. The stuff that they use in their medicine thing, Chuseh', they call it.

Chuseh', like a stick?

It's a long cane, about yay long [gestures].[1] It's all wrapped around with different beads.

Fancy?

A fancy thing. The thing that they use as their medicine. They can't just go like this, they got to have something. Something—Chuseh'—they call it, they got to keep it in one place. And they use it when they do that.

At the time, besides that, this kid is just dancing right behind my Dad, and my grandpa's up ahead. And gee, what a great thing. My Mom and them talking to them. I don't remember what they were saying, but they were talking to them. They thank them and stuff like that. That's a long time ago, and I was a really young kid and I don't really remember what they were *saying*. But my Mom and grandma and them guys are talking to my Dad and grandpa.

And did that boy have a long life then?

Oh, after that gee whiz, long, long, long. We was raised up together. We came back down together later on and he [Alfred] was all right, fine. Besides that, when we were up in Mansfield, sometimes somebody was sick. Them days, I see that people were all healthy, really healthy. I see the people are really healthy and very, very few people got sick. They make medicine, and I see them take something out of their stomach or wherever they're sick. They pull it out and they show it to them like this [gestures], and I see it in their hand. They let go like that [gestures]. "This is what you sick from." I hear them say that.

Is there a name for that thing in your language?

No. They say, "This is what you sick from," and they take that out, whatever it is. Whatever make them sick, that's what they pull out. And that's what they let go. They let it go someplace else. And I see some people is better after that. No more sickness after that. I *see* that. I *seen* that. I know it's really there. The power is there. It went [on] for a long time when I was a kid. Gee whiz. I don't know how many years that I seen that. Long time, this is my young days.

Not very many of us are medicine people. But I seen they do good things. They have the power to make one another well from sickness. They make medicine to see if there's moose somewhere in the country. I've seen that. They make medicine to see which way that moose is. I seen that. My grandpa would always say, "Maybe you should go upriver." He'd always tell my Dad, "Maybe you should go upriver," to a certain place.

Do you remember years ago we made that map?[2]

Yeah.

Every little hill or creek or lake, everything have a name to it. My grandpa would always say, "Maybe you should look right around *there*," and he names where it was. And I always see that. He always tells my Dad, "Maybe you should go there."

And that's medicine, too?

That's medicine thing, yeah. One time, me and my Dad we went up with Walter Isaac, Jerry Isaac's grandpa. My Dad, he was sleeping, and me and Walter Isaac, we got up. Old Chief Walter Isaac, he used to live over here [gestures]. We got up and we were making tea and were cooking. Pretty soon my Dad was singing. I remember Walter Isaac had a pan and he was hitting the frying pan while my Dad was singing. And he [my Dad] said, "I seen it today. It's going to be you, Walter," he told my Dad, "that's going to see this game. The game come from way down, I don't know, far away, and it's going to be in that creek somewhere."

And we went up there and sure enough there was tracks. He went down the creek and there was a lot of brush there. Anyway, why I was way, way behind, trying not to make any noise. And he told Walter Isaac to go this way and he [KT's father] go that way. *We* went this [other] way, me and my Dad. We heard shooting, and Walter Isaac, he shot that cow moose and that little calf run towards us so my Dad shot that one. And he told Walter Isaac, "From there, you might see something again," he said. "We might see something again."

I was a small kid. I always had a .22 single shot [rifle]. After they cut up that meat, then they go back down to get their stuff where they left it, and there was another cow moose standing in the lake on the way back. Just exactly what my Dad had told him [Walter]. So we went out and shot that one, too. This is things that I seen, and I believe the medicine people really have the power.

Just men, or women, too?

Well, I never seen a woman like that. My old grandma say she dream, dream about things and that's all I ever heard. But no, she's not no medicine woman. Anyway, why I seen that. I seen medicine people make people well. They have their own thing that they carry all the time in a sack or whatever that they use in their medicine.

What kind of thing do they carry?

Well, Chuseh', they call it. I don't know how they call it in your language, but we call it Chuseh'. They leave it in their sack with something that grows in this country. It's something that's really got sweet smell to it, a plant. And they put that in the sack, and sometime before they make medicine they put it on hot stove, and it makes that smoke. Some people does that.

Like sage, maybe?

Yeah, something like that. Me and my Dad we used to look for it out between here and Mansfield. It grows in the moss. It's a looong deal, sometimes it's yay long [gestures]. We pull the moss apart and we follow it and get all we can out of it. And then they dry it. In our language we call it, Tii men. "Tii men," that's the sage that they use. It's really got a sweet smell to it.

You have it right up in Mansfield; there's some there.

Yes. It's not *that*. You know that grey stuff that has a good smell to it? It's not that; it's different thing. They use that for potlatch, too. They use that when they make songs in the potlatch, too. They put it on stove before they start potlatch.

Anyway, they use that in their medicine thing. Ever since I was a kid I study my people. How the heck did people ever make each other well? How did they do that? So I thought and thought about it, and the only way, the nearest I can think of, is God would give them a power to heal one another. But I can see whenever the [white] medicine doctors and nurses coming into this country, then the medicine people are fading away. *All* fading away. No more medicine people.

The last time I seen a medicine man was Tommy John, that used to make medicine, and Ellen's mother, my mother-in-law. When I came back from the army, I had really bad nerves. My nerves were shot. My nerves was really bad. And sometimes I couldn't stand it. A lot of times I can't sleep, I can't eat, just *terrible*. So they got notice that I'm like that. My mother-in-law went to one of the old men, and that night my mother-in-law said to come with her. So me and my wife we went down there with her, and I was laying down with blanket, laying on the blanket. And this old man, he sing a song. That's in [19]47, I think, '47–'48, something like that.

Is there any special way a person could become a medicine person? How would they get that power? Was there a way they would find out that they had that power? Anybody explain that to you?

Well, let me finish this thing first. What I seen happen here is when the white people come into the country, missionary come into the country, and schoolteachers come into the country, nurses and doctors all coming into the country, and medicine people are fading away. Like I said a while ago, I had that old man [in] 1947 or '48, that was the last time.

My nerves was shot when I got back from the army, that [was in] '46. My nerve was pretty bad, and I needed the help. I was in very bad shape, so he made medicine for me, and he told my wife's mother that my nerves was shot when I was in the front, when I was in the war [World War II]. In my language they say, "Shiidza dehnittcha." "Shiidza deecha," I would say. That's, "I *over*-scared," that's how my nerves was shot, he said. And right at that time he told my mother-in-law *exactly* what's wrong with me. He can try and help me a little bit, not much, he say. "Not much I can do about it," he say.

He may be the one that helped me at that time. He may be the one, I wouldn't say, but I felt better after that. But after that I felt a lot better. And then I went to the doctor, the army doctor, where they give me 180 pills, and I was taking that right after that, too. I don't know if the old man really helped me. I know he did help me because I felt good after what he did. And I felt like really something going through my body when he make that thing. It's hard to explain that. I felt something that's going through my body.

Anyway, why, that's the last time I seen it. And like I say, I think what happened is, all the doctors and nurses coming into the country, the medicine people are all fading away. No more medicine people.

Like I say, the last time I seen it was '47 or '48, something like that because I came back in '46. Anyway, I study my grandpa and my Dad. It's all gone; it's just gone away. When people come into the country, like doctors and nurses and medicine come into the country, then it's all gone away.

I study my grandpa and my Dad and them. To me, my own way of thinking is, I study people a long time, and what I see is me, my thinking is, God give each person a gift to heal one another. That's the way it looks to me. The way I see it, that whenever doctors and nurses come in, God takes all that thing away, take that power back away, and doctors and nurses took over. And reason why I say this is, I see that after nurses and doctors and hospitals and things come into the country and took over, medicine people are fading away. So I really think that God took that power back away from them. The power that I see that was given to them sometimes they misused it. They abused it. In my days I can see that.

Did they ever use medicine for evil?

Yeah.

Oh, they did, huh?

I think that's why they were misusing it. They abused it. And some people, they lose it by doing that. Like they can make each other miserable. They can make each other get sick and die; that's how they abuse it. And sometimes they can make each other blind and stuff like that. They misuse that. They abuse it.

Did you ever see that?

Yes, I seen that. I seen that. I see they abuse it. But, before me. Now this is something I didn't understand too well. The muzzle-loader shotgun come into the country must be somewhere around 1915, 1911, something like that. And this old man at Mansfield . . .

[Background noise, dogs barking]

Too much dogs. (Laughs.)

And he was *really* medicine man. My Dad and my Mom, they say [told me about him], and this is what I heard about what medicine men did.

He make himself a big black marker on his belly, and he told them to shoot him there. With that muzzle-loader shotgun they blast him right there, just shoot him. He keep bothering people all day. He keep telling people to shoot him. "Shoot me, shoot me, shoot me there." So one day he come around and someone just shot him in the stomach. Next day he come back alive again. Now this is something that I didn't see, but I heard that. My wife was just talking to me about it the other day, and she heard about it too and lot of times, like Emma [Northway] or them people heard all about this. It's just a story before our days. And that's just how powerful the medicine people were. I seen my grandpa when he was buried, and my grandma they hang a dishpan, yay big [gestures] in there. That's what he told my grandma to do.

In his grave?

On his [grave] fence. He hang it right inside the [picket] fence. At night sometimes you hear this thing [makes knocking noise with his knuckles], dishpan. You can hear it like, [makes knocking noise]. And my grandma would talk to him [makes tapping noise with his knuckles on the table]. You can see somebody hits it. I heard that. *Really* I heard that, my grandpa. My Dad never made no noise like that. My grandpa [was] the only one. A long time later on when my grandma died we took that thing down because I figured nobody [else] knows how to talk to my grandpa.

Just her?

Just her. They lived together for many, many years. I hear him say that we're here and we don't want you to scare the kids. I hear 'em say that.

You actually heard his voice?

No, no, no! My grandma. My grandma talked to my grandpa. I never heard the voice, but I heard that . . .

Tapping sound?

Yeah, tapping sound on that dishpan. Dishpan was hanging there inside that fence. It was hanging high, and I can hear it [knocking noise] like that. My grandma always talk to him. Today, people don't worship that, but that's their [grandma and grandpa's] way of doing things. They believed in that. We believed in one another because, in their time, they make people well and their spirit is around for a long time. They just don't die and are buried. That don't mean that they're gone, but their spirit is still around for quite a while.

Would this last until they had that memorial potlatch?

No, no, no. This one here stayed for a long time. Some of the medicine people stay for a long time. The potlatch thing has got nothing to do with medicine people. That's really a different thing. Medicine people are just [their] one thing. They can tell you that there's a moose back in a certain place, they can make people well, they could tell you if there's going to be a lot of fish, they could tell you if there's going to be a lot of caribou. They *know* all that good stuff.

They can see into the future?

Yes. My Mom and grandma and all them, they talk to them, talk to them in good way. And I see lot of that. There's a lot of good things that they did, and a lot of bad things that they did. They abused it. I see that. They abused it. They not using it right.

Would they get paid for their services?

No, no, no, no. Nobody get paid for it. Nobody pay nobody. We do have a lot of medicines out of the ground here in Alaska, that we use. We use a lot of stuff out there that grows up here in Alaska. And we use some stuff that grows on the spruce trees [for example]. It's the only medicine we ever had. It's good medicine. You know that grey thing that grows up around Mansfield on that hill there?

Yeah.

Really sweet-smelling stuff [sage]? They use that when they had the medicine. They use it all around them, too. Anyway, I really believe in medicine people. They did their thing. I seen they make people well, and I see that they seen the game where it was. At the time there was hardly any moose in the country. I see that my grandpa always tell us where that moose would be. I seen that, and it's a really true thing for me. I've seen it and I believe in it. I think it's a gift from God is what it is. Everything comes into the country; Western things come into the country, and the medicine people are fade away. It's all gone. Today, I'm sorry to tell you this, but I don't think it's ever going to come back. If it's going to come back, I should be the one that be the medicine man. Because it's in my . . .

Family.

Family. And my grandma and grandpa and them, Ellen should be the one, too, my wife. We're the ones [who] should be medicine people if we going to continue. But, I don't think it going to continue at all. I'm sorry to tell you that, but I think it's not going to come back. There's no *way* it's going to come back. What I'm saying is, I think to me, it's a gift from God, and God took that power back away from people. Because the doctors and nurses come into the country, it's all gone. So, that's as far as I can tell you, as much as I know about the medicine people. I believe in it.

There were quite a few here, not only here. The medicine people is all the way up, all [through] the people that I used to *know* around here. Wherever people were. We're not the only people that have medicine man in our village. There's other villages that have it, too.

It's disappeared all over, huh?

All over. That's what people were using. Anyway, I think that's enough on medicine men.

CH'E<u>SH</u>ĬIG': GHOSTS

First I want to talk about there is such thing as a ghost. People seen ghosts, ghost town, or whatever you call it. You see, in our language we call it Ch'e<u>sh</u>ĭig'. "Ghosts," we call it in white man way. You don't see that for nothing. Lot of people see that in our days. In my days they see that. Even today we're believing in that. Today we're believing in that [a] *lot*.

You say, somebody seen a Ch'esh̆ĭig'. That mean this person going to die. That's ghost. Ghost is something that you just see 'em, and then they fade away, and it just goes, gone. When you see something like that [and] you know it's ghost, you gotta talk to them, tell them to come back. "Come back, this is your home here," people always say to them. That way they'll last a little longer, but even though they're going to die.

But the only time you see the ghost is when people are gonna die. Before they die you see their ghost. That's only time you see them. If I see somebody's ghost or something like that, I got to talk to them, tell them to come back, "This is your home here. Come back to us." And maybe he'll stay another couple years. And he eventually will die, but he'll stay a couple more years, maybe. And that's the kind of thing today we're still believing in that very, very much.

We strongly believe in ghosts, people's ghosts. We see [their] ghosts before they die, not after they die. Before they die. That's the only thing that I experienced. I've seen. I heard the ghosts. I really believe in that today, in the ghosts. But some of the people, they see somebody here and they turn around and look away and look back again and it's gone. And we really today yet we really believe in that, the ghosts. That's before they die.

What do they look like? Do they look like real people?

Same, same people. Same man, whoever you think. If you seen Kenny Thomas, and I'm sitting over here but you see me someplace else, that's the way it is.

Someplace you're not supposed to be.

Yeah. That's the only time we see them.

Do they talk to you?

Oh no, they don't talk. They don't say nothing. You just see their ghosts only. No talk, no nothing. One time in my lifetime, I heard [a ghost] in the same village. I heard it. I didn't hear this ghost by myself. But them days there's no hospital, no nothing. And one of our friends, young man like us, he's ready to die. And he's just barely hanging in there every day. We sit up with him. Everybody take turns sitting up with him. This time me and Silas Henry's boy, Drane, we stay there with the kid, our friend. Anyway, why we have just a light.

I experienced really my first ghost. I heard about it, but it never bothered me. And something tells me, "Don't get scared." We were way back there. The windows were out front like that on one side and the door was over there. And knock on the window. And he went around. I could hear him going around, and there's another window back there, and the kids was laying under that window there. I remember we burned one whole candle and another half a candle, that time of night. A candle and a half we burned, when all this thing happened.

And he bang on that window back there. And by that time I wake his Dad up. I told him we hear that. "That's your friend's ghost, so he's going to go, that's why he do that," he say. "No. I wake up now so you guys can go home," he told us. "If you want to you can go home," he says. So I went out there and my friend Drane, he tell me, "Stay with him up here in his tent."

"No, I don't want to stay there."

I got a cabin over across the creek. I got to cross the bridge and up the hill and then to our cabin. Nobody in the cabin. Nobody. Just me. So I went up there. I got a .30-.30 in there, and I just held my .30-.30 right close to me, and I went to sleep, and I never heard *nothing*.

All this time, that ghost just about get him [Drane]. And he went and wake up the next door neighbor and told him about it, and this kid, he's one of our buddies—we're all a bunch of boys—one of these boys went to sleep with him. And pretty soon there's *two* ghosts. *Two* of them! Gee whiz! They were just about getting into that tent frame, getting into that tent with them. So when they get around back, they ran out and they ran to the next-door place.

Anyway, this Drane and Isaac, they both died. At the same time. Right after Richard died. The three of them died. Drane and Isaac, the one that sleep with him? And here I was way over across the river by myself. In our house. My Dad and them's house. And nothing bothered me.

What year was this?

Oh, gee whiz, I was a *kid*. I was small. I don't know what year it was [distracted]. Trouble is, where are we? Where were we? Yeah. We talk about the ghosts. Anyway, right after what happened there, them people that were in the tent, they both died. They heard their own ghosts.

They saw their own ghosts?

Yeah. They heard their own ghosts. They don't know what it was, but that's them. Anyway, nothing ever bothered me. I walk across the creek, on the bridge, and I went up the hill, got into the house, and locked the door, and went to sleep. I held my .30-.30 like this [gestures]. You know, do just about anything when you're scared. But something tells me not to go with him. He told me to go home with him and stay with him. But I don't want to do that.

Who is this guy?

Drane Henry. Anyway, he died too.

Is he related to Gene Henry [of Dot Lake]?

Yeah, he is. Anyways, yeah. Drane's Dad was Gene's uncle. Anyway, why something tells me not to go, so I didn't go up with him. So that's the same year both of them died. And then that kid died not too long after we heard his ghost.

Really today some people still see ghosts. I never seen one, not even in all my life I never did see a ghost. But some people does see ghosts. And that's still here. But most likely when you see something like that my Mom always tell them to come back home and come back here. That's the only way that they can live with us maybe a couple more years. But they eventually will die. But that always was there. People talks about it.

Like up this way, like Northway, Tetlin, and places like that. It's still there.

Ch'es<u>h</u>ĭig', you call it?

Ch'es<u>h</u>ĭig'. Yeah. I thought about that all the time.

GUU: STICK INDIANS

Right now we'll talk about the Stick Indians.[3] Long time ago, when I was
a kid I heard about this. Stick Indians, they call it. That one we call it Guu.
"Stick Indians" is "Guu" in our language. Many times you can hear 'em
out there. Like in our language you say, "Naxaxa'ęh." "Naxaxa'ęh" mean
you can hear 'em back there. They throw sticks, they'll talk, they'll whistle. They do different things, and that's what we call" Naxaxa'ęh." They
make all kinds of noise, but you can't see them. That's what you call,
"Naxaxa'ęh." Many times people hear that.

It's a funny thing that in my days—I'm seventy-eight years old and,
tell you the truth about it, I never hear it not one time. I never hear it. I
been in the country all my life, all over the country, [and] I never hear
that. I never hear "Guu." Maybe it faded away when I was a kid. Gone
when I was a kid, I guess. I heard about it. Many times I heard about it.
I make living off of this country. I been all over the country. I traveled
everywhere by myself. I never hear anything.

I heard people say, "Naxaxa'ęh"—that mean they hear something. . . .
When I was a kid, another thing that I heard is my Mom and them,
they go to pick berries. And them days, you don't have rifles everywhere. We were lucky to have an old muzzle loader years ago. That's
the only one or two people have it in the whole village there. Very few
of them. And most of the time that I know my Mom and them, they
carry this long knife, oh about a foot and a half, two foot long. Long
knife, really sharp one. They make case for it, and they put strings
around their belt, and they put in on the belt and pack it like that. And
that's their protection. And every time they go somewhere they always
carry a rope. The rope that we have at that time is a homemade rope.
The Native people made it themselves, like made out of babiche. They
braid the babiche and sometimes they braid four of them, most of the
time three of them. They braid that and make *long* rope with it. And
that's the only kind of rope we ever have.

And my grandma and my Mom and oh lot of other people went
berry hunting. And gee, people come around them just about to catch
them. They tie themselves together with that rope—four or five of them,
I don't know how many. One of my grandmas was the head of them,
and my other last grandmother, little, little grandmother, she's way
behind. She's a brave one. And the scared one is in the middle. They all

carry that knife. They all have that knife in their hand. They're not going to let anything go. They came back just about to the village, and then they don't hear it no more. Every time somebody go somewhere they hear that noise, same noise that my Mom and them did. They're around [the Stick Indians]. Sometime in the springtime they come in; in the fall time they going back. I don't know which way, but they go back. They go somewhere.

STORY OF THE TWO KIDNAPPED GIRLS

And I hear the Stick Indians, whoever it is, they stole some people from down below us [downriver]. They stole two girls. They stole some other girls that they brought back, and one of the girls that they never brought back because her Dad was really mad, really mad. And if he wasn't that mad maybe they could have brought her back because we heard that one of the women they took, they stole from their camp. They took her, and her Dad plead them to bring his daughter back to him. In my language, you'd say her Dad, "dahwuudetka." "Dahwu-udetka" mean, "Please, please bring my daughter back." That's what it mean in white man's language.

But he's not mad or anything like that. Just every time he talks he'd say, "Please bring my daughter back to me," or something like that. Then they felt sorry for him, so they put him in some kind of house somewhere, and they left her there. And he took some stuff out on the trail for them. Fur, necklace, or something very valuable at that time; he took that out there. He pays them to bring that girl back [a ransom]. They took that and they brought the girl back. And we heard that, and it's a true story, a true story.

Anyway, like I heard that they stole some girls from way down there [downriver]. The true story is this really fine feather on a swan—the big swans. Not the top feather but really fine feather right next to the body [the down]. Look like cotton. She got a sack of that, one of the oldest ones. She got sack of that. They're packing it back. I think they're going this way up north or something like that. But anyway, every once in a while she'd put a little feather in her mouth, and she'd wet it, and she threw it out. When it dries out it gets bigger. And that's how they tracked them. Her brother and them tracked them behind, and they catch up with them some place on the ocean. I don't know which way. Maybe that way, this way, wherever the ocean is. And that's where they were. And this guy, this couple [of her] brothers and other people, they all together, and they [had] a lot of canoes there. They come over with canoe. And lot of canoes down there. And they just cut the things [canoes] open, cut the bottom[s] off.

This little girl was down under a [smoke] hole someplace. And they were lying down and this one man [a guard] was lying there, and she say, "Oh, my brother!"

"Don't say that! Don't say that!" they say.

"What [did] that kid say?" that man say.

"Oh, that kid's just dreaming. She don't mean to say what she say. She's just dreaming."

But she can see that her brother [is] lookin' through that hole. To let them know this is what they did. And people know that they're there. So pretty soon everybody was there, and they just had to kill them off. Cleaned them out and took his sisters back.

When them Stick Indian steals a woman or girls, especially young girls they always take.

What we call "kidnapping."

Yeah. Anyway, they *do* something to them so that they can get used to them. They're that kind of people. So whoever they steal will not be the same person that we know, that left our village. She's just a different person.

When you bring them back [home] you do like this. You use your spit and you do like that [gestures] to them so that they can calm down. Otherwise they're really wild, very wild for long time. They rub them down with their spit all over like this [gestures]; everybody do that to them. And that's how they get back to normal. But at the same time, if it's a woman, she could be the best sewing person, sewing stuff, and she'll be a rich woman. That's what they give her. And some of the people that we know around here used to been. The one we know used to sew a lot and make lots of money for that stuff. I guess when they get 'em that's what they give 'em.

Have you seen people that came back from there? From the Stick Indians?

Well, you see, that's the same people that they stole, that they brought back. Like the man [who wanted] to get his daughter back. They gave his daughter back to him. They didn't give her [back] here; they didn't do it that way. They left her in an old house up someplace, 'round there, close. And that's where they found her. And they took the stuff [ransom] all right.

ANOTHER STORY ABOUT STICK INDIANS

A long time ago, I see right around Kechumstuk country, this is a long time story, long time before time. They're the same people, they're Native people. They look like Native people. But this guy, one evening, he went hunting. He go *way* up the hill. And he was looking *way* out, lookout. Anyway, why he's coming up the hill like this, and this guy track him all the way up there. And way down there, about halfway down the hill, there's brush [growing] together like this [gestures]. He come through that.

In evening time just before dark he was going to go home. He don't see anything, so most of the time he was watching that guy. He went to that place where the brush comes together like this, and he didn't go across. He keep watching; he's still over here somewhere. Soon as he went through that brush he just went like this [gestures] and start getting up. Start getting up, and they don't hit him pretty easy. Soon as he went like this [gestures], he shot 'em right through the chest. He kill that Stick Indian.

Man, I tell you, there was nothing but beads all over him. Just beaded things. And he took all that beads off, and he put it way up in the trees. He put it in the birch bark. He wrap it and put it *way* up there. And he's *scared*. He never tell anybody he killed the guy. After he killed him, he took all the beads off, and what he did is he take him to the creek, little creek, like. Wet creek? He pull all the moss and he just bury him in the creek, put the moss all over him. And he didn't tell anybody for how long.

I think two years later he told people that he did that. So they took the beads and necklace and stuff like that. There wasn't hardly any necklace around this country. But wherever they come from, that's where their necklace come from. Anyway, why he told 'em. So he tell 'em a story about it. He killed one [Stick Indian].

For how many years they [the Stick Indians] look for him. They look for that [missing] guy. They look and look and look for that guy— that one missing. The one that got killed. It's in Kechumstuk area, I'm sure. That's what they all say. That's where they [he] killed him. And for how many years they look for this guy. They seems to know what that guy look like. They're looking.

The reason why I say that is, one of the old man from Mansfield he left stove in Dihthâad. That's way this side of the village about a mile and a half. He left his stove there. He came down here to pick up his stove, and he's packing his Yukon stove back to Mansfield. There was two of them, he say, two of them Stick Indians. Anyway, this [Stick Indian] guy was just going to shoot him, shoot at that guy from Mansfield. And this guy, his teeth is *all* messed up. His teeth is coming out here [and] here [gestures]. Really bad teeth.

And he heard, "Oh, Naxaxa'ẹh!" And he heard them so he looked that way, and he see that that [is] not the guy that killed the guy [the other Stick Indian]. So they all almost kill him; they thought it was him. But after they looked down there, they know it's not him. That's how people know they're looking for that guy.

They're looking for him for don't know how long. But gee, I don't know how many years. That was all when I was small kid, when it happened. During my days, I never heard anything in my life.

I thought about the Stick Indians all the time. [One time] we were camping way out. I was big enough, maybe [between ten and fifteen] years old. I was big enough to handle a .30-.30. So I must be ten or twelve years old. Ten years old or something like that. And I'm going up the creek like this, way up creek. There's brush and spruce trees and all that up the creek and I'm going up one side, the high side. About halfway up I *hear* something while I was walking. God—I hear something I never heard before. Gee, [it's] making all kinds of noise, and this is in September. Oh, all kinds of noise.

I told my wife about it many times, so we could tell it to our grand-kids. We told it to our grandkids before. I hear something, somebody talking. I don't understand what they say. Gee, I scared too, *really* scared. I was shaking. I want to go home, yet I want to see what the hell is making that noise because it's dangerous for my family. I was just a kid, I think. Not too old. Ten or eleven years old. And I'm big enough to handle a .30-.30 good, I know that. In that time you don't have all kinds of shells. I think I have twenty rounds or something like that. 'Cause I know. I put six in the magazine and one in the barrel. I'm ready. And I held some shells in my hand. I go a little at a time, little at a time, up on the side of the hill. Pretty soon I hear it right straight down, almost up at the end of that creek. And it's like this [gestures], way up here. I hear it down here, right straight down here. I go up a little farther.

Now I hear it back *this* way a little bit. So gee, I got to go down. It sounds like people. They're together before they can kill us, I thought. They're going to come into our camp later—that's what I thought, my thought was. Well, I'm going to get a few before they do that. So I walked on [in] high spruce trees. They don't have limb all the way down to the ground. Pretty high, like. And I can see people go down like this [gestures]. Easy, I can see them standing or sitting in that brush somewhere. Sounds like they're close, but gee! I take a quick rest, and I go ahead again [laughs]. I'm getting closer and closer. Gee, I can *see* them the way it sounds. Nobody. I don't see nobody. Pretty soon I crawl a little bit, then they make lots of noise. When they make noise, I go. When they quit, I quit.

Gee, just a little ways I can see them. But nothing. Nothing. All the trees stand up like this, but this one tree goes like this [gestures]. You see a lot of them trees. Limb, like. You know trees that are just about to fall? It's just like that. And there's seven owls [laughs]. Little ones. Seven little owls trying to learn how to talk. That's what they were.

That's what you were hearing?

Ooooh. *That's* what I been hearing. Oh gee, thank God. I sit there sweating, sweating to death. Gee, I felt good. I got back on the side of the hill, and I went back home and I told my Dad. He says this time of year a lot of young ones is trying to learn how to talk. You hear lots of things. They're learning how to talk and that's why you hear lots of things, he say. And I told him about that owl. And they're young ones. "That's why they say that," he say. "You can hear a lot of that." And I experienced that owl.

Another time, I was upriver by myself. I was hunting. And I was hunting way out in the lookout, and I was coming back to the boat. And I got way upriver, and I was coming downside of the bank from way out in the brush. And I hear a whistling. Someone whistling at me. What? I stop. My boat was way down that way and somebody whistling down that way [gestures]. I was way out in the brush on the bank [thinking], "What the hell is that?" Then I go ahead again, and I hear whistling again. Then I go look down the river and nothing. My boat's down there. I don't see nothing. It was a bend like that, and I was way back here. Pretty soon I come to the river. Then I want to find out what it was.

I got to go that way anyway to my boat. Anyway. It was a couple beavers was sitting down there on the sandbank by the river. And they were eating this cottonwood. And once in a while they'd lay out that whistle. And that's what it is. [Phone rings.] And I remember my Dad always tells me that little beavers are the ones that say that, most of the time. They learn how to talk.

But the Stick Indians I heard it's very true about it. I heard stories about it. I was too small at the time; I was really young when all this good thing happen. But we heard lots of true stories about it. It's something that I didn't see. I never heard anything.

But Stick Indians have faded away like medicine people. I would say back somewhere in thirties—somewhere '34, '35 , somewhere in there. Then nobody hear no more [stories] of that kind. Before I went in the army, we seen somebody trying to steal a kid. I don't know what in the heck he was trying to do, but me and my friend, we were sitting up all night. We just got there from Tetlin. We were hunting muskrat up there, me and my brother. Way this side, between Tetlin and Northway. And season was closed so we went back. We went back to Northway so we could get on the boat to come back. And my brother worked on that boat, anyway. And the boat is there and worked on that boat every day and I just waited and waited until he gets ready.

So this guy, his brother have a tent back there with lots of kids, three or four kids, and his wife in the tent. And he's out hunting ducks or something. That night a dog was barking like heck. Gee whiz, we looked around and nothing! We were in the house. He told me, "Don't go out." I wanted to see what it is. And from behind the tent he trying to lift that tent. They put logs around the tent to hold the tent down and they peg it. He trying to lift that. And I can see his butt sticking out one side trying to pull that out. Pretty soon I see the whole man with blue coat, with blue overalls. And I can just see that he's a Native person. I told him, "Gee whiz," and he took off. The guy's brother, Esau his name, I went behind him, and [laughs] he *really* running after that guy.

Did you holler at him?

No, he got that gun. He want to shoot him! But that guy is running too damn fast. He just lost him already, not too long away. That night we waited for him. We waited a long time for him, and he never come back. This time we just stayed and stayed and watch, watch, watch. He never come back.

What was he after, do you think?

I think he was after the kids. I'm sure. That's what we thought. He wanted to steal something, somebody. That house is like this [gestures]; that's where he was, where my friend was. About the length of this reach here, we're up this way. That's where we have our tent. Right across from the store here [gestures]. Over here was close to the store, Herman Kessler's store. And the boat was right down here [gestures], on the bank. And that's where my brother work, evening time. High banks down in front of that village.

We have little tent, eight-by-ten tent, is all we had, me and my brother. I think my sister was with us that time, too. And three of us was in there. And me and my sister, we sitting outdoors in front of the tent. We have a stove out there. My sister cook on it. And I see a man hid just to the other side of that bank. Once and a while he come out like this [gestures], all the way down. Gee whiz, I told my sister about it. She's scared to run down there. So she went back behind like this [gestures] and she holler to that girl that was in the tent—she was outdoors. And she told the people. They went like this [gestures] to the river and they couldn't find him. They didn't see nothing. They figured he went in the river.

(Laughs.)

I was positive I seen a man. Two or three times he come out. He'd look around and he'd go back down. He'd go a little ways and he'd do that.

And that's how I seen him. During the bright daylight, evening time. And that's the time that I seen that. It's not a ghost.

What do you call it in your language?

Gu̱u̱.
   And Herman Kessler he have a store in the old village. That's the same year, the same spring. We all sitting around in front of the store. He have a *big* tent, and they have the store inside the tent. And people were buying all the time. They buying the fur and stuff like that. We can see the trail a long ways. Somebody was walking and coming this way. We were all sitting in front of the store. Somebody was walking, just coming up this little knoll, and you can see them coming up into the village. He came across over a little flat and he was gone. That's the same year that I seen him in the village. That's the same guy, I think. And they saw it down there. Me, I was there when they seen him. And I'm sure that's the *same guy.*

He's Indian, do you think?

Yeah. Looked like it. But I didn't see what kind of clothes he was wearing. All I see was his head that time. Anyway, why this time he was wearing those blue jeans, bib overalls. He was wearing that, I'm sure. That and a blue shirt, I'm sure. The one that coming in to that old village, to the store. And we thought he was going to come up pretty soon. And Matthew says, "Gee whiz, where's that guy?" He's not going back, and we didn't see him going anywhere. So we all run down there and . . . nobody! And everybody got scared.

(Laughs.)

Now we don't know if somebody going to kill us or what. Then I told my brother, "Let's get the hell out of here, go back to Northway." That time, Nabesna, they call it. We went back to the village, and we stayed there after that and don't hear anything more. All that time we were down there between Tetlin and Northway, and we never heard any-thing when we were muskrat hunting. But when we got to the village, that's when we started hearing things. But anyway, that's what the people call "Gụụ." "Naxaxa'ẹh," they call it in my language. It mean, "You hear them out there in the brush but don't see 'em." Sometimes they throw stick at the people, and all that. They can hear 'em, but they can't see 'em. That's what you call " Naxaxa'ẹh." That's something that you don't see, but you hear 'em. You know it's Gụụ.

I don't know. It fade away somewhere around [19]34 or '35. Somewhere around there it quit. No more. You don't hear that no more. Like I say, all my life I been out in the country and I don't hear nothing. I never see anybody. But Northway I have seen [ghosts] a couple times. That's all the experience that I have.

Do other people tell you about it, too?

Oh, *lot* of people talking about it. They *hear* 'em. *All* the time.

But not recently.

No, not since '34 or '35. Somewhere in there. That fade away, too.

CHAPTER 4

Greetings from Uncle Sam
World War II

In 1942, when he was twenty years of age, Kenny was drafted to serve in the U.S. Eleventh Army Air Corps. He was first stationed at Ladd Air Force Base in Fairbanks, now known as Fort Wainwright, and was then shipped out to the Aleutian Islands. Military historian John Cloe estimates that "Approximately one thousand men died in battle or were counted missing in action during the course of the Aleutian Campaign," which lasted from June 10, 1942, to August 15, 1943. From the Aleutians Kenny was sent on to Okinawa, an island in the Western Pacific south of Taiwan. Following the amphibious invasion of Allied forces on April 1, 1945, Okinawa claimed the most casualties of any Allied campaign against Japan in World War II. In the following three months over 14,000 Americans died, while 35,000 were wounded, and the Japanese suffered more than 107,000 dead. Another 42,000 Japanese civilians were killed by artillery shells and bombs. The bloody and bitter fighting finally came to an end within a few days after the United States dropped atomic bombs on Hiroshima and Nagasaki on August 6 and August 9, 1945. For a young man sent far from his family and culture, it was indeed a terrible time.

ARMY DAYS

You want to tell me how you got in the army?

Well, I used to trap from here to Kechumstuk. All the way to Chicken, I would say. I have a camp at Gold Creek, I have my base camp would be at Kechumstuk; from there I travel away to set my lines [to] Dick's Ranch all the way down, like Long Cabin, Big Hill, and I run my line up there. I came back 1942, early '42, in February. About the middle of February, because I used to work [in] '41 when the war broke out, and I used to drive a Cat [Caterpillar tractor or dozer] for Adam Green and Morrison-Knutsen [construction company]. I walk the Cat from Delta all the way to Northway.[1] A whole bunch of Cat, about twelve Cats, I think. That's before I went in the army. I made good money.

Then I walked a Cat all the way from Slana to here. I was using all our trails, our Native trails. And I just follow that, so it made it kind of easy, but this one here from Delta is a guess. I know where Robertson, Johnson [Rivers are]. I knew all of that because I ran the boat between here and Delta. I know where Robertson, where Johnson, Gerstle, Big Gerstle, Little Gerstle. I know all of that creek. I know where they at. And that's how I brought that Cat through here to Northway.

Anyway, when I came back in February of '42, early '42, when I brought all my traps back in. I mean I picked up my trap and put it away for the winter. I came back about the middle of February, about the tenth of February. Then my sister and my cousins said, "Kenny, they're going to want you in the army. I think they going to draft you. You got a greeting card here." A greeting *letter*. The whole letter got a big deal on it that says, "Greetings."

Anyway, after I tie up my dog team, my sister was so scared. And the whole village is just praying about it. And I notice when I got back from the army they had one flag up there in [the Tanacross Episcopal] church. People were so scared that I was going to get killed. They had one flag in the church. I went to church after that, after I got back from the army, and I asked that man, "Why you have that flag here?"

"That's supposed to be *you*!" [laughs.] "Every time people go to church, they pray for you. That's why it's there," he said.

American flag?

Uh-huh. Gee, before I went in [to the army] I didn't see no American flag there, but when I got back there was one there.

Anyway, why gee whiz, I didn't know what to do with it [the government letter]. There was no telephone, no nothing. I was drafted. So the road [Alaska Highway] was just starting to build, and there's no way I can get in [to town], and at that time a plane comes in once a month with the mail. And no transportation between here and Fairbanks.

Is this wintertime?

Wintertime. It's in February. And I got no way to go in. So, hell, the day I came back and I got to go to Fairbanks to Ladd Field. That's where my physical [exam] is going to be. They want me there for my physical.

And you're the only one from here?

I'm the only one between Fairbanks and the border with Canada. I'm the only Native person was in the army for the Second World War [from this area]. There's a gentleman who went with me at the time; he joined the army because I went in there. He wanted to be with me. He joined the army, but his health was bad so they turned him down. He came back, and I stayed. I didn't want to stay, but I did [laughs].

Anyway, why they put me through the physical and, gosh, the army [said], "You're the one we're looking for" [laughs].

(Laughs.)

I'll go back a little bit. I got drafted and I got no way to get to Fairbanks, and I went to the biggest company commander here that just moved in over here [at the Tanacross airfield].

The road crew?

No, no. The army crew. The army guys come in. Then plane and everything landed on that [airstrip] . . .

You mean right here?

Yeah, and I went to the company commander, I guess, what they call it at the time. I don't know who he was. I told him I wanted to see the biggest boss there. So they took me there, and I told them I got drafted and I have no way to go to Fairbanks, to Ladd Field.

"Oh, I'll get you there in a little bit," he said. So they get one of their planes, I guess, and they flew me to Fairbanks, to Ladd Field. That's how I got to Ladd Field.

Before they were building this airstrip, right here?

That's already there. Like I told you about that air base long time ago that was built by hand. The army, when they come in, they made it bigger with a dozer and stuff like that and [airplanes] land on the gravel. And later on in the days, I guess they did blacktopped it, later on. But at that time they were just using the gravel field.

So they took me into Fairbanks and Billy Paul went with me. I got my physical and I was in. From there I went to Fort Richardson [Anchorage]. At the time when we got it, there was hardly any soldiers. Not many soldiers. They needed the soldiers very, very bad. Not too many soldiers when the war broke out. Not very many. So they put me one week in training. One week time. I was in perfect health, and I was just really tough.

You got to be tough to live in this country. I was making a living off the country. And this is what they need. And I was raised with a gun in my hand. I don't miss anything. I was trained not to miss anything—rabbit, grouse, or whatever, the game. I was raised with a gun in my hand. I understand how to use it. I know to use gun, and I know what to do with it. I got in the army, I was in boot camp, and I was a sharpshooter. I got medal for the sharpshooter. I was teaching the people, like you, from the Lower 48 that comes, that never seen a gun in their life. I was teaching them. Right away I got three stripes, Buck Sergeant, for doing that.

I didn't tell them about the time I was home. I used to work in a mining camp, I used to run Cat and stuff like that, heavy equipment. But when I was in the army I wanted to be a flyer. I wanted to fly up in the air. And I got in the Army Air Corps, Eleventh Air Corps. It's the same thing as the air force today. That's my company, Eleventh Air Corps. And later on, they find out that I can do heavy equipment. That's when I was in Adak.[2]

They find out that I can run a Cat in the wintertime [through] a lot of snow. I'd start the Cat and got on, and could do all that stuff. They're trying to plow the airfield, and they notice that I handle that before. What happened is, from there, they stuck me in the combat engineers because they found out I was heavy equipment operator. I was in the air force. But I was detached to combat engineers. From there I went to Kiska [Aleutian Islands]. You know, Kiska was the last when Japanese already left? I got there.

Did you fly down, or . . .

No, no no. I went on a ship. No, I didn't fly at all. After I got to be a combat engineer, I was still in the air force but I was detached to the engineers. From there on, I run equipment, mostly building the roads, is what I did. And from there, we went to Kiska from Adak. Shemya first, and then to Adak, and then from Adak I went on a ship to Kiska. We attack Japanese. We got to Kiska. And we just got on the island and then we went. We got radios on us.

Did you land on the beach?

Oh, yes. On a tugboat. Just *nobody!* Nobody on there. All Japanese took off. I'm sorry to tell you this, but there was more American kill each other than they did Japanese. No Japanese there.[3]

I see that because little while ago I told you I was teaching the people, like you, that never seen gun in their life and never been out in the boondock like I did. I was raised out in the country. I was raised with a gun in my hand. These people never saw a gun in their life, never went hunting in the brush, in the thing like this, and they don't know how it is. And they know how to pull the trigger, so they shooting at something that they don't see right. They shooting at anything that move, them people. That's how they mistake, killing each other.

But I was trained not to do that kind of thing. You know, me. All my life my grandpa, my Dad, my mother [said], "Don't shoot at something that you don't know what you're shooting at." Anything could be moving, could be man. You see, them days we're not trained to kill people. But we were trained to be ready for the war. Like when we stay in our camp, in our tent, we can't throw our jacket in one corner and our shoes over there, and our socks over there. We can't do that. We got to put it somewhere where we can just grab it now and put it on right now and ready to go. That's how we were trained.

Handling a gun, my grandpa and my Dad at the time, [said], "For the game, you got to see the head. You got to see the ears before you shoot. Don't shoot something that move. Somebody might be over there. Even if you're scared, don't shoot something that you don't see." And that's the way I was brought up.

It was tough, I tell you. I was okay then, I was brave. I was brave. I was with a couple guys that always are like brothers to me. When I went in, they were there at the boot camp, and we went . . . no, Clark is only one at the boot camp. Victor, he was in the combat engineers. All three of us were together all the time. They're white people, but they're like brothers to me. For three years I been with them. Two and a half, three years we were all together all the time. We did lot of things together. We fought together, we play together, we sing together. Just like brothers.

I left there after we find out that Japanese left Kiska. They pulled out and there's nobody there. So we went back from there to the boat and from . . . where was that? Shemya , I think. I don't know where in the heck we got to. I think it's in Shemya or Dutch Harbor.

Well, after we got back from Kiska, the boys is all together. We're all together, three of us. Nobody shot at us, but there's a lot of Americans killed each other [more] than they did Japanese because there's nobody there, they pulled off. Anyway, after we got back to Dutch Harbor, I'm pretty sure it's Dutch Harbor is where we took off on the ship. Then from there we went to Okinawa.

What kind of ship was it?

Gee, I don't know. I remember USS *Yukon,* I'm pretty sure. You know that USS *Yukon.*[4]

A cruiser or battleship or . . .?

No, no, no. It's cruiser. They were using that before the war, but they were [also] using that for the war. It says on there: "USS *Yukon.*" I guess I don't know what the "SS" stands for, but I remember I got really [sea]sick on the damn thing [laughs]. Anyway, why we were all together; we're still together. Oh, we're going out to the front. We're going to have fun! And sometimes we feel sad, but you know all three of us taking [care of] each other. We're all hold hand, trying to be happy all the time.

OKINAWA

Anyway, after we got to Okinawa, we find out it's not piece of cake, you know? We find out we don't get no bacon and eggs every morning. It's terrible. And we were out on the [battle]front. Those engineers, combat engineers, is always out on the front. And Clark was a truck driver, and I was a Cat driver. I was in all trades, like heavy equipment operator. Like I was running the grader, I was running the front-end loader, and everything. I done that back home, you know? They got everything. They got stuff to build the roads with, at the time. We were building pontoon bridge across the river, getting trucks and stuff over there. And we do that at night. And the time we got back, oh two weeks, I guess we were there. Two or three weeks I would say. We were building lots of roads, and we were going to the front all the time, going ahead.

And Victor went. They were taking five hundred at a time. Five hundred people at a time to the front. Five hundred from different groups: five hundred from air force, five hundred from infantry, five hundred from signal corps. You know, just put them out on the front. And the second group that went out, Victor went out [with them]. Victor went in this five hundred group. And later on, maybe third or fourth group, Clark went out. And the few people that I know, the camp that I was in that came back, few of them. First, Victor didn't come back. We notice that. Some of them came back. Some of them got shot. And we know that he's gone.

Anyway, well Clark finally went. It don't take one day. This is long, long, long world war. We're out there on the front, gee whiz. While you're out there in the Cat, or you're out there shooting somebody all the time. Either way, I'm all over. I'm not on the Cat all the time. Only time I'm on the Cat is when we have to make roads. And I got shot at on the Cat many times, but I made it back. I had gun and stuff like that on the Cat. And hand grenade and stuff like that.

Anyway, why we fought and fought and fought. Me and Clark were together for a little while after we lost Victor. And we're in a foxhole, and I was just shooting all over the damn place and people getting killed, and some people just so damn scared, crazy. People don't know what the hell they're doing. I've seen first lieutenant from the foxhole shooting damn .38 pistol up in the damn air, just hollering like hell. I have to throw him back into the damn hole. That's just how bad it was. I'll just say a little bit about it because my nerve was bad when I got back. And I'm afraid that my nerve will come back if I . . . you know.

But I was there many times when we're in the foxhole together, me and Clark. We're the only ones left. And I remember one time these people was shooting like hell at us, and he was singing: "Jesus Hold My Hand." He was singing that really loud. "KENNY!" he said. Oh, he make me so happy. I was scared, and you know, we all sing together in the foxhole. He was singing, "Jesus Hold My Hand." And gosh that really make me feel good for the rest of the day. Make my day.

We made it through that day all right, but you know we're together. Pretty soon I got back. Then we went back again, and he got into next group without *me*. Next five hundred was without me. And I was building the road. And they don't need him for [driving] the truck. So he got in and went ahead with this group, and I find out that Clark didn't come back.

Oh did I come . . . I just didn't give a damn. I lost my brother. I felt like I lost my brother. I felt really bad. Clark didn't make it. Where is Clark? If I found him I could have buried him. But there's so many people that got killed, so many people that never was buried. It's just something terrible.

Like today. Like me, I grew up in a different world. I'm not trained to kill, but like I say, before that when we're all [three] together; we used to pray together. We used to laugh together, pray together, and we ask God for help many times. And after I lost him, I didn't do that. I didn't care. I didn't care if I make it or what. I just went for it.

But later on down the line a ways, we went and they pulled us back after, oh God, about a year or less. I would say about every two months or so, they pull us back.

You were living in tents then?

Oh yes. They pull us back and let the other people go ahead. You know, we make change. So anyway, why that's what they did to us, and like I say, after Clark and Victor I lost them, I didn't care if I got killed or what. I just went for it. I just got really mad. I shouldn't have, I guess, but I did.

Could you explain what you meant, "I just went for it"? I don't quite understand that.

Well, I felt really bad. Two of my buddies never come back from the front. And with the third bunch I went out with, I really went out there to kill. I don't care if I got killed or not. I just went. I want to get all I can.

I see what you mean.

Yeah, Craig. I don't like to talk about that today. I'm trying to be a good boy and trying to read a good Bible today, and I ask God for forgiveness for what I did, and I'm not proud of what I did, but I really miss my friends today yet. They're white people. I live with them people for three, four years. They're just like brothers to me. I don't have brothers. They're brothers to me, and I lost them, and that's why I really got mad. I didn't care. They took my buddy. I like to go on with them, but somehow the little man upstairs got me back.

I got a lot of buddies that's good friends, but they're not close like me and Clark and Victor, you know. We were together for three years! I know a lot of other people, but like quite a few of them people I used to live with in the barracks and stuff like that, and I met them and I know lot of them that went out together to the front.

But it's something that some of my buddies did after everything quiet down. Some places they cut [off] Japanese ears and they put them in vinegar [laughs]. I seen that. I took the money. I brought [it] back. Remember that money that I brought back, Ellen? Them little bitty money. Them bills? Just small. It's smaller than ours, Japanese [yen]. I brought back whole bunch of that, and that's all. And I trying to take one of this gun that they had. I wanted to bring that back, but I had so much things on my way back, when I was coming back for discharge. I was going to bring one back, and I was only allowed 150 pounds. But too much load and hell, I didn't care if I didn't bring it back anyway. I'm worried about *my* life. I was really in a bad shape. My nerve was so bad.

When did you leave Okinawa then?

Oh, I was there for VJ Day, from '43 to VJ Day.[5] See I got in the army early '42. February 20, 1942, about three months after the war broke out [with the bombing of Pearl Harbor on December 7, 1941]. And I didn't get back until '46. And so that's been quite a few moons in there. Anyway, why it's something that I had a good experience, and my nerve was pretty darn bad.

You saw that little air base [now an FAA airfield] in Gulkana? I spent thirteen months there.

In Dry Creek?

Yeah, in Dry Creek. Then I served time in the army here in Alaska, most of the time. But I went down the chain. I went to Shishmaref, Dutch Harbor, all over. From Shishmaref is where I went to Okinawa.[6] I was in Kiska. We was going to shoot all the Japanese off Alaska. They got that and they took off before we got there and there was no Japanese in that country. More Americans kill each other than they did Japanese. It's a shame to say that, but that's the way it went.

You told me one time that you got wounded too, huh?

Yeah. I got wounded here in my arm. I just got Purple Heart about six weeks ago.

Really? Oh, congratulations.

See where I got shot here [demonstrating with sleeve rolled up]? I got shot from here to here. You see that, huh? That's where I got shot. And they just find out that I was in the war, and I just got a Purple Heart here not too long ago. And you see that picture there? Bring it over here. Get it. This is the time when I was receive my Purple Heart. That's about six months ago. And this here is my friend, Richard Frank.

I don't know where that Purple Heart is, but you can see some of my pins here. I have more pins than that, but when we had fire across the river in our other house that burned up [in old Tanacross], I had all these medals. Like good conduct medals, I have sharpshooting medals,

Family photo of
Kenny (right) receiving
the Purple Heart from
Richard Frank in
Fairbanks, 1999.
Photograph courtesy
of Kenneth Thomas Sr.

and other medals that I had. But I only have just two or three that I
saved. Anyway, that's the only thing that [was] saved out of the whole
thing that I had. But I lost a lot of that in the fire over across the river in
our house. Anyway, this is time about six or eight months ago when
they discover that I was shot in the army and war.

And I really was hit in Okinawa. And this gentleman who took care
of my wound here, he's a medic, and I met the gentleman at the time,
and he said he was from Delta [Junction]. His name was Robert Johnson. I know the Johnsons. I know Walter and Lawrence Johnson and
them before I went in the army. And this Robert Johnson is Lawrence
Johnson's boy! And I met him in Okinawa. He's the one that patched
my arm when I got shot. And we got to be friends because, well, it's
hundred miles [from Tanacross to Delta Junction], but I felt like he was
from home. So close, you know. He made me feel good when I talk to
him. Oh, somebody from home, ha! ha! Hundred miles away, but still
then it makes you feel good.

Anyway, he's the one that patched my arm, and then really I was
sorry that I didn't get to see him. I missed him by two months or something like that. You know I go by the place. He had that big sign like,
big sign: "R. L. Johnson, Tractor for Rent." Rental. And I see that all the
time. And I told my wife, I say, "I know the gentleman here that when I
got shot, he took care of my arm." And I want to see him. How many
time we look for him; he wasn't there. But the last time I went there to

look for him he [had] died. He had a stroke or stuff like that. He died, and I was real sorry I didn't see him before he died, but he's the guy that really took care of my arm.

Did they have like a field hospital there?

No, no. Hardly. In the tent is the only thing we ever have. We don't have hospital in a house like this. No, we're just in tent on a bunk bed or something like. Sometime we don't even *have* that, just mattress maybe. And they took care of us good. But, a lot of times we went places where we have rest camp and stuff like that, to different place where we can be relax, for month or so. Then we hit it again. And I'm glad to see that VJ Day, I'm telling you. But I'm not the same guy as I was when I went out. I was really tough when I went out, and I wasn't very tough when I got back because my nerve was *bad*.

You probably saw so much.

Yeah. Anyway, I never thought I could be a man like this again. I was so bad shape. I couldn't stand nobody behind me. I couldn't stand to see blood. Oh, just terrible. I couldn't go in the brush by myself. So little while ago I told you about how that medicine man did that; that was back in '46 or '47. [Phone rings.] Anyway, I went in the army. At first I thought the army want me to stay in the army, but I didn't want to. They want to send me over to Germany, someplace in different country, just for me to stay in the army. I didn't want to. I told the company commander that I really had a problem with my nerve, and I wanted to see if it going to do me any good if I get home. If that might do me some good if I get home. So I'm all for to go home, you see, what I can do for my nerve.

Anyway, I keep going back to the army hospital in Ladd Field. And they keep giving me some pills, and this time last time that they gave me pills, they gave me 180 pills, a big bottle. "Kenny, you got to take this every day. If we're going to help you, we're going to help you. You ask God to help you with these pills," he told me. And I asked God. I wanted to be back where I'm at years ago. And I keep taking that pills every day, every day. I'm getting better and better all the time. Sometimes it comes back; sometimes I just don't feel it.

What kind of pills?

It's a nerve pill, nerve pill. Anyway, why pretty soon I got to be by myself. It don't bother me at all. But once in a while I get nervous, but you can tell that I've been somewhere [laughs].

Oh yeah.

Anyway, why it's nothing to be proud of. I'm not proud of what I did. But I did something that I didn't want to do, but I did. But you know I was brought up in my lifetime that I wasn't trained to kill. You know, I love people. And I always love people whether they're different from me or what. But I love people because we're all just like one. And I ask God for forgiveness today for what I did, and many times, I think, a lot of missionaries tell me God will forgive me for things that I did. Now I don't worry about things that I did. I did for a while, for quite a long time.

And I always say, in the Ten Commandments they say, "Thou shall not kill." I brought up with that in my hand when I was a kid. My Dad always tells me; my Mom always reminds me of Ten Commandments. "Thou shall not steal; thou shall not lie." You know, all that good stuff that's in there. And my Dad say, "If you obey this, I don't have to worry about you," he say. He always tells me. And my Mother tells me same thing. So now my Dad always say, "Don't take something that don't belong to you. You ask somebody before you take this."

But now today you see breaking in. Lock the door. When I was a kid there was no padlock that I remember of. We just put all the stuff in the cache and no padlock. We don't even know what padlock is, and all the food. Next person comes you don't even *think* about looking in there. They're not going to take anything unless they ask. But like I said a while back, the world is changing, bad. I mean different world from the time I was a kid until now. I seen a hell of a big change. So anyway, I thought this [was] going to be okay when I got back, but for two years I couldn't stand anybody behind me. I'm always on alert. I got five years [in the] reserve. I can go back in the army anytime. And I go to army place where I can get anything I want, like . . .

PX [Post Exchange]?

Yeah. Oh I was good about that, and in the meantime I'm trying to forget. I just work, work, work all the time, and I'm okay as long as I'm on the Cat or truck or something like that. That way you get your mind off of something always, not remember about army days. It took me while not to think about what happened, but I'm mostly on the Cat and making good money. Trucks and graders and stuff like that. Heavy equipment operator is what I am. I helped build all these roads up here.

So that was good for you when you come back, to get work?

Well, yeah, that helped me quite a lot. It really did help me quite a lot, for my nerves. And pretty soon I got to feeling pretty darn good, and we got married, me and the wife. And we have childrens, and like I say I work all the time, and we had some good days and bad days, but we made it pretty darn good, and we've been married for fifty-three years right now, going on fifty-four. So three years ago we had our fiftieth anniversary, and we celebrate that with bunch of my friends from down lower Yukon, from all over the country. And we had seventeen musicians come up here and play violin. And people from Fairbanks, Anchorage, Minto, Northway, Tetlin—everybody came—Copper River. We had a big time to help celebrate our fiftieth anniversary. We have a tape of that.

Well, when you were in the army were you homesick for Tanacross?

Well, I did for a while.

You missed speaking your language?

Yes. You know a lot of times at the front, I wish I had somebody, that guy can talk my language to, on the other end. And really you always talk back and forth. If I had somebody that can understand me back there, it will help me lot talk back and forth on the radio. Japanese they understand damn English too. But for my language, it help me quite a lot.

I guess they had a lot of these Navajos; they called them "code-talkers."

Well, that's what they say. All the time. All the time. How many years
that I was there, at the front. I never seen one Navajo or outside Indians at all. All I see is Spanish. Mostly Spanish I see.

No Eskimos from Alaska?

No. I don't remember seeing Eskimos, really. Like I say, I wish I did. I'll
feel better if I see anybody that is from Alaska, at least. Like this
gentleman here, from Delta, he's a white guy, but we got to talking
about Delta and I knew his Dad and uncle and them, and he make me
feel like I know somebody from home, even though he's a hundred
miles away from here. I never saw him before, but even then he make
me feel good. He give me big lift, and I felt good when I talked to the
guy. So anyway, why I never saw any Eskimos. I really don't remember
seeing them.

Do you want to stop [talking]?

No, no. It's all right.
    Anyway I seen a lot of white people, a lot of white people. More
white people than anything else. There was a few colored people,
mostly white people. But there was 250 or so many people in Shemya
were colored people. But they got different camp than us, and they
keep them one place.

Oh, they segregate them, huh?

Yeah. You know there's so damn many of them; 250 is a lot at the time.
And they killed their company commander. They hang him. They
don't know who did it, so damn many. That's the time I was in the
[Aleutian] Chain.

Shemya?

Shemya. Anyway, they couldn't put anybody in jail because they can't
prove who *did* it. So they have to restrict them in one place. At the
time, if it was me that took care of the people, like a boss, you would

say, I would send them to the front. Would you? I'll send them to the war where they can fight, right? I mean, would you do that?

I don't know.

I mean, they killed their company commander. Why keep them at one place during the war? And here I'm fighting down there. Why restrict 250 people when you can use them out in the front? I can't see that. You know I seen it, but it happen. They restrict them to the camp. They can't go nowhere. They can't get out of there. Whatever. I don't know how long they were like that, but at the time a lot of people were talking about it. And there's a few colored guys. Not very many, mostly white people.

Do you still stay active in VFW [Veterans of Foreign Wars]?

I belong to VFW.[7] I belong to American Legion. I belong to DAV, Disabled [American] Veterans. I belong to that too. So my wife, she's auxiliary, women's auxiliary. She belongs to that. So my army days is something that I'm not proud of it, and I'd like to say that I always kind of afraid to talk about it, and I never told my kids that I got shot until they saw me here in this thing here [points toward photo where he was awarded the Purple Heart].

This was just recent, huh?

Yeah, about six months ago. Anyways, "Gee Dad, were you in the war?" . . . "Yeah."

Well, like I say, it's nothing for me to be proud of. I always worry about it, and is God going to forgive me? And the reason why I say that is I'm brought up with the Ten Commandments in my hand, all the way till I grew up. It was in my family. My Mom always reminds me about this, and my Dad. And I felt like I broke that law. But it wasn't my fault. It wasn't my fault that I did that. And I'm not proud of it, and I *try* not to think about it. I'm trying to forget it because of my nerve. And there's some things that I see that's terrible.

I did some reading about that. When you told me you were in Okinawa, I did some reading about it. They said forty-nine thousand Americans died there.

Oh quite a few wounded and quite a few more that died. God only knows how many. But like I say, you seen people all over, laying around all over. And a lot of people have never been buried in that country. Lot of people that we just scrape them together and just put them in a hole. That's all we ever do. That's when you have time.

I guess Japanese, a lot of them died too.

Oh yes, got to be. Yeah. That's why the war is over. We killed quite a few of them. They know that we're tough. But today, like I say, I'm not proud of what I did. And I don't want to talk any more about it, and I never told my family what I did. I'm not proud of it, and they know I was in the army. And I don't want to say any more about what happened. And the only thing that I wanted to say is that my family was so surprised when they see me [get] that Purple Heart. You don't get Purple Heart for nothing. So I must have went somewhere to get Purple Heart, and I deserve Purple Heart. And when I got out of the army, I didn't care if I got a Purple Heart or what. I didn't want to wait for it.

But later on they found out that I was there, and I deserve this Purple Heart, and one of my brother's kids in Northway have a Purple Heart. So we in the family, we have two Purple Hearts. One of my brother's boys, my nephew, he have a Purple Heart—Sherman [Thomas]. So, yeah that's the thing when I come back. Right now I see people in the army is just peacetime thing, you know? They're there to get training or go to school and get a good education now. The days when I was in, you were out there to fight, not to get training or school or something.

COMING HOME

When I got back, I tell you, when I come back home, this thing was just *oh man!*[8] Right around here, right around the [Tanacross] airport, just nothing but buildings, hangars, hospital, store, PX [Post Exchange]. Oh gosh, the army, just warehouses. You name it, they got it up here.

All that is fallen down now?

No, no, no. They tore it down. Anyway, why when they left, they just let it go. When I got back I come in to a big place. Gee whiz! The army was in full swing yet. I come back through here, and they have a gate out here on the road, MP [Military Police] gate.

You have to go through MP to get to the village?

Yes.

You're kidding me. Really? (Laughs.)

That's the way it was. I come back in to my people, coming through with the bus. The bus got to stop there, and the MP have to check us.

"Congratulations, soldier!" they say. "Glad you're getting out!"

Well, later on they come over, and they always come over and see me and visit. But I don't want to see them. I'm just trying to get away from the whole thing, get away back in the camp. And then the old lady and I got married in [19]48, something like that. And she helped me through my nerve, quite a lot, you know.

Did it feel good to go out and hunt and fish again?

Oh yes, really. After I got back I wasn't shaking that much. Anyway, why gee, what a great day! I come back in that bus. Oh, Fairbanks. I land in Fairbanks. Old John Hajdukovich was waiting for me. I was coming back from Anchorage. Old John was waiting for me, and he got me a room at the Pioneer Hotel. Lacey Hotel, I think.

How did he know you were coming in?

Well, I called. Only thing I remember was the Pioneer cab. I called from Anchorage. Tried to get a reservation in the hotel there, and he happened to have been there in that hotel, and someone told him about it. He stayed there, wait for me. Man, he was just glad to see me. We been together for many, many years, me and John, Herman Kessler, and lot of old-timers in [Big] Delta. Some of them still alive the time I got back. And old Rika [Wallen] was still there.

Was Milo [Hajdukovich] still alive then?

Oh yes, uh-huh. Lot of people still alive. Lot of people died. But like I say, I stayed there a couple days with old John at the Lacey Hotel, I think. Either the Pioneer Hotel or Lacey. Anyway, why he say, "I wanted to get back, but the plane wouldn't go till later on," he say. Well I told him, "I'm going to go up to the army air base and just catch a plane from there." I got to Ladd Field, and I told them about it, and shit right now they get me airplane and take me home.

It's a long, long time. Gee, quite a few years. But I never could forget my language. I talked my language all the same as I did [before the war]. And I understand my language, never lose it all my life. And even today, like how many years that I was in the army I never lost my language.

And like I always say, it doesn't matter. I live with white people most of my life, and that's why I always say, I don't feel any difference between the races. Many of them is just like brothers to me. I got along with many good white people, *good* people. Just like Native people. Lot of [white] people they give their left arm, to be Native people, to live the way I live. They like that. That's the way it is. Like I always say, today I see today that our Native people's kids is lost in this country between two different cultures. The white culture is over here, and the Native culture is over here, and we're all lost in between two different cultures. I see that quite a bit.

And I see most of my people are going over here, quite a bit. Which is good. I like that. They got to have the education. I want them to have the education today because we need that to run our village. They have to run the [Tanacross] Corporation so they can take care of our land, the big money that they have there in the corporation. Somebody got to run that. Somebody got to be the one who fight for our land and our villages, and for right now that I see the way it is today that we got to have education to get a job. If you don't have the education you cannot get a job. And that's the reason why that I like to see when Native people get graduation. It make me feel good. And this is what we need.

I see lot of changes. Native people are changing quite a lot. More of my people is getting educated. More of the people is going to the college. And down lower Yukon, I see in Fairbanks for many from Fairbanks on, I see a lot of Native people are lawyers. I see Native people teachers, and when I see something like that, you know, like in the future, there's going to be more and more of this. Lot of our Native people are graduating from college, and lot of our Native people are getting educated, more than I ever seen in my life. Like I say, maybe next ten years I see everything is going to switch around.

The white people is going to work for the Native people. Right now it's already happened. Right now it's already happened. And we've been working for the white people for how many years? Now the white people is working for the Native people. I see that coming up a lot in the country. Even right here in this little village here [at the Tanacross Tribal Office]. White people is working for us. Not only here, different places. Lot of white people are working for Native people all over.

Long time ago in my days I work for white people all my life. Now they're making changes, that they're working for us. That changes I see. And like I said a little while ago, and I didn't want to say too much about my veterans [days]. I was in the army. Sure I was in the army, and I'm kind of a little bit afraid to talk about it more. Talk about something else, you know.

CHAPTER 5

Changes after the War

Marriage, Road Building, Firefighting, Drinking, and Recovery

Like many soldiers, Kenny's readjustment to civilian life was as stressful as the war itself. Some of the post-traumatic stress he encountered seems related to the profound social and economic changes that took place in Tanacross following his return from overseas. For the village, this was a time of economic prosperity, with many new job opportunities in highway construction and firefighting. Kenny benefited as much as anyone from these opportunities but strayed into several years of hard drinking that drove him into debt and deeply hurt his family. He attributes his remarkable recovery to a Native minister who visited him in the hospital and inspired him to become an alcoholism counselor.

CHANGES IN THE VILLAGE

One thing I'd like to say, is, after I came back from the army I see lot of changes. At the time when I got back people were still trapping. Oscar [Isaac] was trapping, and Julius Paul was trapping, David Paul was still trapping, Billy. A lot of people were still trapping when I got back. But in the summer they always looking for job. When I was kid we didn't even know what *work* is, but what a change when I got back from the army. People always looking for job. Everybody works in the summertime. So that's a big change for the people. We getting away from the subsistence life. The law is coming in. The law is coming in.

The people I left here in '42 were different. When I got back they were different people. They was more modern than when I left them, more in modern way. They have more things. Anyway, the big change was the [Tanacross] airfield. From there on, everybody is looking for job.

They probably had radios by then, huh?

Yeah, they have radios, phonograph, guitar, violins, and stuff like that, that they didn't have when I left. More money came to the village. The biggest change for the village here is when they built this [Tanacross] airfield. That changed the Native people hell of a lot. And I see big change when I got back home. More potlatch, more money.

More gifts at the potlatch?

More gifts in the potlatches, and people start getting booze, getting into the booze, not that much, but some of them do.

Where do they get booze then?

Right here at the airfield.

At the airfield?

Yeah, they have beer at the PX.

And it's open to Natives too?

Yeah. They had it there and they had it in Tok, at the liquor store.
     Anyway, you have to work there before you can get stuff like that. You're entitled to it when you're working at the air base. That made a lot of changes to Native people here, more money and more things. They got more things, that I can see.
     Anyway, when I got back after the war in 1946, I see the changes, quite a bit of changes. Native people are changing because of a lot of money. When I left, most of the people used to live like Native people a long time ago [the subsistence way of life]. But when I got back from the army there was a lot of changes. They live mostly like the white people, try to live like the white people. More money, more money for the food, more money for the different things. Lot of people is working on the [air]field; lot of people, about 50–60 percent working on the field

Aerial view of the Tanacross airstrip and Tanana River in 1950. Old Tanacross appears in the distance on the far bank of the river just to the right of the end of the airfield, on what is today an island. New Tanacross is located on the near side in the heavily wooded area to the left. B86.28.3752. Photograph by Walt Smith, courtesy of Anchorage Museum of History and Art.

and brings in the money for their family. And this place when I got back, oh my God it was ridiculous from what I seen when I left here.

People are changing. More sickness in Tanacross. More people are using [Western] medicine in Tanacross. More people are using eyeglasses in Tanacross. They even have a public health nurse there in Tanacross when I got back. Man, people are using aspirins. Some of that medicines they got no use for. That's what people use all the time. That's quite a change. When I left here there was none of that kind of stuff.

ROAD BUILDING

When I got back out from the army it was 1946. When I went in the army I was 174 pounds. I was just tough, just pure muscle. And when I got out of the army I was *still* 174. I spent three years, eight months, and twenty days in the army, so I came back.

After I got back home in '46, Ellen was really young at the time, and when I got back home, in '47 we got married. And five years ago [in 1997] we just celebrate our fiftieth anniversary.

You knew her before you left, though?

Yeah, I know her. We wrote back and forth, back and forth, [while I was] in the army.

Like sweethearts?

Yeah. And I never thought of going back to trapping, never did. And I look into it, and I wanted to go out and trap, but the [price for] fur is not too good. So I just let it go, and then I didn't trap at all, just work, work, work.

By trade I was a heavy equipment operator. When I apply for the job they notice that I was an operator so they grabbed me right away. And they need me for that road. I'm pretty handy on a Cat. I operate the Cat, I operate the scraper—like a grader on the road, and I run dump trucks, I run drag line, I run low boy [a flat truck for hauling bulldozers]. And mostly I starting out I haul freight, like a low boy to every camp in Alaska. Wherever the road commission were. And I did pretty darn good. I haul to Livengood, sometime I haul to Glenallen, sometime I haul down to [the Canadian] border, wherever the road commission were. Alaska Road Commission is what it was.

Anyway, why I got to be their right-hand man and try to do my best. I was running a low boy all the time, for a long time. Later on, when that Fortymile country start, I was the first one to strip up to Fortymile Roadhouse, where that Taylor Highway comes into the Alaska Highway.

Anyway I start stripping from there, me and my friend. My friend just died the other day, few days ago, few weeks ago. About a week ago, I guess, he died. His name is Vern Johnson. Vern was an operator. He goes that way, and we were just stripping the road, back and forth, back and forth.

When you say, "stripping the road," did you . . .

Survey sticks would be right here. Then another one would be over here, and another one over here [gestures]. That's how wide we have to strip the top layers of that stuff that we have to push over.

The trees and everything?

Trees and everything.

Stumps?

Stumps and the whole shebang. Somewhere you get really big timber then they get laborers. They come in and they knock down all the big trees, and we just push the stumps. Anyway, we went right along. Sometime we bury the damn Cat down in the mud so damn deep and spend many days on it, trying to get it out. And sometime we have to take half a stick of dynamite and just put it on the side and blow that stuff off the side so it'll drain out. Oh, we had a good time. Gee whiz! We would just strip and strip. Same thing every day, every day.

This is for the Taylor Highway?

That's for the Taylor Highway [to Eagle and the Top of the World Highway to the Canadian border]. And we keep on going, keep on going. Some days we get stuck. Sometime it take couple *days* to get out. I remember one place way down Mile 17, we had to have a Cat come in to pull us out. I been on [with] the road commission for a long, long time. Pretty soon I got down to where I can't come back. Seven-twelve is what I'm working.

Twelve hours a day, seven days a week?

Seven days a week.

Holy smokes.

No way to get out of it. Sometime, what we do is we have a base camp here, then we use Cat to go to another base camp, and another one.

Tanacross kids playing on an old D-7 Cat similar to the one Kenny drove. Photograph by Craig Mishler.

When did they sleep?

[Laughs.] Not very much. We have to have a camp here, here, and here [gestures]. People have their own stretch to work on. But us, we just keep on going, keep on going, stripping, stripping. Some days is really nice. Up at Fortymile [River], in that area. All it is, is a tailing pile. We just level that out. That's the easiest part, that Fortymile where that [gold] dredge went through. The easiest part there.

It don't take one day. It take a few moon to do that. Like every season we goes up there. And I start out April, and I never get out of there until December, close to Christmas. I was their right-hand man, really. What I do is every [piece of] equipment on the Taylor Highway, I'd have to haul every bit of it back to Tok for maintenance. They repair everything, all winter long. I don't want to work all winter. I could work all winter, if I want to. Them days, I want to spend time with my wife. We just got married not too long ago, and we just do what we want to do. And I come back after I haul everything and I get laid off, I ask to.

Then I bring everything back, all the Cats and everything. Sometime I drag dead Cat for miles and miles. You don't have that many big low-boy beds. I think we had only two in the whole area. All the steam thing that we have to bring back in, points and everything.

Were you using D-9 [Cat]?

D-8 is the biggest we had. It was a cable blade. Not like today. Today you have this hydraulic and pow-pow, you know. But them days, we use this cable-drum, cable operation. But it went on for years and years. Back in fifties all the way into sixties I worked for them.

Pretty steady work, huh?

Pretty steady. Things got really old. We could run a car into Eagle, then I go just here and there to the spot where they really needed me. And I was down to where I can grade that road with a D-8. When you start grading that damn road with a cable operation, you're doing great. That's one of the best operation you can get. Not very many people can grade road with a cable blade.

I guess I never seen a cable blade.

It works by the drum in the back, behind you. You got to stick that back and forth, here [gestures].

It's on a big spool, the cable?

Yeah. It runs out on top of you and the drum behind you. It goes up and down. It got that blade.

That's how you lower your blade and raise it?

Yeah, that's how. But now they have hydraulic that goes up and down. I went for long time, back in sixties, I would say, and I got an offer from old Bill Adams. I was working for the road commission at the time for the season.

FIREFIGHTING

And Bill Adams was stationed here on the [forest] fire. Bill is a pretty good friend and I tell him what I know about the fire. Long time ago, when we had the fire up on the hillside here. They didn't have C-ration or anything like that back then. We have to bring our own food and everything for firefighting. [Phone rings.] Anyway, Bill, he's the expert on the fire, and he teach me a lot.

This is BLM [Bureau of Land Management], is it?

Yeah, BLM. "Well, I wanted to hire you," he [Bill] say, "to be a fire boss in Alaska." I told him how much money I was getting, $3.50 an hour. Top price an hour for Cat operation. For drag lines and all that stuff.

"Oh, this is no good, Kenny. You just as well work for $10 an hour. You gotta be the boss. You gonna be the boss and fly all over Alaska." So what I do is I'm up there [in an airplane] with a [fire] spotter all the time. I forgot what year. It was in sixties, anyway.

When you started this, it was in the '60s?

Yeah, somewhere in sixties. Anyway, I took him up on the job and I stayed for fifteen damn years. I fly around in the summertime and watch with spotters. Whenever there's a fire, then I man it with people. I land. If the fire is close I hire the people.

You did the hiring, too?

Yes, everything. You know I was making damn good money. Some days I make seventeen hours, eighteen hours, twenty hours. I hire people from way in the hell down in Gambell. Gee, way in the hell down the Kuskokwim [River]. I land at Red Devil; we went up to that Native village there and I hire people.[1] I did all this for fifteen lonely years. And I made damn good money.

Sometimes I take a couple days to train the people. How you can operate water pump, and what to do when you're building trench. All that. I knew exactly what to do, and I train people as I go. When there's no fire I do that. I train people for a couple days. And I make Number One firefighters out of these people right here in Tanacross. You remember that, Ellen?

Ellen: Yes.

Number One fire fighters out of here.

Always call them first?

First people on the fire. I bring the experts in. That's how they go fire to fire till we man it with other firefighters. But they're the first ones to be on the fire, the Tanacross people.

Did you go up in helicopters, too?

Oh, you bet. Every *day!* That's where I'm at all the time, up there! *All* the time. *All* the time. I could be a fire boss over here, and I could be a fire boss twenty miles down that way. I could be fire boss over there too. I tell you, it's really a lot of responsibility. Some places I go to, I had three or four fires, and I had to take care of that as a fire boss. Every day I'm up there; I don't walk. In a helicopter. Every day I got to be on one fire to another.

More than one fire at a time?

Oh, yes. That's how bad it was. I really train a lot of people in Alaska. And I got people from down in Lower 48 come up here. Their ball game is a little bit different. What they're doing down there and what we're doing up here is a little bit different.

Anyway, I took two hundred men from Alaska into Wenatchee [National Forest] down in Washington. I took the fire over in Wenatchee area. When I got there and I got in the helicopter, and I wanted to see the fire. And he said, "Well, I'll take you around."

"What's this line here for?" I swear, they're five miles behind the fire line. Five miles! "What in the hell are you guys doing way the hell back there?" And I know damn well that they shouldn't be way in the hell back there when the fire's not going too fast. It's coming down the hill.

They're just trying to be too safe, huh?

Either that, or they don't know what the hell they're doing. So I told this fire boss—I got him on the radio. I told him who I am and I got two hundred men here. "I seen the fire line way in the hell back there. What in the hell you guys got the fire line way back there for? It's not supposed to be that far back."

"We're fighting this fire, sir."

I said, "We want to get it *out*. That's what I'm here for."

"What would you do?"

I said, "Just follow the fire line, the fire. Get in front of the fire and then burn into it. That's what I'd do. You got any Cat?"

"Yes, I got nine of 'em here," he say.

"Well send 'em down here."

They walk all that Cat down in. They went "chuu, chuu, chuu, chuu." They got one hundred, two hundred people behind us burning into it, backfiring.

Backfiring?

Uh-huh. Gee whiz. From there I took over the whole damn fire by myself. That's a *big* fire, a big fire. We went around that damn thing with a Cat and the people. I took some Idaho people, supposed to be the best. They got the best people from Alaska. We got the best fire-fighters in Alaska; that's what I took.

I was down there for about a month or so. Got the fire out. And gee whiz, they gave me big thank-you from everybody. From there I went to Boise, Idaho. I went down there too, for the fire. Took some men down there. And every time I go, I take a hell of a big responsibility. Every state you go to is different. The ground is different than up here. Here, you build a trench through moss. The moss will smolder, and you build a trench through that. Back there, you just scrape it. Just get all the limbs, them roots that grow in the ground? Just cut them. That's all you got to do. And hell, you can just scrape and go like hell. You don't have to build trench. And all you do is just scrape it away from the fire.

There's bigger trees down there, too.

Yeah. They got good people for that in some places. Like Wenatchee, they had these loggers ahead of us. They had *big* timber, *long* timber. They gotta have a wedge with a chainsaw that's yay long. They going through that. They can put that thing in between a couple trees like that. They were so well trained for that, in Wenatchee. Gee, they burn like gas, them pine trees.

Anyway, up here when I'm not flying up here, I go to villages and train people. I go one day to Fort Yukon. Next time I'll be way the hell up there in Arctic Village or some place. Train Alaska people how to use equipment. Equipment I understand it really well. I could use that for many, many years. I was *trained* for that, I know exactly what to do with it. And this crew here, my village people was Number One. I use them as Number One crew.

Did that smoke ever get to you? Breathing all that heavy smoke?

Oh, yes. Heavy smoke, yes.

Boy, I'd be worried about my lungs.

I didn't have any lungs then.

(Laughs.)

To worry about. It doesn't bother me at all. I did that for fifteen solid years. At that time I had enough money, tell you the truth. All this time while I'm doing this, I wanted to oversee the operation. And God, I want to buy airplane.

Your own plane? (Laughs.)

I really wanted to buy airplane. I had that in my mind secretly. And I had enough money to do that. I got home one day, and I told my wife to sit down and said, "Ellen, I wanted to purchase a plane."

"What you wanna buy airplane for? No, I don't think so, Kenny. You can do something different. I don't want you to go up there any more."

Because that's where it all started from. After fifteen years and the good time that I had.

Ellen say, "Kenny, you got to stay home this year. You're not going back up there."

"Well, that's all right. What you want me to do?"

"Find work someplace else. Do something different. I don't want you to crash up there," she said. "Do something different. You're lucky enough that you didn't crash for fifteen years. Thank God for that," she said.

Kenny and Ellen Thomas, ca. 1971–1972. Photo by Bill Simeone.

Well, I thought about it. My wife loves me, and my family loves me. Why the hell should I break whatever they want me to do? So I just stayed home—and the hell with it—and back on the Cat again.

So I spent fifteen seasons up there all the time, training people. And that's what I did for a living. At the time I want to buy that airplane and I thought oh gee whiz, I thought the GI Bill would get the money to train me. I could have taken training on the GI Bill, and then, well, that went down the drain. I had enough money to buy the airplane and that went down the drain. I was going to rent it to the BLM in the summer, for the summer season. That's what they do at the time. I rent private planes.

Somebody private?

Yeah, private planes. Someone's big enough owner. I thought about the mail run to Tetlin. I thought about the mail run to Eagle and Chicken and all that stuff, and I got it all figured out what I'm gonna do with an airplane. Then I bring it up to my wife and she say, "Right now, Kenny. No airplane for you."

Laid down the law, huh?

Yeah. So that went down the drain. I could have owned whatever Warbelow had today.[2] But that's the way she want it.

Well, you probably lived a little longer that way. A lot longer.

I thought about that. That's what my family want me to do. I could do
lots of things. I got a lot of trades of all kinds.

DRINKING DAYS

So I tell you the truth about it. Back in [19]70 I fell off the wagon. I'm
the kind of guy who work all my life, and I had everything I wanted.
My wife and I had everything we wanted at that time. We had some
bad days. We had some good days—*lot* of good days. But I own everything I needed. Only thing we don't own is airplane. And you tell me
why I started drinking.

Somewhere around '60-something, a lot of people [here in the vil-
lage] are boozing. Gee, every Friday everybody goes up to Tok, every
Saturday. I felt like gee, I was left out. So one Saturday, 1968, I joined
them. In the army I didn't have problem drinking. So I drank and
drank and drank. I never lost a job in my life. I work because [I have] a
good job. And gee, first I started out, I used to drink up there [in Tok]
and come back, and gee whiz, got a lot of butterflies in my stomach
next day.

Hangover?

Oh, terrible. But even then I go to work. I work for eight-inch pipeline
down here in sixties. I was the maintenance man on that. The pipeline
between here and Haines. Every weekend I start drinking. Pretty soon,
I miss a day, Monday. I lie about it. I made a fool out of my wife. I tell
her to call my boss, "Tell him I'm really sick today, can't get to the job.
Don't say I'm drinking. Call the boss and tell him I'm sick." Here I am
with this big hangover.

And that went on and pretty soon I go Tuesday, I can't go to work
Tuesday. Then, finally, I have to quit. So that went on like that. I quit

the job, and pretty soon I just went every day drinking, every damn *day*. I'm just not the type of guy that buy a bottle one day and buy another bottle the next day. I don't do that. I buy the stuff by the cases. You know how them case of booze is? I buy [it by] the cases. Within three months I spent eight thousand dollars. Just went *crazy*! I never let up, not one day in three months—ninety days. Oh, God, that was terrible. I bought stuff by the cases, four or five cases [at a time].

You know, Craig, I have plenty of money. I got all kinds of money. I got money in the bank. And pretty soon after I quit working I go to the bar and I ring the bell and, oh, God, the next thing I know all the check stubs [are] coming back in—four, five, six thousand dollars down the drain. And she [Ellen] hides the checkbook. Everybody knows me, and I go to the bank and I get another [check]book. And hell, you know? All this time she never said anything to me. But, even then, everybody knows me. They take the car key away from me. I had a car, I had pickup, snow machine, boat, everything. I had everything but an airplane. I don't have an airplane.

And this is what the booze does. Pretty soon my wife takes all the car key away from me. I get on the bus—*school* bus [laughs], that's just how much people knows me. I was a popular guy. I get on the mail truck, I get on the school bus, I go with [Alaska State] Troopers.

Just to get to the bar?

Just to get to the bar or just to get to the bottle. After two years off and on, I quit one time again. And I went for about six months and I went on again. This last time, I was drunk for three months, three months straight. I'd just *live* on the booze. Before three months was up I wanted to quit. But I can't quit on my own. I was already throwing [up] blood and stuff like that. I was throwing [up] blood and trying to hide that.

You probably had little kids here, too, huh?

Yeah. Young kids. I was throwing [up] blood, and one day they find that out. I was out there throwing up blood, and they seen that. I had bleeding ulcers in my stomach. Oh, really bad. And what I did is I tried to hide it. And I don't want anybody to see it. So one day she [Ellen] find out that I was doing that, I was heaving the blood.

Oh, I want to quit that booze so bad and there was no help for me. There was no alcohol program, no nothing in the country to help me, and so I went to the doctor. There's no doctor, no nothing here. There's an old man down there; he was doctor just coming into the country. He give me a shot, and it knocked me out, but it didn't do any good.

RECOVERY

Finally I had to go to Glenallen to get sobered up.[3] I was down there for thirteen days in the hospital. Never was in the hospital in my life, and that's the first time I been in a hospital, there thirteen days. From there they help me and put me to sleep. Up here I couldn't sleep, I couldn't eat, I couldn't do *nothing!*

And I think that's where my turning point was, is that preacher coming in every day. Minister, a Native guy.

Really?

Athabaskan. He come in every day.

Who was that?

Harry John.[4]

Oh, yeah. I know him.

He comes in, he always have big smile on his face, "Kenny, how are you today?" Oh, he'd laugh, and here I'm dying on the bed. And I thought to myself—I asked God for help—I told Him, "Why can't I be like that guy?" He's not sick. He's always happy. I don't have to lay here and die. Why can't I do that?" He prays with me and all that stuff.

So, I made up my mind from there, after I got up on my feet, I going to be like that guy. I want to be happy the rest of the way. I'll never be a preacher, but I'm sure gonna give it a try. I believe in the Lord, and I wanted to be a leader of my people. And I wanted to help my people before they get down as far as I did. I know I went down almost to the death, one foot in the grave already. And I want to help my people before they get down as far as I did.

So I come back home, and I thought about my wife. Oh, I didn't know how much I hurt my wife and the family. I didn't *know* that. I thought all the time I'm hurting myself. But I didn't know I was hurting *her*. So, right away I went to work.

I was shaking a little bit but I got on the Cat, and I was working here, right here in this village. This was a new village at the time, and I was digging all this water and I was putting the water in for PHS [Public Health Service].[5] I was digging and put the pipes in for the PHS. I work up until October. Two years I work here. Then finally, one October I got laid off. We got everything done. Everybody was ready to move in. From there on, I just start to working. And I work for, oh, three or four months. And I never seen a bottle again after that up till today.

Up until today I haven't touched anything [alcoholic] yet. I want to prove [my sobriety] to the people. I been called a wino all of my life. Not all my life—all the time that I was drinking. People called me "Wino," don't even trust me at all. Just nothing but an old wino. And I told Ellen, what I wanted to do was I wanted to build myself back up to where I were a long time ago. I want to show these people I'm not no damn wino. My name's Kenny Thomas. I want to show them people out there that I'm not a wino. I'm a better man than that.

So I went ahead and went to work all this time, and I show the people out there today that I'm not a wino.

What year is it you quit, then?

1971? '70 or '71.

And you started in '68?

'68, yes.

So you had three really bad years?

Two bad years. All my life. *Really* bad ones, I would say, almost took my life. We went ahead and do whatever we had to do, just work, work, work, and pretty soon we got all that stuff back. We lost the car, all broke down and can't do nothing no more. We go ahead and buy new ones and new trucks. Gosh, no more "Wino," just trying to start new. But some days we had bad days, some days we had good days, all our life. Sometimes you don't get good job or something like that; we had some bad days.

And then you went to work for a contractor?

Yeah. Later on, after four or five years down the line, I thought about myself. I thought about the people in the village. This guy, good friend of mine, came from Anchorage. He always come to visit me. His name is Charlie Pedro.

And I told Charlie, I said, "Charlie, is any way we can help the people out here that have a drinking problem?" And I see a lot of problems here in the village. Lot of fighting, lot of breaking doors, and I wanted to help people from that.

Charlie said, "Oh, some way. Maybe we should write a grant. What do you think? You tell me how to write it and I'll write it," he said.

So I just sit down and talk with him like this, and he wrote that grant for me. Gee whiz. We sent it to Juneau, and by that time that money come back—they okayed the money—we have $126,000.

(Laughs.)

And I don't know what the hell to do with it, and by that time, before the money come in, Charlie starts *drinking*. And Charlie killed himself with that damn drink. And I don't know what the hell to do with the damn thing [the grant money].

So, me and my daughter Mildred, and Al Woods, and Cassie O'Pollack, the four of us we started something. We wanted to do something. We wanted to get [a] place and the village council didn't know what to do with it. They don't know how they could help us. Anyway, we rent a place in Tok, finally, without pay we're trying to get started. And I'm the only honcho, I guess, in the whole thing trying to get the thing going.

One of us—we had a meeting there one day—and he said, "We should get somebody from Anchorage that knows about alcohol program."

So we did. They help us get the thing started, a couple of them came up. Then we got couple people from Lower 48, NIAAA [the National

Institute on Alcohol Abuse and Alcoholism] for two weeks. We got on our feet from there. And then that's how I got to be a counselor. There was hardly any pay in it. Anyway, I took the job. I was heavy equipment operator; that's my trade. But I took this job and I thought to myself, "I want to help these people before they get down as far as I did with the booze."

And I worked for twenty years in that damn field [alcohol counseling]. Twenty years, trying to help my people. I set a treatment center up in Mansfield; I set a camp up in Mansfield where I can take [clients] away, where they can get away from drinking and all that stuff. And it went on for twenty years. After twenty years I had to quit. I wanted to do this for the Native people, *my* people.

I'm a heavy equipment operator, and I could have pulled tractor for somebody on the [Trans-Alaska] Pipeline, make all kinds of money, but I didn't. I want to help the people. The pay wasn't worth a damn but I stuck on. I hang onto it.

What did you do with those guys when you had them in treatment?

Well, we would teach them every day. We would have a class every day. When we go up there, we have different classes. I did the best I could. I didn't like the idea[s] [from] the people who do it by the book from the Lower 48. Our ball game is much different.

Different than AA [Alcoholics Anonymous]?

That's right. A lot of the Native people I work with don't have the education. The technique I got from the Lower 48, that don't work with my people at all. Lot of people I have to get down to *their* level to make them understand what I'm trying to do. So that went on and went on. I did all that and . . .

Do you think it was successful, for sobering people up?

It did a lot. It did a lot. It helped a lot of people. It helped a lot of people. A lot of people are still sober out there; a lot of people who quit drinking died. But it really did help the people. I didn't do it for the money. I did it to help the people. That's why it's really good.

Even today, I talk with people out there, I tell them, "Maybe you could do something different than what you're doing. You don't have to do this. This is bad for you. If it's good, I could use it, too, like you, but it's no good, that's why I don't use it." I always talk to the people out here, even today. I'm just Kenny Thomas, but I wanted to help the people.

What would you do when you run into somebody who's got a big problem? How would you try to handle it?

Well, it all depends on what they want, how they want help. There's lot of people who try to play games. I can't help you when you want to play games. You got to let me know what kind of help you want. I could do anything for you. I could make you arrangement in the hospital. I could make arrangement on your traveling [to get therapy]. Do you want to get out of it? I can't control what you want to do. It's up to you. I told 'em, "This is the best way to do it." The best way is not to drink at all, but we all have that problem, drinking problem. But what I'd do is I'd help people to get jobs. I'd put them on good jobs and find jobs for them. And that's how I'd do it. See, it works out pretty darn good. I held a treatment center in Mansfield. So it worked pretty good for me.

CHAPTER 6

We Don't Say Potlatch for Nothing

In this chapter Kenny talks at length about the all-important potlatch, an elaborate ceremonial complex that involves close cooperation between clans, speech making, singing and dancing, and the strategic giving of gifts and food. Only a few elders, such as Kenny, have a detailed knowledge of kinship and family history. This knowledge allows them to advise persons about what gifts should be given and to whom. Many rules must be strictly observed before, during, and after the potlatch, and any mistake in protocol can be disastrous and lead to hard feelings between relatives of the same or opposite clan. Every summer Kenny and Ellen and their daughters hold a culture camp at Mansfield Village to teach young people how to potlatch one another. Potlatches that are done correctly help to heal the family and the community, especially following a death or recovery from a major illness.

THE POTLATCH TRADITION

Potlatch is a tradition thing that been going on for many many years, way before my days. We learn it from our people, my Dad and my Mom, my grandpa and all them. We have to learn it from them. What we doing today is, we carrying it on. My Dad, my grandpa and my grandma, they teach me about the potlatch. This is the way it should be. This is the way everybody should handle it. At that time, and today, it changing, too.

What I mean is, way back then when I was kid, you know lots of Injih. "Injih" mean you can't have a woman or everybody handle all the stuff you have.[1]

It's what we call "taboo," I guess.

Yeah.

Things you shouldn't be doing.

The girls are not supposed to handle [men's possessions, especially guns and hunting equipment]. That's what you call, Injih in my language. Anyway, the boys always handle their [own] stuff.

The gun shell, yeah. You know, how you treat it. You don't just throw it anywhere. Take care of it so the woman won't step over it or nothing. What you hunt with, keep it in one place in your packsack. Don't let somebody else do it for you. Like this country, everything is alive, alive. Even the tree. You see these spruce trees are green? There's life into that, right? We respect that. We don't cut it down for nothing, [just] because it's in our way.

The flower out there, there's a medicine come right from this country, right from this land here. And some of us don't know what it is, and some of us know what it is. That's why you respect these flowers, any living thing you respect. You know on the mountain up there? You shoot at sheep, long time ago. We shoot at sheep. We got to pick up that shell can [case], bring it back. We don't leave it up there; it don't belong up there. That's how we respect them mountains. We don't throw away stuff like that up there. We bring it back. That's our traditional way.

You got lots to learn. You can't learn everything in one day. It don't make sense to you, but that's the way it is. That's the way it is with us. That's how we got to take care of ourselves. Right now today, women are really Injih. Young woman are Injih. She can't wash your clothes right with woman's clothes. You can't do that. That's our traditional way.

Injih means like young woman every month they have a period, every month. That's really Injih to us. They don't eat on the same table. They don't eat on the same plate. They don't eat and drink out of the same cup, and all that stuff. They trying to stay away from young boys. They make the luck. They make the luck change if they don't care about that Injih. Then to bring bad luck. That's why we respect these people. Just like we leave them [young girls] over here [in isolation] till they get over it. Then when they get better they come back to our table. That's when we're trapping and make living out of this country. You know the animal can smell you if you're around people like that, around young girls.

My grandpa, my father, and my mother and grandma, what they teach me is how I related to the people. We all know each other in this village, or when the village was over there [across the river], we know how we related. We were trained. We were teach how we're related to those people out there. *That* we got to know, we *got* to know. This is the first thing in this country that we got to know before we do any potlatch.

Today, we carry that on, between me and my wife, and we teach that to our kids. At the time, we have to know how we related to each other to carry the potlatch on. If potlatch is not from the Native people you have to learn how you're related to the people before you can do any potlatch. Potlatch is a very important thing for us. It's very important for us that we respect the potlatch a *lot*.

OUR WAY: THE BIG COOK

We don't say potlatch for nothing. You go down lower Yukon, I guess you've been around the country, people they get together and eat together they call it potlatch. Us, we call that a "potluck." We don't say potlatch for nothing up here because it is very important that we really respect that. Potlatch is a thing that you have to put blanket out there, you got guns out there, money, four or five days of food. Every day you eat three meal a day, for maybe five hundred people I would say, maybe less. But there's a lot of people from all over. If we make potlatch here in Tanacross, people from Fairbanks, Minto, Stevens Village, all the way down the Copper River, Tetlin, Northway, Fairbanks, Nenana, all will come.

You send out invitation?

Most of the time we do.

Cars and people gathered
for the Tanacross potlatch,
August 2001. Community
hall is on the right.
Photograph by Craig
Mishler.

And how do you send invitation?

We have to go in person. Like if I was inviting my wife, she's Dik'aagyu
[clan] and I'm Ałts'ii Dendeey. [When] I'm making potlatch, I have to
get [the people], on my side of clan. I have to give the potlatch to *them*
[people in clans of the opposite moiety]. So I'll go to her boss [Ellen's
clan elder]. In the village here in Tanacross, they always come to me
for invitation. They talk to me and I'll send the people to *them*. That's
the way it goes, for us.

Is there a certain way you're supposed to make the invitation?

Oh yes, yes, yes.

A real formal, high language?

By their language, yes. They tell us what they're going to do and who
it's for. Like for people who passed away long time ago. Sometime you
can't make potlatch right after they die. What we do is, when someone
had died, we just put them away. We bury them. Then we give away
what we have. Lot of people will donate. My relations will donate stuff
to me. If my brother died or something like that, people related to me
will donate to me. I'll give [my brother's possessions] to the people. It's
a gift. Sometimes we have to give to our own relations, but we have to
tell them that you got to use this as the "kaii" [gift]. "Kaii," they call it.

What's the meaning of "kaii"?

Just like my gift to you to remember me by. If my wife give you something that I used to own, if I died. "Here, Craig, this is your friend Kenny Thomas's thing." You take this to remember him by. That's what it mean, "kaii." Do you follow me? It's a gift that's given to my [own clan] relative. Otherwise, all the gift will go to others of opposite clan.

Oh, so there's two kind of gifts then?

Yes. The first gift is, sometime we give to my relation. If my brother or sister died, then I can give some to my relation, but I have to use this to tell them, "Take this as a kaii." It's the only way. Otherwise, you can't do that. You got to talk about it before you do that. In potlatch you can't do that. No kaii in potlatch.

You mean in memorial potlatch [as opposed to funeral potlatch] you don't use kaii?

No kaii. First gift is when they first die. But a year or two later, you going to make memorial potlatch for the same person, you don't do that no more. That's first one [funeral potlatch] only. First thing you have to, is, you have to learn how you're related to the people out here. This is what you have to teach your kids, your family.

This is when it's really good when it comes to culture camp up in Mansfield. Last year [1998], you [Craig] went up with us, and at the end you see the song that I sang, the potlatch song I sang before the start. The old days, when I was really young kid, that song is very strong. Sometimes up there maybe you must feel the power when we're singing that. You can feel it sometimes. You can feel our power that's working in there in that potlatch. That's why we don't let any kid go on that canvas that we put down. We don't let kid go on that because the power is in there and the kid will have a short life.

Really?

Yeah. They might die right away.

Blankets and guns
(center left) being
readied for gifts at
Kenny Thomas Sr.'s
honorary potlatch in
Tanacross, August
2001. Photograph by
Craig Mishler.

That's like Injih.

Yeah, Injih for the kids to go on there. Anyway, you really got to take
care of that, and then you have to take care of yourself after you make
potlatch. You have to watch what you eat, where you go to bathroom,
and you can't cross the river, you can't walk on trail because the girls
all walk on trail. What my Dad always tells me is, "Walk on the side of
the trail. Because girls are all walking on that trail all the time." That's
how you take care of yourself. What that does is, it gives you luck.
Whatever you put out, you get it back, easy.

Or you mentioned that power, too. You got a word for that?

Gee whiz. "Ho'te." You know how you take care of yourself, like I said?
"Ho'te."
    You got to take care of yourself like that.

Power? Dadukneh?

No. You know Ho'te. Power is . . .different thing. Long time ago, there
was power in there, like Chuusi'. Lot of Chuusi' going around then.

Ellen: ***Uh-huh [affirming].***

"Chuusi'," you say. That's the power. Lots of power in there.

Ellen: ***They use that in their house.***

That's why the kids aren't supposed to go on that [canvas or tarp]. Yeah, the Chuusi' is a strong thing. A lot of people use it. That's as far as I can go with that because I don't want to give myself away.

Okay. (Laughs.)

Because that's something that I shouldn't talk about. I guess I shouldn't talk that deep about it now, but I did. Anyway, I'd like to say that we have to take care of ourselves after we make the potlatch. There is a power, like Chuusi' that is in there, that's why we don't let kids walk on that tarp, because they [would] have a short life, you see. First thing you got to learn is how you're related to the people, which clan are you related to, and which person you're not related to. This is what I teach up in Mansfield at the culture camp. That's why the end of that teaching in Mansfield we have little potlatch. Everybody make something they give away to their friend. Not their relative, their friend.

That's very important that we should teach how we related. I got people in Northway, I have people in Tetlin, I have people in Copper [River] on my mother's side. I have people in Dot Lake; I have people in Mentasta. This is how I was trained; I was teached that way. My Mama and Dad pass this on to me. This is what I'm trying to do, pass this on to our young people today.

You see that little walking cane I had while I was there in Mansfield? I give that to a young girl there, pretty young girl.

Diamond willow?

Yeah. Anyway, you seen that one. In my language, that's my *grandma*, that young girl.

You're kidding? Really?

That's my grandma. One of my grandma, last of that tribe.

What do you call her in your language, then?

"Stsuu gaay." That's "my little grandma."

(Laughs.)

She's the last of that tribe. Not very many of them in that tribe. She's the last of that tribe; that's why I did that. You got to understand some things like that. It's not easy. You got to teach the young people today. Some people are really interested in learning. Lot of people here in Tanacross that understand what we're doing.

I guess then that you give gifts according to how you're related?

That's right.

I give a blanket or rifle depending on relation.

That's right. We have to go opposite clan from our clan.

And how many clans you got? Three? Two?

We have maybe two or three right now, like her [Ellen] Dik'aagyu. I'm Ałts'ii Dendeey. And Dennys and them is Ch'echeelyu. So, there's not very many, maybe three [major clans] left. It used to be seven.

Seven clans in the old days?

Oh yeah. The old days when I was kid, before the epidemic flu they had over there in the villages they had anywhere from fifteen hundred to two thousand people in one village. I would say about two thousand people because there were big village in Mansfield. Then on this side of Mansfield, Dihthâad they call it, there's people there. Then back on this way a little ways, another mile, is the Fish Creek. People used to live there, too. Three different place where people live. Mansfield is the biggest place and that's where they held the potlatch.

EARLY DAYS POTLATCH

In the old days they have a tripod, like what you got there [pointing to the video camera and tripod]. They go like this and they put a pole across and they hang their blankets on it. At the end of them, where it comes like this, they hang the gun on it.

If it's that many gun today. Them days, those things [potlatch gifts] are hard to get. It's not one of them ten-dollar blanket like they use today. Them days, it's Hudson Bay blanket *only*. They use lot of fur for the potlatch, too. Fur and beadwork, too, like moccasin, gloves, mitts, and stuff like that. They use that, too. The women use that for potlatch and them was greatest thing. You never go without that in a potlatch.

Diane [Kenny and Ellen's daughter] was telling me that, what she heard was, you're only supposed to give away five guns? Is that right?

That's what I'm talking about a long time ago. That's the time when I was really young. It's a deal like when somebody die. We're talking about the days [when] it's hard to get anything, not easy. But long time ago, when I was really young, my Dad said, "There's only five guns that you can put out there."

"Why?" I say. You take a person, like the one that died. One arm is one, two, three, four, and your whole body is five. Five pieces on your body, that's all you can put there. That's the first one, that memorial potlatch. That *funeral* potlatch, that's what they call it.

Five guns. Now today, people are bringing thirty, forty, fifty guns. They bring it in like you bring handful of wood or something when they're making potlatch. I come from the days when it's very hard to get anything. You're lucky to get five guns sometimes, at the time when I was kid.

Shtaa'in. I want to say little things about Shtaa'in.[2] My Dad, he talks about it. My Dad and them, they make big potlatch in Mansfield. They used to put the blankets out there [outdoors] on a stick like this, they put [up] a pole, and they put a brace like that [to make a wood tripod] and they hang that blanket on it, and each clan got their own pole. *My clan got their own pole.*

This is outdoors, you mean?

Yeah. That biggest potlatch in Mansfield have two different clan that making potlatch. Sticks like this [gestures with fingers to show a tripod]. Sometime [people think], "Gee that guy [has] more [gifts] than us." You know, the clan. And still it's not a competition thing. That's just [a measure of] how many [people] there are [in the clan]. You and me, [if] our clan is very low [in numbers], we're not going to go very far. More people is alive with you today, more than me. And my people, not too many live with me. I can't go [give away] as much as you can. You go farther with your stick. It don't mean competition or nothing. More people. You have more people than me; that's what it mean.

More relatives?

More relatives.

THE FUNERAL POTLATCH

When you're ready to make potlatch—potlatch is especially when somebody dies or loved one goes—then what we do is we have funeral. They call it "funeral service." I mean if my brother or somebody dies, what they're going to do is I'm going to put [out] maybe ten guns and fifty blankets or something like that, and four hundred or five hundred dollars cash, but yet my relative will donate some to me. My family will donate some to me. There's a lot of times when my family give me something because I'm their Daddy. They make their money my money. They don't want their name to be mentioned about what they donate to me. I can use it any way I want to. I can use it for food, mostly for food. That's what I use for food when my kids donate that to me. But, you've got to be very, very, very careful about that.

Usually when the funeral time [comes], like [if] my brother died, my relative [fellow clan members] will give me something. My kids will give me something for the food. But my wife can't give me nothing because it's the law that we shouldn't do that—different tribe [clan]. My kids are different tribe [clan], yet they're part of me, too. They want to help me, [but] I can't use that as a potlatch [gift], but I can use it for food. So that's what we call, "funeral potlatch." That's just

Frank Gene of Tetilin dishing up moose head soup for Tanacross potlatch, August 2001. Potlatch guests are being served in the background. Photograph by Craig Mishler.

like a gift to one another. You got to talk about this if you think you're going to do it on both sides. The relative, you going to give a little something to them. Okay. You got to talk about it. You got to talk about it before you give [a gift] to somebody.

Let's say we're going to give you "kaii." Some of them [speaks in Tanacross]. That means, "My clan, my people, will give them a little gift." If I already say something, they can't say "No" to me. But on this side [different clan, opposite moiety] is all of my friends not related to me. Them are the people that bury my brother. You see, they have a right to get the gift. It's a funeral gift is what it is. That's why we give some to some of our family sometimes, not all the time. But we got to talk about it before we do that.

I've got one question for you. When you talk about relatives and your relations, we have a word for that in English. We call it, "kinship." We talk about our "kin." In your language, would you have some word for when you talk about all your relations?

"Huutsudelken" is "the ones who help me, the ones I'm related to."

On your side?

Uh-huh, on my side [my moiety]. I related to them. "Huudeeken," that's why they help me with the funeral. Or, "Ludeeyakiinen," when they give me little something, when they help me with the funeral service.

But on the other side, what you call those people?

This is "Detł'een'įį." That's the ones that bury my brother, the ones that bury me. They bury my brother. Them, they have a right to get anything. But over here, some of them "Udeega kanen," we give them little something, too, but we got to say something before we do that. Some of them do the "kaii." "Kaii" means "gift," a gift from me to remember my brother, like that. Just the special people get that, not everybody. It's a good thing to pass it on to the kids today.

I was raised when we had no material things. What we had was handmade. It was not purchased in a store like we do today. My father and the elders told me during the potlatch or during the time when someone dies, funeral potlatch, don't put a whole bunch of gifts out there, like you would during a memorial potlatch.

I have five girls and three boys. I try to teach my kids what is the best thing for them. I want them to learn how they [are] related to the people. I want them to know that. Some of them like Mildred and Diane and some of my kids are really good about that. In fact, some of my kids are helping a lot of people in Tetlin, Northway, Mentasta. You know, they understand who to give the stuff to when people making potlatch. Right away we know which side the potlatch is for.

THE MEMORIAL POTLATCH

Two or three years after that is when you're allowed to put out as much as you can afford to. Much more than during the funeral pot-

The Thomas Family, Christmas, 1996. Left to right, Top row: Roy Denny, Chris Denny, Michelle Emerson, Kirby Thomas, Delbert Titus, Gabe Jonathon, Ray Thomas, Richard Thomas, Kenny Thomas Jr., Sarina Northway, Derick Titus (partially obscured); Middle Row: Betty Denny, Diane Titus, Ray Titus, Nancy Thomas, Kerchelle Thomas, Debbie Thomas, Marci Ann Titus, Kenny Thomas Sr., Ellen Thomas, Coleen Denny, Karen Jonathon; Front Row: Dalen Titus, Michael Thomas, Sarah Denny, Kyle Allen (in Santa Claus hat), Stephanie Moe, Mildred Jonathon. Photograph by John Rusyniak.

latch. It takes a very long time to accumulate gifts to pass around during the potlatch.[3] *Really last one.* It all depends on how long it's going to take you to pick up ten, fifteen, twenty guns.

You're talking about a memorial potlatch now?

Really [the] last one. But this is what we do. Nthee neeshu'dee'aa. That means, "What we have in us, the grieving," what you call it in your language. The grieving is with us many, many years.

You're hurt.

We're hurt inside, and what the potlatch is doing is to make ourselves feel better. When we have potlatch, that's only way we feel better, and from there on we got to try to help ourselves to not remember no more, trying to forget from there, from this last potlatch. And it *does* help us.

My grieving is longer than yours because you don't have grieving at all, hardly. I mean you [white] people. The grieving stays with Native people *so long*. There a lot of love for each other, for us. Thing is, we know each other so many years and we used to live among each other for many years, and up this way in Northway, Tetlin, Dot Lake, and Mentasta, Copper River, we know everybody. That's why the grieving is there all the time.

Of all my friends, the white people that I know that their mother died, and few months later, they don't *talk* about it no more. It's really different from us. It's *our* way. You've got to understand *our* way of doing things *too*, you know. It just stays with us, ever since a long time before my Dad and them.

You said before that you don't have to give away lots to make it important, huh?

No, no, no. You see lot of people, like my sister-in-law over there, she wouldn't have so much, so that they get up maybe ten gun [and] they go ahead with it. But somebody will help, their relative will help them. Like [if] he's making potlatch on my brother, my cousin that's married to her. I can give help her in ways, too, and my wife can't put nothing there.

But you said it's not competition to give away more than the next guy.

No, no, no. Not that way. Gee whiz, I hope you don't understand it that way. It's not competition thing. It's a *grieving* thing is what it is, grieving that stays with us a long time that we want to get rid of, that's all it is. And we don't try to put out more [gifts] than one another. No, we don't do that, don't even think about things like that. We just go on with what we have, and let my relative know before I do that, too.

Are you broke afterward?

Maybe—no, I don't think *that* broke. But, some things you just put on the side here and there, maybe a couple of thousand dollars, maybe three or more.

And you said that even an old widow could still have an important pot-latch with just a few things?

Oh, yes. Few things that they have, it's got a lot of power, my Dad always say. More power than *big pile* of potlatch. Just little piles of pot-latch have more power.

"Chuusi'" means—I don't know how to explain it. People had that Chuusi'. Long time ago, lot of medicine people [were] in there too, and chuusi' too. Hałii usi'. That's why the kids can't go on this canvas [tarp] that we put out there for that potlatch. The kids don't last too long after they get onto that because of that Chuusi'. Hałii usi' and there's medicine in there for that potlatch.

Even right now, today, there's a lot of spiritual things in there; it's very strong. Some people still have it, just a spiritual thing. It's not got nothing to do with potlatch or anything; it's just a spiritual thing that's strong, very strong. Some people have it very strong, and if I make potlatch you can sure feel it because I don't want to lose all my stuff. I'll get it back easy that way. That's why they say there's a song for it. There's song for all the potlatch, really potlatch.

How do you mean you'll "get it back"?

In your luck. The luck, the song that go for that.

Yeah, you said something about looking after your luck. How do you look after your luck?

Well, you got to take care of it. You got to take care of your luck. Today, [this] thing in our language, Injih, that goes along with us. If I make potlatch, there's lots of Injih things I got to be careful of. The womens are really Injih. Lots of things that young people, young woman, young girls can't [do]. They can't grab you like this [gestures]. It's something that's different from your culture. You got to be very careful around young people, like young girls.

They can still go to the potlatch, though? Young girls?

No.

Training potlatch held at the Mansfield Culture Camp, July 1999. The tarp area is off limits to young children during the feast and the gift giving. Photograph by Craig Mishler.

No? They're supposed to stay away?

When they have their monthly period they can't [attend].

I see. Even today?

Even today. Today, I don't know. I don't know that any more. I think that's really Injih, though. *Lot* of Injih. They just don't use that no more today. Injih is something that you got to take care of yourself when you make potlatch.

Abraham Luke was telling me that if you say "Injih" to somebody and they go ahead and do it anyway, then they're really in trouble.

Yeah, that's what I mean. That's what this means. That's why you don't want it to happen.

GIFTS

When somebody die, like my relative die, all my relative will give me the stuff. They give me blankets, guns, money, and stuff like that, to have memorial potlatch with. All the stuff were mixed. That's why they call it Memorial. It's not a potlatch. It's a gift thing, you know. Gift thing. Because too many people from different people have put in money there. That's why we don't sing song for it. But right here the last one we do is that I collect guns. I collect blankets for many, many years, and I'm doing it by myself.

Just you?

Just me. Sometime my people will help me too. My own people, not them. Not Ch'aadh, not Tandîidz altsiil, just Ałts'įį dendeey, Dik'aagyu. I mean Dik'aagyu and Ałts'įį dendeey and them kinds are different people. I'm one of Ałts'įį dendeey. Them people will help me.

That's what you call "really potlatch"?

That's what I call the "really potlatch." That's the one that really really respects that. *Very* respect it.

That's because you have to sacrifice?

Uh huh [affirming]. Anyway, it's a good thing to learn, and I teach that in Mansfield, in our culture camp. I teach people how we're related. You've got to be very careful right here, how you're related. And the people you're not related [to] is the one to give the gift to. If I related to somebody, that I'm making potlatch on my Dad, then he can't be related to the person that's going to get the gift. So you got to be very, very, very careful with that.

If you make a mistake, what's going to happen?

Well somebody's going to refuse it. "Who the hell? That man is old enough. How come he don't know?"—somebody's going to think. Somebody's going to say. That's why you got to be very careful. That's

Kenny dancing with Jerry Isaac (right) and youth at the Tanacross potlatch, August 2001. Photograph by Craig Mishler.

why you got to listen to me all the time. When I teach my kids, I want you to listen to me. I'm teaching you not to make no mistake in your potlatches. This is what I teach.

And I don't want nobody to tell me from different village: "Did that guy ever teach his kids?" This is something I *avoid*, trying to avoid, All these people here—my wife's clan, all my kids, and whoever lives here, I got to make damn sure that they don't make mistake. Because I live here in this village, and I'm the one [that's] supposed to teach these kids today. It's not easy thing. I got to do that all the time. I got to see these people. I got to let them know. I got to let the kids know. This young person want to make potlatch, I got to tell them who is not related, [and] who is he related to. All that I got to tell him that.

For the potlatch.

That's right. So that they don't make mistake.

If they make a mistake . . .

It's my fault.

Could somebody get mad?

Mmm hmm [affirming]. You know the clan, like my Dad's people. My Dad and my Mom is [from] two different people, two different clans.

And I'm on my Mama's side. And if my Mom gets something, I'll get something [a gift]. Like if my Dad gets something, she'll get something [pointing to Ellen]. That's the way it is. It's not an easy thing, but you got to learn it. But most likely, you got to be very careful about me. I got to think all the time. They're making lot of potlatches, and I got to be involved in *all* the potlatches. They got to come see me.

Even if it's not your side?

That's right. Because I live here. I'm the elder that knows how we're related. I got to tell them who to give to, who not to give to.

You've got to know everybody in the village.

That's right. I know everybody in Tetlin. I know everybody in Northway. Northway is pretty hard place. That's the only place I have trouble with. Very hard place because what we do in this village, they're different. They're doing different. What I mean is they related, and they marry each other. Same clan will marry each other, same people.

EAGLE FEATHERS AND FACE PAINT

A long time ago, just like the other day when we had a potlatch down here, we use the eagle feather all the time for many, many, many, many years. In my language they call it, Ch'ṭaa. We use that all the time for our clans and what not. Eagle is our main boss. He's the head of us. He's the one that give us the name. He's the one give my wife his [her] clan's name. What Eagle did, he's the one that tells me, "Kenny Thomas, your name will be Ałts'ịị dendeey." Naltsiin you call it. [To] Ellen, my wife, he say, "Ellen, your clan's name will be Dik'aagyu." And so on and so forth. Like, "Tsesyu," he give name to other people. Checheelyu, Wudzisyu, Ch'aadh, Tandîidz altsiil." All different names he give us, that Eagle. He's the one that give us the name[s] for who we are.

That's why today, the Eagle is the one who give us who we are in our clan. That's why he's way ahead of us. We have a right to use the [eagle] feather. The [Native] people in Alaska have a right, anybody in Alaska has a right to use this feather.

Each clan, Mansfield people. The one that making the potlatch will have the feather on. If I'm in part of that potlatch, like last night, a few days ago, we had potlatch here—and this one guy I see, he had feather back here [points to the back of his head]. And I say, "That's a different clan." Not the way from what I learn. In my clan, I'll have one just like that, I would say [makes a V with his outstretched index fingers and points to the right side of his head]. And Ch'aadh people, they have one on this side, the left side, back this way [points toward left side of his head with index finger pointing back]. Back years ago, if you remember right, you've seen Andrew Isaac? He have one in the middle, like this [makes a V with outstretched index fingers and points to forehead]. Do you remember that feather he had?

No. I remember he had something that looked like it come from Woolworth's. It had a whole bunch of feathers around his head.

Oh, that's the bonnet, they call it.

Bonnet, yeah. He looked like a Great Plains Indian.

But he always wears one in the middle like this [again makes a V with outstretched index fingers]. Today, they call him Tradition[al] Chief. That's why he do that. Yet he should be over here, that feather [gestures to the right side of his head].

But he wears it up front?

Yeah, because he's the tradition[al] chief.

How about the Dik'aagyu? Where do they wear it?

They wear it back here [points to the back of his head]. When you wear that, that's just to show you what clan I'm in. If you're smart at all, you know I'm Ałts'įį Dendeey. If you can read the Native education, you know darn well that Ellen is Dik'aagyu. That Checheelyu, Ch'aadh, Tsesyu. Tsaih, they use that tsaih paint [reddish orange ochre] [gestures to indicate horizontal stripes on cheeks and vertical stripes on chin].

They paint different for each clan?

That's only thing they can use is tsaih. They rather use tsaih, even though they have a right to use that feather, the Tsesyu people. Tetlin is a Tsesyu place. They always like to use that tsaih.

You want to talk about the tsaih a little bit?

I don't know too much about it, but I know that my Dad and them call it, Tsaih Tł'iig. Tsaih Tł'iig is a place where Native peoples go to pick up tsaih. Between the rocks [is] where the tsaih would be, in here, you know [gestures].

My Dad talk about it many times, and I ask him lot of questions about it, and he always say that you had to build a big long ladder to get up to it. And when they get up there, like my Dad always say, my Mom will make something like a big bag, like moose-hide bag or caribou bag. And they fill that thing up, as much as they can pack because they don't go down there every year or whatever. Every once in a great while they goes down there. It's down that way somewhere. And when they goes there they take something with them, always. They take like a necklace, for one thing that I remember. They take bone necklace that they use. And that was very valuable thing for Native people at the time, and it's just like money to Native people. Sometimes something like fur. They take tsaih from there and they replace it with something.

In our language, you know that place, Walti' dun iiyuu ziidii.[4] That mean that place is just like a living thing to the Native people up here. It's just like a living thing: you might think something bad for them and people die fast if they don't put anything [there]. What they took they have to replace it with something. That way, that place wouldn't feel bad about what they took. So they replace it with something very valuable where they take the tsaih.

During the time when I was a kid, I never heard anybody [who] went down. I remember using it when I was a little boy, when we were into dances. It don't take very much, just a little. Not even half a tea-spoon and you mix it with some kind of grease, like lard or something, and they put it on their face. Some of them are really dark red and some of them is kind of light red, reddish-colored orange, three or four different [colors]. I noticed that my grandpa, Big Albert, he use that for snowshoes. Just a little bit. [For] just days like that, you never lose color or nothing, it just go right in the wood. You'll never lose that color. For many years that I owned those snowshoes I never lose the color.

They say you have to go at least one week to get that stuff. I wish I knew where it is. But it's here in Alaska somewhere. Toward that way, they say, but I don't know where.

Downriver?

Downriver, or down below Eagle, or towards Eagle or somewhere in that area. They say that it takes one week, five or six days to get there. That's really walking. You take tsaih from there, you replace it with some kind of deal, like you "make a deal." You get tsaih and you got to replace it with some kind of necklace or fur or something, because Native people always say that place is really a living thing, just like a person is there that you're buying the tsaih from. That way, this place wouldn't feel bad against me as if I took that tsaih for nothing.

Does each clan make different markings?

No, no. That's just them [the Tsesyu clan].

That's the only clan that uses tsaih?

They want to use that. We got right to use it, too. But they're the first people who got that tsaih. There's big stories about all of this good stuff. They're the first people to find that tsaih. Little while ago I told you about the Eagle that give them a name. You have reason to call people what they are. You have reason to call me "Ałts' įį Dendeey" because I make lot of potlatches. That's why you call me that. There's a reason about what you name the people, what you name the clan, I would say.

And then last night too, you were talking about what happens if your feather falls out [on the potlatch dance floor].

Long time ago, at the potlatch when we wear that feather, we wear all them feathers. If I have two here and while I was dancing I lose that feather, if it drops on the ground. Them days there was a power, a very spiritual power out there. Today, you call a ceremony. We have ceremony for what we do. At that time, our ceremony is really powerful. There were Chusii' in there. There were medicine thing in there, there were Chusii' in there that were so powerful that they don't want people [or] a young kid to go on there. Because after they go walk over that canvas thing that they lay down for their guests, the one they made potlatch on? You cannot walk on that, young kids. Because in the future they'll just die from it. It don't kill them right there, but in the future they will because of that Chusii' in there. Lot of medicine thing.

Today, you wouldn't know who in the hell have it. But there's people have it. Lot of times I'm sitting in a place like a potlatch, man, the spiritual thing is so powerful out there. Just phhhew shhhew, going around like. Even I can feel it.

In your body?

Uh-huh. That's what we got to have when we have a ceremony. We got to dance around that feather if I lost a feather on the ground. We got to build up that spiritual power. We pick it up with that power [hands outstretched with palms up]. And it'll give back to me, if it's mine [hands folded together pulled in]. If it's yours, it'll give it back to you. That's how they pick it up. They don't just grab it like this [leaning over with right hand outstretched as if picking it up] and [say], "Here." No, it's got to come through the power that our ancestors used before us. Even today, we respect that, when it drops. You're not supposed to drop anything. I make damn sure that people wear that thing [so] you don't drop it. Because it's very hard to just pick it up and [say] "Here." You don't do that.

You got to have power for your ceremony. Things that we do is very, very valuable. It's just of few of us that carries it. That's what we're trying to teach to the kids today of Mansfield. That's why we have a culture camp and them kind of things. Whatever we do, like singing and stuff like that, it's got a lot of meaning to it.

THE HONORARY POTLATCH

You talked before about the funeral potlatch and the memorial potlatch. Can you tell about the get-well potlatch and how that works?

Well, we'll talk about how people honor me.[5] A while back after I got back from the hospital [in July 2000], I came from Anchorage to here, and what my people did is they had a big cook ready for me here, and the next day people come from Tetlin with all their food, and then they held an honorary potlatch for me. I guess people have a lot of respect for me, I would say, in the white man way. The people have so much respect for me that they don't want to see me go right now. But that's the reason why they have people all together, and a lot of people are praying for me. Lot of people are praying for me, and we don't know how we can thank them.

So they really think the world of me, and they don't want to lose me now, and so they pray lot for me. Everybody really prayed lot for me, and it's a miracle healing is what it is, and my people don't know how to thank everybody, so they just have one big potlatch, just to honor me. And that's when all my friends came to my potlatch, one of them is Craig here, and them guys that brought me back from Anchorage. They all got little gift from us, from my people, my daughters and them. And lot of my relatives they put stuff in with us too. So that's how they thank the people. That's why they honor me with the food, and the gifts that was given away, and lot of people that visit us. It really went good. I was really proud of my kids for doing that for me, and not only my kids, but my relatives also that helped my kids.

They went in together with some other families. Some of it was memorial and some of it was for you?

Mmm hmm. And one of my mother's sisters was up at Tetlin, and he was raised as kid, Danny Adams. Danny Adams's grandkid was born. Danny Adams's daughter had baby boy, so he's one of them that they make cup of tea on. And Danny Adams's little bigger boy, Danny Adams Jr., is another one they make potlatch on.

Did he pass away?

No. He [Danny Jr.] got hurt, and he got back on his feet again.

I see.

Just like me. So he was in at the same time they had the potlatch. Me, Danny, and that little boy. Three of us.

And the little boy, he had trouble too?

No, the little boy was born, for his birthday. So we welcome him into our culture [with that potlatch]. So that's why we did that. In our way it's very important for us to do that. We just welcome the boy into our culture. And that's supposed to bring him lot of luck. And this is one reason why my people did that. I'll tell you what. They spent a lot of money on me. And that's how they thanked the people that prayed for me, and I'm glad that they did that.

KEEPING YOUR LUCK AFTER THE POTLATCH

You got to really take care of yourself after you make potlatch. You can't go across the running water, this [Tanana] river. You can't go across that for month or so because your stuff will go down the drain. That river will take your stuff. Don't ask me how, but it'll go downriver. That's why you don't walk on public trail, go on side of the trail.

This is after a potlatch?

Uh-huh. Because girls are walking on that trail. Don't walk on the trail. Go on the side of the trail. You don't go across the river because you'll lose all your stuff down the river. It'll go downriver.

How long do you got to watch that?

About a month or so. And you can't go to bathroom where the young girls go to bathroom. You got to go someplace else. That's the way it was, long time ago.

This is just for the person who makes the potlatch?

For the people that make potlatch. This gentleman here [who makes the potlatch], he have to be very careful. [There's] lots of Injih for him. Different things that you eat, different things that you do. Being around the young girls are very Injih, lots of Injih.

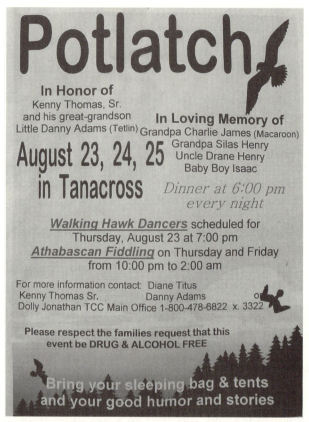

Poster advertising Kenny Thomas Sr.'s honorary potlatch and the memorial potlatch for others (In Loving Memory of), August 2001. Photograph by Craig Mishler.

Young people especially, huh?

Yeah, especially. We got to try not to feed this gentleman different parts of moose or caribou. You got to take care of the meat that they kill, and you got to take care of that head. The first kill that he does, I got to make big cook with it, to hang onto that luck. I make big cook with it to their grandma out there, and I feed all that meat to them. And I give them little gift with it and little meat with it, and that's what we do. That will bring the luck back to them. They keep their luck that way.

CHAPTER 7

Becoming a Song
and Dance Leader

Here Kenny talks about how local song and dance styles have changed in his own lifetime. He observes that dances, performed in the context of potlatch feasts, are important to the emotional and spiritual life of the Indian community and do much to bring together families, clans, and villages. His decision to record elders and become a song and dance leader, drummer, and composer is also discussed, as it is central to his emergent social identity. He is largely responsible for the continued strength of traditional song and dance in Tanacross and for the active participation of young adults. In addition to singing and drumming, Kenny also plays the harmonica and sings popular crossover songs such as the "Eagle Island Blues."

HISTORY OF THE GANHOOK

When I was a kid, when I was a young boy, there was people come from Moosehide [Yukon Territory]. They came to Mansfield to this big potlatch, and they brought with them the dance, Native dance and the song.[1] Boy, what a great thing came in to Mansfield, and they brought a Ganhook with them. Ganhook is a long stick with a bunch of beads on it, and when you shake it like this, it rattles. Makes good sound.

And what happened is that was the first time we seen dance like that. Us here in Mansfield, when I was really young there was no dances, no Native dances like that. There were sorry songs. When somebody die or

Sorry Song performed at Tanacross Memorial Potlatch in August 2001. Left to right, front: Emma Northway, Debbie Thomas, Kenny Thomas Sr., Jerry Isaac. Back: Ellen Thomas and Kenny Thomas Jr. reaching for handkerchief from clothesline. Photograph by Craig Mishler.

something like that, then they sing sorry songs, that's all. No such thing as a dance, up until the people come from Moosehide that brought the dance to Mansfield.

It was a very big potlatch and [Han] people from Eagle come with Moosehide people, and they all got together and then come to Mansfield, and they brought the dance to Mansfield. And what happen is they got a big potlatch from Mansfield and they wanted to give something in return to Mansfield people, but they don't know what. But their chief, they call Chief Isaac from Moosehide, he thought what he brought was the dance and the Ganhook, so at the end of the dance and the potlatches at Mansfield, what he did is he give that song, he give the dances, and he give the Ganhook to the Mansfield people, us, everybody, not only one person. It goes to everybody at Mansfield. So that's how we got the Ganhook and right now I am pretty sure, the way my father use to say is we have the right to use the Ganhook because it was given to us. Ganhook is not [for] everybody to use; I think we are the only one that have right to use it because it was given to us from Canada.

Another thing I'd like to talk about, and I don't want to change the subject, but I want to say that most of the Canada people come and always my Dad and them talked about it you know, Canada [people] come down Yukon River, and some settled in Eagle. They were coming down from Moosehide and Dawson, that country, and they come into Moosehide and into Eagle. Then later on, way later on, from Eagle, they heard there is caribou crossing up at Kechumstuk. Long time ago, way before me, Kechumstuk was settled there, and it was called Sages Chaeg, that's our language. Sages Chaeg, that's Kechumstuk.

Anyway they settle at Kechumstuk, the Canada people, half of the Canada people from Eagle come to Kechumstuk, settle there for that caribou crossing there. Long time ago that is the only way we can make a living, is following the caribou and wherever the game is, that's where we settle. So half of the Canada people settled there and then from there we found them from Mansfield. So later on they were inter-married to Mansfield people, and Mansfield people were married to Kechumstuk people. And they all intermarried to each other. That brings some people to Mansfield, and there were a lot of people that came to Mansfield from Kechumstuk, that's all from Canada.

There is a song from Dawson. Long time ago, this dance and song and things like that come from Canada people. So that's the reason why Native people long before us invited people from Dawson for their dances. They really dance good. In this country there was no dance. There is a sorry song that we always do. *That* one we have. It's here already. Yeah, that one. But the good-time dance that they have over in Canada, we didn't have.

The first time we invited them from Moosehide. The Eagle people, they're all in the same group [Han Hwech'in] anyhow. They come into Eagle and then picked up their people in Eagle and then they all came on down. When they come into Mansfield that time I figure it must be sixteen people. They say it was the third or fourth time they had pot-latch for them. Many times they came down, three or four times, I'm sure. From what I hear. This is before my days.

They get potlatch all the time in Mansfield. Big gifts, *big* gifts. They come from long ways so they give them good, big gifts.

The Dawson people?

Yeah, Dawson and Eagle both. And many times they got a good, big potlatch from Mansfield. And this last time I think Chief Isaac is the one who came down with them. He always come down with them, they say. Somebody named Silas and Taylor, and all them guys come down. And Juneby from Eagle and Elisha Lyman and all them guys all come down from Eagle.

And what happened with this dance is, people they like that, in this country. They like that. So what they did is the last time they had a potlatch, they had a big gift from Mansfield people and this gentleman here, Chief Isaac or Chief Silas or whoever it was, feel really guilty about it, I think. And what he want to do in return of this potlatch is he want to give this song, dance, and the Ganhook to the people of Mansfield in return for the potlatch.[2]

Like payback?

Canada wants to give Mansfield people something. They don't have anything. They told the people, "We'll give you this song, we'll give you this Ganhook, we'll give you this dance. It's yours, in return of the potlatch that you always give us. Use it," they said. So we have a right to use that. Just like we bought it. What people call trade. That's how it is. That's how we have right to use this Ganhook and the dances and all that thing.

And today, even if today someone make a speech and say, "The dances come from Canada," I'll believe that. That's where my Dad said it all come from. So you know the song [sings]. This song here is one of the song that we still use today from last time when Canada [people] got to Mansfield. And we used to use two or three. After we took over the dance here, then we're making our own song.

Your own dance song.

Our own dance song. Right now we're using this song that I just sung. Okay. That's only one [that] come from Dawson. That's the only one that we got left. Only one we use, anyway.

There's one that they do up there now, that's the "Canadian American Flag Song." Was that one that you guys got, too?

Tanacross dancers performing a Han dance that came from Dawson and Eagle Village, August 2001. Women are in the center of the circle with hands on their hips or holding bandanas. Photograph by Craig Mishler.

No, no. In the old days they didn't have that. We have song for American flag, our own, right here in Alaska. But I never heard anything about Canada have any songs about the flag.

They do.

Maybe they do now, but I never heard about it until now.

So that's the way it is. That's how we got this dance. This is how we got this Ganhook. It was given to the people of Mansfield in return for the potlatch that we give them. We give them big potlatch three or four different times, and they feel so guilty that they want to give something to the people in Mansfield, and they don't have anything to give. So this one old man said, "Give them the song, dance, and Ganhook."

So that's the way it went. That's how we got this Ganhook. This is how we got the dance. This is how we got what we have. And we have really right to use what was given to us in return of the potlatch that we give. That's how we got it. In other words, we didn't get it for nothing. It wasn't Christmas present or anything. In return of the potlatch, that's what we got back in return of our potlatch that we give. So that's the way it is, and I hope that there's no misunderstanding. And this is the way it is and there's no way I can change it. And that's the way it is for today.

DANCE REVIVAL

I'm a dance leader to this village all the way up Upper Tanana. Wherever, the whole Alaska, I would say. To start with, I was in army years ago [during] the Second World War. When I left this country in 1942 there was little bit of dance going on. Not very much, but little bit. We used to have clothes costume when I was a kid. But it died off for quite a while when the army and all the good stuff that comes into the country, that dies off. People all went to work and make lot of money from the field and whatever the army was doing and what not. All the Native people are working, and the more money that comes into the country the more the people went modern, and some of the people quit teaching how to hunt for their subsistence. They don't try to teach their kids all that. They went to this easy way, the modern way. The big change, *big* change to the easiest way. They went to the white man way. With the world war everything went booming so our Native people quit that dancing.

So when I got back from the army, I didn't want to lose that, really. Northway still had it. Them old people, Walter Northway, Bill Northway, Frank Sam, Bill John—all them guys that still have that song. I bought a tape recorder and I bought some tape and I took it up to my aunt and my uncle. I'm related to them people up there that still have it. On the way up there there's a liquor store. So I'd buy them two or three bottles and I give my uncle [a] few shots and tell them what I'm doing. I tell them, "I don't want to lose this. I want you people to get together." We always sit down, have a cup of tea together. My uncles, my grandpa, and all of them, they come together with me.

They always liked me. They always called me, "Soldier." They all come together and they start singing and here I'm taping them. Really I don't want to lose that. Steven Northway, you remember him—Walter Northway, all them guys. They were my uncles, that's why it went really easy for me. They know what I'm trying to do. They're smart people. I told my uncles that I don't want to lose the Native dance. This is something I want to hang on to; I want to bring it back to this country.

This [singing] is something I want to hang on to. I want to bring it back to this country. And then two times I went up there, to get different songs that I want. But there are two ways of dancing. One way is good-time dance. And one way is sorry song, when somebody died.

Well, all that song that were made. It's not easy to make a song. It takes time, and you've got to be a very smart person. Like I study. I study all this song, and I learn it, and pretty soon my wife, she always let somebody know that I'm singing, or somebody, you know. So they could come. Like Abraham Isaac and me, we used to sing. I'm learning from this tape recorder. I play it all the time. And I go back to my uncle, and I ask him, "What does this song mean?" There's a meaning, something. The song is there, but it mean something. This is the thing that I got to find out. It's all there on tape, and I have to put it together. And it's not easy.

Just the same thing as what you're doing now, that you're trying to . . .

Record?

Record it. And then you *learn* from it. That's how *I* learn it. And pretty soon I find out what the words *mean*. Every song have meaning to it. And I learn that. Then I sing it. I sing it all the time. Pretty soon I got help. Like Abraham Isaac, he help me a lot. Pretty soon Andrew come, Andrew Isaac. Me and Abraham, like holiday we used to sing it really happy song together. We really get together and sing it, really happy songs for the holidays, like Christmas?

Yeah.

Then *everybody* start joining us. Pretty soon when they have potlatch, we [were] dancing. We find ourself dancing. Because song is so happy that everybody start joining just automatically. I try to teach our younger people the songs and the dances, and it goes on all the time. Like today, you'd say I'm trying to teach these young people. I got three or four guys, they're trying really hard. But nobody *ever* get as good as I am right now. They could try, but without me the potlatch is not a potlatch.

Is there anybody who's learning from you that's going to take over after you?

They going to try to take over. It's going to take time for them, it look like.

Ellen: Jerry Isaac.

Yeah. Jerry Isaac is doing that right now. Larry Jonathon is doing it right now. My daughter here is doing it, Debbie [Thomas]. And all my girls are singing. And one of my boys, but he's kind of shy to get out there. And he was drumming since he was that big [gestures], one of my grandkids, little boy [Christopher Denny]. Him and I went to Washington, D.C., to dance for five or six thousand people.

So that's how people [are] getting started again. Dance getting started again. If there's a potlatch somewhere, they call me. They want me there. Without me the potlatch is not going to be a potlatch. That's the way it is. I'm trying really hard, like you would say [sings]: "Onee, hee hee. Tanacross danii hee. . ." You know them kind of songs mean: "We're the Tanacross dancers—watch us." It means something. *Everything* means something.

Have you ever composed your own song?

Oh yes. My daughter, we're making potlatch, all of us, and my late father and mother were buried over across the river [at the old village of Tanacross]. The [grave] fence is so old, I got opposite clan for my mother, opposite clan for my Dad, to build me a fence for them. Rebuild that fence. So they'll have new one.

So therefore we got to make potlatch. I can make potlatch on my Mom, but I can't make potlatch on my Dad. That's her people, my wife's people. My Dad is my wife's people [Dik'aagyu clan]. Same clan. My kids have right to make potlatch on my Dad. They can't make potlatch on my Mom. I'm only the one that can make potlatch on my Mom. So my wife and my kids, they're making potlatch on my Dad, and I'm making potlatch on my Mom.

So, we had a whole bunch of guns. Gee, I must've bought thirty or forty guns. My Dad have lot of people on that side, you know. And I have a lot of people on my Mom's side. All my cousins. Everybody help me too. And my daughter comes in here, "Well Dad, I'll tell you something." I wanted to come in with a gun, dance into the community hall with a gun. "We got to have a song, Dad. Our own song. What can I sing?" she said.

So every day I thought about it. Every day I thought about it. What can we do? What can I do? I got to make some kind of song that can stay with my kids. So I thought about it and thought about it, and one day it just come into my mind—shewwww! Just like that. So it stay every day for a long time, and I thought about it. What kind of word I could put in there. The right word that I can use to finish that potlatch with.

So the one we want to go down with, come up [referring to body movements up and down during the dance] to make people happy. That's what my daughter want.

Happy song.

Uh-huh [affirming]. So we all mixed, my Mom and my Dad. All the guns were mixed. After that we're separated, but when we come in [to the community hall we were] mixed, [all at] one time. Just happy thing. But we were singing [sings]: "Hee haa hee, hee haa. . ." That's the song that I made.

For your mother.

For my mother and my Dad. I give it to my daughter [Diane], and they [are still] using it today. This is one of the best songs that everybody likes. That song, you see everybody get out there and dance in it today. Yeah. That's the stuff that we come in with, strong song. Very strong. And it means a lot of things in my language, my way. We had a lot of guns and stuff. Like you say, spiritual power is in there.

When you sing it, do you remember your mother that way?

Oh yes. That's what it means. Yeah, it's really something. Like today is one of the top songs in the country. It's not easy to make song. We got to think about it for many, many, many, many days. Each day I put a little song in there. I take some [words] out, put some in. Take some out, put some in. Take some out. You know that's why it's not easy. It mean something. It means something in each song. Sometime the word don't fit in there—we'll take it out. To make it powerful, it's got to be just right.

The song we use when we bring in the guns on the last night of the potlatch is a good-luck song I made for my daughter Diane. We do that song when we come in with the rifles, but sometimes we also do it without the guns. When we do it without the guns, the women go into the center of the men and dance with their hands on their hips. It's the same song.

And how about your drum?

Well, drum is the circle of life. It's very important to us.

For the potlatch.

For the potlatch. All we're in the circle of life. When they hear that drum, people comes.

What do you call the drum in your language?

Ch'elxal. Xal is a noise. Hitting the drum.[3]

Do you have name for the stick too?

Ch'elxal tįį. Yeah. Like white people say, it's the circle of our life. [Sentence in Tanacross.] Us, in the middle. We're in the circle. That's what it means. It brings the people into that circle all the time. When you hear something, you got to go there and see what it is. And this is how I learned to get this thing started, get the people started again. I always think that God has given me that gift to share with the young people.

Another question about your dance. When you come on the dance floor for potlatch, do the clans separate from each other?

No, no, no, no, no. Mixed together. Only time we're separated is when you have a song of their own for their potlatch. She [Ellen] have a song for her own potlatch. I have a song for my own potlatch. My clan. Different clans have a different song for their own potlatch. This is the last song. There is memorial potlatch, which is different thing, that we can't sing the [same] song that we sing for the last one. There's another

Kenny Thomas Sr. with drum (Ch'elxal) and drum stick (Ch'elxal tįį) at the Mansfield Village Culture Camp, July 1998. Photograph by Craig Mishler.

Tanacross women
doing the Calico
Dance, August 2001.
Ellen Thomas is
second from right.
Photograph by Craig
Mishler.

memorial potlatch here. You don't have to sing potlatch song for that
one. You can sing sorry song for this one.

But when you get to really potlatch, you got to have your own song.
Like a little while ago I told you there is powerful spiritual power in
there. That's the one that have power in there. That last potlatch [song].

There's power in the song, huh?

Oh yes. Very powerful.

The Calico Dance and tug-of-war that we do on the final night of
the potlatch was something we used to do a long time ago. Then we
stopped doing it for a long time, and I worked to help bring it back.

STORY OF A POTLATCH SONG

There was young man living with his uncle, but he was lazy and good
for nothing. He couldn't hunt, he couldn't trap, he couldn't do anything. Three times his uncle beat him with a stick, and after the third
time he just left and went out into the woods by himself.

He was walking along feeling ashamed when something or someone came over him and landed behind him. Anyway, whoever it was
told him, "Don't look at me. I'm here to help you." And this person or
thing hit him across the back with his cane, and right away the young

man threw up. The second time the cane hit him, he threw up again and spit out all that bad luck food he had been eating.

And from then on he really got lucky. He began to catch all kinds of game and lots of fur. He got so much stuff that he made three pot-latches on his uncle.[4] And at the first potlatch he sang this song, "I was ashamed . . . Yowshe'," which we still sing today.

FIDDLE MUSIC AND SQUARE DANCES

Anyway, when I was a little bit older, I seen my Mom and them dancing in the old fiddle music. The white people comes into the country at that time. And Native people are learning how to do the fiddling and harmonica. I remember they have square dances. Ellen's dad, Joe Joseph, was a caller, and my uncle Charlie James was a caller too. You talk about good time, without alcohol and drugs; we don't even know what the hell that is, and people really have a good time.

Who were your fiddlers those days?

The white people, some white people do that, and they were teaching the Native people. Finally they picked it up, and they went on by themselves. So that's what we do.

I heard Silas Solomon was a fiddler.

Silas, yeah. And Julius Paul. That is really something for people. Long time ago, the white people played for the Native people; they used to live here, some of them white people.

Did that start before your time or when you were a kid?

No, I think, it start when I was really young.

In the 1930s?

Before that I think. I just barely remember that I used to sleep in the dance hall waiting for my Mom [laughs]. So it must have started in late twenties. Anyway, why it was a lot of fun without drugs and alcohol.

Gee whiz, when I was a little boy—that must be back in the twenties somewhere, early twenties, I remember that the white people are going through, stampeding in Fairbanks and Dawson, them places. Lot of white people come through and they bring fiddle. And they plays for the dance all the time. All the times that I seen the dances and square dances that they had and they played violin, I never seen guitar. I just seen either harmonica, maybe banjo four or five times. But most of the time [what] I seen was violin. And I noticed that everybody's practicing when I was a kid. I didn't know one of the best thing people like in my area is square dance. They dance square dance all night long. I remember Joe Joseph and Charlie James doing the call.

Callers?

They're callers, yeah. And I seen my Mother and them was all dressed [up]. They wear a black skirt with white shirt, and my Dad would be wearing suit with white shirt. Everybody, not only my Dad. Everybody dressed up. They all dressed the same. The women will have black skirt and white shirt and moccasin, and it's just everybody dressed for it. Anyway, I remember sleeping down there waiting for my Mom and Dad, in the community hall. And I watch. Sometime they're up to about eight couple, but I seen maybe up to sixteen couples.

You were talking about how they dressed up, huh?

Yup. You know people *really* like to square dance. I seen *good* square dance, very good square dance. You know how they right in command, how they call? They're just right in there with that. They're doing it so long that they just like fall in place.

Do the callers dance too?

No, no, no. He was standing over on the side.

Over by the fiddlers?

Yeah. And boy he just blah, blah, blah all the time and make people just happy. I notice that and gee whiz, it's really going strong. You don't see that today. I see Rabbit Dance, Duck Dance, and all that stuff.[5] Them days I didn't see that kind. But this square dance that I seen way back there in the twenties, it's not like the square dance they're doing it today. It's really different. A lot more fun. More fun, more people, and they have more than one fiddle. It goes a long time. They don't do it for ten minutes. They're going maybe half-hour, forty minutes, hour, or something like that. It seems like to me an hour or better.

For one dance?

Yeah. Long time. Gosh, I like it when the guys go zig-zagging. The guys go this way and woman goes that way. Zigzagging between each other. And then you get to your partner; then you swing one time, then you dance around. Oh gee whiz, it's really something. They were really all trained for it, I think. And it's a lot better dance than today. I wish I could just go back to that. A lot more fun.

How did the women dress up? Did they have long dress?

Long dress, yes. Long black dress, really black dress, way down to ankle. You know when they swing like that they just shooooooh, just like umbrella.

Their skirts are swirling around?

Yeah. So, it's a lot better than what it is today. And people are really dressed the same. Everybody dressed the same, and like brand new slippers and black suit, and white shirt.

And necktie?

Necktie. You know, some of them old-timers, my Dad I remember right on his tie he had a gold pin, big gold pin. Some of them they have gold chain. My Dad I remember he had a Hamilton watch, railroad watch he called it. Gold chain on it. They put [on] all the best they got. They put all that stuff on. It's something you'll probably never see it again. I don't think I'm good enough to start anything like that. I don't remember all what the [dance] call was. Some of them I do, here and there. I was little bit too small that time.

You mentioned the other day that Arthur Wright was one of the fiddlers. What do you remember about him?

Oh, he was one of the players. I remember him playing square dances. He was a schoolteacher at home. Arthur Wright was originally from Minto.

Was he Native?

Native, part Native. And he has a wife, white woman for wife. And I remember Gareth Wright and Alfred and Don [Wright]. I remember all of them at home. I used to play around with them all the time. We grew up together, and we had a good time. Arthur Wright was a player, good player. And I remember Silas Solomon was a player too, and Matthew Paul, at that time. Mostly the white people play that used to live right around there. Some of the Native people got into it. But I seen not only fiddlers; I seen harmonica. Five harmonica, five people altogether. Someone over here goes down, someone [else] picks it up. It's just really good how they got set up.

Could they dance for that?

Oh yeah. They play a square dance song.

Gee, I never see that.

If they brought that [harmonica] thing down with me, if I brought that harmonica down then I could play you some square dance songs, but I forgot it. And when there's no fiddle, I see them dance with that harmonica. Gee, like "Turkey in the Straw," gee—"Comin' Around the Mountain When She Comes" and all that good stuff, "Soldier's Joy," all that song was there. I remember them dancing with that harmonica.

Did you have a community hall in those days?

Oh yes. Big community hall, big son-of-a-gun. I never seen any guitar. Guitar would sound good with that harmonica. I remember some banjo, old banjo. And later on I remember a few mandolin. Many people are using. But I'm pretty sure they're pretty active in dance in that area. They wanted to keep that up all the time, practice, and just before Christmas and places like that.

They do it for every holiday?

Yes. Every holiday. Sometime they just do it for practice. They just sit around and watch. I remember my older sister and older brother was in it. My older sister Lena was in it, and my brother Silas was in it. And my other cousin, Silas Solomon, he was in it. They're young. They're young people. But they got so they're pretty darn good. And them are the people if they're alive they could carry it on. But all of them deceased; they died. But anyway it's a great thing for the people living in that area. That old man who used to live in Tanacross. He one of the fiddle player. He teach the Native people how to play.

What was his name?

Old Flannigan. Anyway, it's a great thing for the Native people. I notice them Tetlin people come all the way from Tetlin to come to dance. Northway come for holidays just to see the dance or to get into it. They practiced too.

Would you have that kind of dance, square dance, with a potlatch, or was that separate?

You know that last time when they had that potlatch up there for me, that's the first time we ever got fiddle there—I mean [Western] music there. My kids are doing that because I like that music. You know lots of people who don't dance Indian dance, they dance in fiddle dance. So they made it so everybody will have a good time. So anyway, I remember a lot of people from Tetlin. Titus David, Walter David, and a lot of other people come from Tetlin, I remember it.

Did they have dances up in Tetlin too?

No, they come to Tanacross to dance. Sometime if they're going to practice, they send word up there. They come two or three nights, two or three days to dance and then go back. Just like here [in Fairbanks] what they're doing [for the Athabaskan Fiddle Festival]. During holiday, twenty-fourth night they start dancing.

December 24th?

Yes. All night long. I don't remember how far into the night. I remember sleep and wait for my Dad and Mom in the community hall. Anyway, it goes on and on and on. Square dance is just only thing they do. No two steps or nothing. All they do is square dance.

But you said they did what we call contra dances. Men in one line and women in one line.

Yeah, yeah. Oh they did that too. Mostly square dance though.

In a big circle?

Big circle. I seen up to sixteen couple. It takes a lot of room for sixteen couple. You know that Tanacross community hall that we have there, it can't hold sixteen couple there, I don't think. And you were talking about sixty-four couple. Oh my God!

(Laughs.) It could just be talk, you know.

That's what I think, 'cause I seen up to sixteen couples, and they were crowded. We seen how at culture camp, and [sings] "Hold hand, hey, hey, hey," etc. That song, you know, how they go up there and hold hands, four couple[s] [referring to square dancing to drum accompaniment]. That's part of it, I remember. They swing their arms; that's part of it. But I'm trying to find more. There's lots more to that. You go zigzag in between. What we need to do is we need to practice that, practice.

Who made that Square Dance? You made that?

Yeah.

Yourself?

No. All of us. All of us did that. It's a sorry song is what it is. Sorry song that we made into Square Dance [sings]. You see we just make up from one song to another. Into Square Dance or Twist.[6] Twist is Chubby Checker like, and Two-Step song, we made that up too, you know. Just to have a good time. Just for the people that don't know how to dance Indian dance, we're doing that for. We go together like that, man and boys together.

Oh, when they cross over?

Yeah, uh-huh [affirming].

Is that kind of like some kind of square dance?

Yeah. That's part of it.

That kind I never saw before.

That's part of that Square Dance I'm talking about.

Is that from a sorry song too?

No. That's a really one. Chubby Checker is a really one too. And that come out of *his* song.

Right.

So anyway, why we do lots of things, like I think in my area we are really rich in our culture, that we understand what our language is, and we can combine that with English, kind of put it together and put it in *our* language, go from there. Yeah, it's hard; it's hard to do things like if we can get some fiddlers and maybe we can try to go back to that old-time square dance. We got to get in practice all the time, till we get to as far as we want to go.

So you remember these dances when you were a little kid?

Well, I couldn't say that I remember all of it, but I remember lot of it. We can try to go with it. It probably will come back to me, but I know I remember lot of it. If there's good song that we can get four, five, or six couples, and just try.

Start small.

And just go from there.

Add more couples.

Then people will get to know what it's all about. Then they can go for it. I think what we need to do is more practice. And we have to sit down with the people and tell them what this is all about. This is what I seen. I got to tell them stories about what I seen. It's so popular that people from way in the hell different villages come long ways, I remember. They come from Kechumstuk to Tanacross just for fiddling dance and square dance, and things like that.

CELEBRATING THE HOLIDAYS

And I remember one time six families was on the way down. Got snowed in at Long Cabin. It's about seventy miles, I would say sixty miles from Tanacross. And they got snowed in, and they can't go any farther. So they got on the lake. Oh, they shovel all the snow off with snowshoes. And they build a big fire, and that time they bring some meat. Them days two or three families get together and cook every day till seven, eight days, I guess. The second-to-last day to cook, January 2nd. Anyway, why they can't go any farther, so they got onto the lake, and they haul that snow off, and they put big Christmas tree there. Nothing on it. And they cook that meal, cook a big meal for six families. And my Mom tells stories and some guys do like this [gestures] and make it look like they're playing violin. Looks like they're doing a square dance. And that's how it was at that time.

But they got no fiddle.

No fiddle, just [sings a few vocables]. They make it look like they're playing, and that's just how important that thing is to them. And I always tell stories about that. My Mom tells me about it, and that's just how important square dance [is] to them.

So I think, Craig, what we can do is, after we get the fiddle music going, why we can try to start it. Even before that I'd like to try. If I can get some good fiddle music and get some kids together. They got good idea how it's going to be because we do a little bit of that [in our drum dance]. But we have to practice. We have to practice.

Long time ago, people are just getting ready right now for Christmas. Everybody will be out on the trapline. Christmas Day they call Nalchin bal dhen. "Nalchin bal" means "today," in white man's way, you would say it's "a gift exchange." That's what it means—"Nalchin bal dhen." That's the day that they exchange the gift. Like you come in here and you bring that thing through the door like this, with a little hook on it with a lot of paddles on it, and you come through and you got to put it.[7] At that time there was no such thing as pencils, no paper, no nothing. All they had was charcoal or something like that. You draw something like a gun or something you want. A gun or whatever. They don't say no to nobody. If that is what they want, that is what they're going to get. Then you go back. If you did that to me, then I have go to you [with a gift]. Something like gift exchange, and that's why they call it Nalchin bal dhen. Anyway, gee it's a lot of fun.

Is there a name for that hook?

Yes, that why they call it Nalchin bal dhen all together, the day, and all that stuff. Anyway it's a lot of fun, like they start December 24 up until January 2. Everybody's cooking. One day it will be me and my family [cooking]. Next day it would [be] somebody else. Next day, it will be somebody else, and all the way down, lots of good time.

Could you tell about that solstice? The shortest day when you change your socks?

Yeah. Anyway, they respect the day. Christmastime. Right now you people call it Christmastime. Nalchin bal dhen—Christmas, how we call it. "Dzeen ni' xodl" just means "short days," and "with winter approaching."

Kenny with masked friend attending a Halloween ball at the Tanacross school, October 31, 2000. Photograph by Craig Mishler.

Twenty-one [December 21]. They used to tell us during this time, "Exchange your socks from one foot to the other." That means "You go from one foot to another." You change your socks to different foot. Because they respect that day that we're going into the wintertime. Then it goes all the way into winter and back into June over here. June 21 is the longest day in Alaska, in the world, I would say. Us here, longest day. That's the day you see the midnight sun, I guess. That's what they call it today. And there you go again. You change your socks again. "Don't forget," they used to tell us. When you're exchanging your socks you're supposed to be mentally preparing yourself for the change of the season. That's what it means.

When you say, change your socks, do you mean put on clean socks?

No. Just switch.

Switch your left to your right and your right to your left.

That's right. You don't put no clean socks on.

Okay. (Laughs.)

That's what it means. That's when we change all together. We're supposed to change with the world. Change from summertime into wintertime.

CHAPTER 8

Living in Two Different Worlds

Subsistence and Cultural Preservation

Of all the things that help define Native culture, subsistence hunting and fishing traditions lie at the core. Alaskan newspapers have almost daily headlines on subsistence issues, and debates over Native versus non-Native and urban versus rural rights are incessant, setting the stage for an ongoing legal and political debate. For thousands of years, before there were any white people in Alaska, Kenny's ancestors found ways to live off the country, but Kenny realizes that in order to preserve subsistence, it has to be taught to each new generation and practiced every day. Species by species, he talks about the pivotal roles each animal plays in shaping Indian life and explains why each must be respected. In this context, grandma's walking cane and grandpa's caribou fence are enduring symbols of leadership and continuity.

CULTURE CAMP

After I came back from the army I see there's a lot of things changed, mostly not my way but the Western way of living. And people are getting away from our traditional way, our cultural way, so one day we just sat down, whole bunch of us, my daughters and whole bunch of us, and we just thought we could start a culture camp up at Mansfield. That's what we did; that was seventeen or eighteen years ago. And it seems to work out very good for us; people from all over the state of Alaska comes to see us every summer. We don't say no to nobody.

And you are very welcome to come there if you have time, whatever. And last few years we have a little help from Tanana Chiefs. Before that we have to do that on our own. We have to raise our own money. The reason for that, for raising our own money is, I am trying to keep the big wheels and politics out of there. And I don't want anybody to tell me how to run the camp. I want to run it myself, the way I think is best for my people. So what we teach there at Mansfield is our languages, our Native songs, our traditional way of making spoons, birch-bark baskets for the girls, and sewing slippers and bead work and stuff like that for the girls, and we carve a lot of diamond willows, different things. And we teach a lot of subsistence, how to fish and what to do with it after you catch it, and how to dry it, how to smoke it, what material you could use to smoke the fish.

And sometimes we get a moose. [The Alaska Department of] Fish and Game let us take a moose [with an educational permit], and that's what we dry, and we teach how to dry that. We teach the boys how to hunt, and we teach them how to set fishnets and stuff like that. It's a great thing—how to pick berries. And we teach lot of our young children about the potlatches and a lot of good things that we teach up there. A lot of people from different villages are there to learn from us, so that they can take that back to their village and try to start something like what we're doing.

I think this is about the best thing that ever happened to anybody in the country is our culture camp because we are losing it, and right now I can see it working because lot of kids when they have potlatches, they understand how they [are] related, and they understand who to give it [their gifts] to, and most of the time they come back to me for their relationship, and I help a lot to my people here in Tanacross. Not only here, but in Tetlin, Northway, Mentasta, Dot Lake, elsewhere, like I tell them who their relations is because I know their background from them. Their old mother and old Dad, and I know how they [are] related to each other. So that really helps for our potlatches.

Now today, what I'm trying to do up [in] Mansfield is let those kids know where they're coming from, where their Dad come from, where their Mama come from, where their grandpa come from. And I let them know who they are; *this* is what I teach.

Aerial view of Mansfield Village, September 29, 1988. Photograph by Craig Mishler.

FINDING GRANDPA'S TRAIL

So what I'm doing is I start blazing trail for these young people. Young people today are so hungry to learn the old ways, our old people's ways [speaks in Tanacross]. They got nobody to teach them what the thing [our culture] was, years ago. Right now today, I'm trying to help the young people to find our grandpa's trail again, the trail that was lost a long time ago. This is what I'm trying to do. I'm trying to help these young people to find this trail again, and I'll keep blazing this trail up until my time is up. But what I want to do is I want to leave what little I have to these kids.

What very little I know and remember is what I want to leave on this earth for them. That mean that I going to leave a little something that I know with them before I leave. But today, I see younger people who really want to learn a lot of things. What I do is I teach the songs of Mansfield, I teach the stories, I teach how the people [are] related. That's what you got to know—how we're related to different people.

Like I said a little while ago, Tandîidz altsiil is one of the very important persons. That gentleman is related to the both sides, like Ałts'įį dendeey [Kenny's clan] and Dik'aagyu [Ellen's clan]. He can bury either one of us and get potlatch from either side. That's Chaadh people, Tandîidz altsiil, he's the same as Chaadh and Checheelyu. All three names is the same as one. Mostly they [are] related to Chaadh and Checheelyu. Mostly are related to just two [clans of] people. But he related to us on both side. That's why they call [him] a Middle Man, Tandîidz altsiil. That's why they call him Tandîidz altsiil.

My father and them used to make speech to each other. One of the things they used to make speech to each other is the Old Mansfield Hill, and that's where I'm from. All the people who used to make speeches, my grandfather, my uncles, all those people used to make speeches about these mountains and Mount Sanford, and all those. That mountain up there, Naadain Xu' or Tanacross Mountain, that's always [been] known; it's always been called or referred to for people from Tanacross.

That's just like American flag for the village, them hills, what I'm talking about. That mountain up there has often been used in speech as well, to indicate or identify people from Tanacross. All these mountain, Mansfield Hill, and all these other mountains, during the potlatch speeches they were often used, so it's just like they were inscribed with the names on each of these mountains.

Today I'm trying to bring this thing back and I'm trying to tell the people what this hill is all about. As far as I can figure what it is, the hill is just like American flag for us Native people, for the village. I don't know how else you would call it, but each hill represent the village. Dihthâad [Dhel'] is Mansfield, Naadain Xu' is Tanacross, Tetlin Sheddh is Tetlin, Chendeł is Northway, Copper River is Keltin, Dot Lake would be Chiin Tsedl.

Tetlin Hill, and the one in Northway, all those are what my uncles and grandfather and all of them used to bring out during their potlatch speeches. Nowadays, all these symbols, all these names, are lost. This person I'm telling a story to, I want him to know, too, there were people that lived down towards Salcha area. Even up [Goodpaster River] there used to be lots of people.[1] There is nobody left there anymore. Even up around Kechumstuk there used to be a lot of people, back then. Out of all these people there aren't very many left, just what you see right here, only a handful. That's all there is. Just a few people from Northway and Tetlin, just a few of us together.

Each summer when we take these young people to Mansfield, these lessons are what we're trying to pass on to the modern Native generation. "Hua uniil tin" means "teaching the children about the meaning of potlatch." "Huhtiitł." Today they call it "potlatch." That's what we do each summer at the culture camp. During the culture camp too, the young people including my grandchildren are taught about the relationships within each clan.

Relationships and how you're related to people is very important to know because during a potlatch you need to know the relationships within each [Upper Tanana] village. All those people who are related and not related come together at this time. That's why you need to know relationships. In white man's way it's very important for the kids to know that. It's very important they learn how they related. Lots of ways you don't want to make mistake.

Because during potlatches, we give gifts only to people who are not related to us [that is, to people of a different clan]. The people who are not related to us are the ones who give us gifts during potlatch times. The people of Northway, Tetlin, and other villages around here and how they are related is known by my children because I have taught them since they were small who their clan relations are and who their nonrelations are.

THE WALKING CANE

I started the culture camp because I was so sorry for my people. My Dad, he blaze trail for me up to this far. My grandpa, he blaze trail for me up to this far. My Mom, my grandma and them, this is how far they cut the trail from here and across to the old village. My grandmother and them, it's just like they stuck their [walking] cane there in the ground for me. We should be holding up that symbol, we should be holding up that meaning. That's the kind of people we should turn out to be.

I wonder if we going to haul that cane up there. If it fall down, that mean we lost all our culture. My people, they put that cane in that village for me over there in Mansfield too, and I don't want that thing to fall. That's the reason why. I don't want that cane to fall over. That's

Flat-bottom riverboats, looking down the Tanana River from Tanacross, August, 2001. Photograph by Craig Mishler.

why we have that culture camp at Mansfield for our young people. That's what the camp is.

Grandma's cane standing upright represents the old people's way of life. Morris Thompson, the president of Doyon, took his cane and stuck it in this land.[2] I'd like to see that cane stand up straight. He stuck it there for us to follow. It's up to us to keep it straight for as long as we live. If that cane ever falls over, the whole country is going to go broke.

I always work with young people most of my life to keep them away from drugs and alcohol. And that's the reason why we trying to keep this culture camp going. Just me and the wife and a few other elders that we have to hire from different villages. Trying to get back to some of the things that we did. Why alcohol is bad. Maybe we could do something different. How to learn to survive. That's why we teach survival. We teach arts and crafts. You seen it up at Mansfield. It's a great thing for the people, the young people. And I think sometimes we think it can help the young people to stay away from stuff.

Our clan today—I'm Ałts'įį dendeey. I'm a high man, really high man. She's pretty high woman [pointing to Ellen], Dik'aagyu. They're high people. We all have high people. Our people were higher. Our ancestor was *very* high people. You don't want to break that down with that alcohol and drugs. You don't want to play around with that. This is the thing that we're trying to teach. Not to play around with who you are. Don't forget who you are before you take that stuff. This is the thing that we're trying to teach.

"Diichah" is our word for "high people." High people are those who are respected. "Tiitaih" is our word for "low people." Low people are not respected because they have not been taught properly.

COUNSELING YOUTH

Tell me about your way of counseling.

They say "Chaxdaenii," which means "I'm teaching you how to be a man, how you can take care of yourself, to be among people."

Explain how you do that.

I got to tell you. Like, if I don't say anything to you, you wouldn't know anything. That's why today I blame myself before I say anything. Before, you hear a lot of people say, "The young generation don't know nothing." You heard that. You don't hear *that* from me. Me, I have to blame myself because I think I'm the one [who] should be teaching these kids already, long time ago. In fact, I'm teaching my own kids. And they know it. And this is the thing that we have to do, to teach them how to be a person, good person.

If you caught your kid doing something bad, when they're little . . .

Yeah, I got to remind them. I got to remind them. This is no good for to do that. I don't want my kids to talk about somebody else, criticize somebody. I don't want they talk about you when you're not around— bad, I mean. Gossip. I don't like that. I told my wife, my kids many times I don't want to hear it. I don't want to hear it. They always tells me about something, but I don't want to hear it. I told them I don't want to hear it. None of my business. Maybe I take care of myself, just the way my Dad taught me. That's the way I taught my kids to be. Chaxdaenii. That's what I recall. They train us. We listen to this. How to be good person. How we can stay away from people who talks about, gossip all the time.

You do that just with kids, or you do it with friends?

I do that with friends too, now. Last twenty years that I been with the culture camp, I share that with the young people. Before that I was just doing it with my kids. I figure *you* can take care of your kids, just the way I've been doing. That's why I didn't share it with the whole [community]. I know today, last twenty years that I remember of, them old people I study them.

Did you ever use paddling or anything like that when you raised them? Is that something you believe in?

No, no. I don't believe in that. I don't want to do that.

You'd rather talk to them, huh?

I want to sit down with them. I want to sit down and talk. Better to talk to them. Sometime they getting about yay high, it's too late to paddle them. If they can get big enough to understand me, they know what I'm trying to say. That's what I figure. What good is paddling them? I don't believe in that at all. No, I don't like that, and I don't like to say, "You don't know nothing." I don't want to say that.

You ever shout at them?

No, no, no.

You don't do that either.

Nobody listens to you. I wouldn't listen to nobody when I was a kid if someone shout at me. "Hell with you, I'm going." That's the way they are.

Out the door, eh?

Yeah. You got to be nice so kids can understand you, and we got to make them understand by sitting down and just listen to us. It's going to do you good somewhere down the line. It probably wouldn't do you any good today, but it will be down the line somewhere you're going to fall back to it. Like many time what my Dad, my grandpa, my grandma, my Mom and them told me, it's coming back to me today.

How they used to teach me. How I should act. Like people, old people, old people in Tanacross. I see them. I help them all the time. I pack water. I pack wood. I do anything for them. Lot of time I go, grandpa, grandma will be praying for me for doing that. Maybe that's why today I'm still here. My Mom, my father, my sister, my brother, all died off except me. I do lots of good things for people. I try to help. All my life I trying to help people. A lot of love in me. We talk about love. I have to show them what the love is by doing it. I can't just say "love." In my heart.

What do you call "love" in your language? What do you say for "love"?

Maldintįį. Maldintįį. It's got to come from your heart. You got to do like I told you a little while ago. Do a lot of things for the old people. Right there that shows you the love that I show love to you for these old people. I love them; that's why I do that. If I didn't give a damn then I just run around out there. That's two different things. So that's what they call Chaxdaenii. Teach all the time. People teaching you. Older person will teach you how you should do this, how you should do that. How it's good that you can help elders.

Just one on one?

Yes, one on one.

You wouldn't do it with a group?

No, no, no. Sometimes I get out and tell everybody, whole bunch of kids. But most likely if the kids just don't listen I go one on one. There's lot of kids that listening all the time at home. But the kids are pretty good.

SUBSISTENCE LIVING

Today, there are two worlds. We got stuck in between two different worlds. As I speak, we are the ones that are stuck in between these two worlds. We would really like to live in the white man's world. That's our wish. I wanted to live like the white man, and I walked with them so very far away. But now I've changed my mind. It's just like I turned around and came back to our world, to our own world. It's just like collecting all of you, gathering all of you up and showing you my grandfather's way. That's why I'm telling this story.

We cannot go all the way to their culture. We might go a little ways over here. That's as far as we're going to go. I want to live like the white man all my life, but I'll never make it all the way over there. I might be over here, but that's as far as I gonna go.

This world that we're taught about, I don't even know what my grandfather and them knew about it, so I can't say very much more than what I know. I want to go back a little ways over here. I can't take you all the way over, but I'll take you part way over here [to our traditional culture]. But I will teach you what I know, and I'll take you that far. We were taught how to hunt, how to trap; all of this is what I know.

That's what I call living off of this country. You make a living off this country. We have to learn how to do that. That's what people used to teach us, how we used to make a living. Today they say, "You make mistake." We were teached not to make mistake, not to shoot something that's just moving. You got to see the head before you shoot something. You got to make sure that's moose before you shoot him. You don't just shoot something that moves because [its] track went that way. Them kind of thing is what we really been teached to do. That's why there's no mistake. I don't believe Native people will make mistake if he's hunting. There's no way he can make mistake from what we learned. We learned how to make a living off this country. And if you don't learn anything about it, you'll get very hungry. You'll never make it. We got to learn how to hunt, how to fish, how to get the food. We got to learn how to do that.

When I was a kid I seen a depression for the white people [the Great Depression of the 1930s]. We didn't know there was a depression going on because we live a different way from you. Over here the white people are just going so dead and hungry they can't buy anything, even if they got money. But you can't eat money. So you can't buy anything because of depression. They go to the Native people and get dry meat and dry fish. They help a lot of white people that come through, cold and hungry. Many time I see my Dad hunt for white man. They come up here and they think that they going to get a pack full of gold and go back. That's not the way it is. A lot of people that died up here starved to death. [They] don't know how to make a living off this country. If you don't have no experience in how to hunt or anything like that, you going to go hungry. And that's the way it is for many people. I noticed that at the time, Native people really helped a lot of white people out. If it wasn't for Native people, a lot of white people would go hungry.

About five miles out of Kechumstuk there's a hill there, a long hill. At the end of the hill there's a big tower where they have a lookout. In that hill you have to dig and try to find vitseh taih, that's the flint rock that you build a fire with. You find it there in that hill.

You see, all of that is *lost*. I know where it is, that one there. I always go there and I never try and dig for it. I seen it, and David Tega, he had some in the house. You take a couple [flint rocks] and they're, oh, about that long [gestures]. You can hold it and hold the other one and you hit it like this and chhhhoo! Chhhhoo, sparks. Sparks just flies from it. You put grass together like this [gestures]. You mash up some grass. You go like this [pretends to strike two rocks together] right over that and the spark will go into that grass and it'll start the fire. That was before the matches.

MOOSE

During my days, during the seasons like this is when moose is start running, looking for one another, mate. When I go out what I'd use is a shoulder blade, the shoulder blade [scapula] from a moose. It's about yay long and about that wide [gestures]. I use that all the time to call them in. I get their attention by doing that. If you go down like this, then they wouldn't know [gestures downward]. What you do is, you go up, like that [gestures upward]. Up, all the time, up, when you use that shoulder-blade bone. You use it to go up. If you go down this way they'll hear it different.

You can just about estimate how far he is from you by hearing him talking. I can talk to the moose quite a ways. I can bring him to me. The moose is not dummy. They're pretty darn smart animal. [When] they're coming to you, they stop and listen. I try to estimate how far it is, and then I go easy on this [shoulder] bone. I try to ease off my calling. I want him to hear me just little at a time, not really loud, so he knows that I'm in the distance. That way you get 'em really close to you. Anyway I talk like a moose all the time. I can call like a cow. I can call like a bull. I can use that bone.

Later on in the years I thought about it, and I got myself a three-pound coffee can and I bored a little hole right in the middle of it. And I get that parachute string about yay long, and I tie a knot at the end. This thing will be wide open, and I shove it through here and I shove it through this little hole here. And the string'll be hanging out maybe yay long. And what I do is I take this coffee can and I put it under my arm here, and the string'll be hanging out like this [gestures] at the end from the coffee can. I use my thumbnail, and I haul that string and I pull it like this [gestures]. Whomp! Whomp! [imitates bull moose call]. That sound *just like* a moose. And I use that a lot in my days.

This is a secret that I don't hardly give away and I had to make my living to do that. And I don't want to give away all this good stuff to the people that are coming in from Lower 48. I think to myself, "They can just learn from the hard way." They're taking my moose anyway. So that's why I don't share with hardly anybody, how I call moose. So far, this is what we do to make a living, and our subsistence today was taken away from us now that we that have to go with the law. We have to go by the [open hunting] season.

You wouldn't believe this, but [Indian] people when they get a damn moose they don't waste nothing. They even take the skin in them days. They take the head. They take all the eyes. The eyeball they take it out and throw it away, but what's behind that eyeball, there's a lot of fat in there. And there's a lot of meat on the jaw and back here [gestures], and all that tongue, and they chop it up into small pieces. And same thing with the nose. They throw it in the fire and then burn it and scrape it and clean it up good. Then they slice it. Then they dice it up, and they throw it together, put it together like this. That's what you call a moose head soup nowadays. You heard about it.

You throw in macaroni and stuff like that?

Well, you take whatever. If you have a bunch of rice and dry soup and things like that, just throw it in there, and it'll come out to be one of the best.

Is that like part of your religion almost, to have that moose head soup?

Yes, yes, really. It's our old traditional way. Our old traditional way is moose have to be there. Without that moose meat it just looks bad.[3]

BEAR

And then in the fall time, late in the fall, my Dad and them goes out for bear. Just tallow, you know. We don't eat bear like downriver people do, but I notice all my life that people never eat bear in this country. I ate bear sometimes, but there is nothing wrong with the bear but just some people. I don't know why they don't eat bear. Anyway why my Dad hunted bear in the fall time just for the tallow, for the fat. And what my Mom does, is she cut it up in small pieces and she fries [it] and makes grease, and that what she takes is grease. She mix that up with berries sometime and most of the time we eat it with dry meat and stuff like that.

CARIBOU

What about caribou?

Caribou is long ways from here. Right now they open up the season in the Forty Mile Country. It's a long ways from here, about one hundred miles, anyway good one hundred miles where the caribou is, and the game warden will say, "Well, we will open it [the hunting season] up for subsistence use." But it's all right for the white people that have an airplane and the equipment to go way out there to get their caribou, but us Native people we don't have the equipment to go way out to get the caribou. The only thing we would get out with would be a truck or car, but the road is closed when they open up subsistence, out there on Forty Mile Country. The road will be closed. It will be snowed in, and no way we that could get out there unless you have a plane or whatever. If you have four-wheel drive, or Cat, so that subsistence is not doing us any good at all. Caribou is quite a ways from us, a good one hundred miles from here.

Once [in] a while Nelchina [herd] goes through Northway and they allow us one caribou a year down there, and this year it has been closed, so we don't benefit from the caribou much. Yeah, long time ago that is the only way we made a living up here about fifty miles, where the caribou used to go across all the time, same route. They come down in the spring and they go all the way down somewhere, and then they come back in August. Gee whiz, them things is fat. Caribou has fat on their back about that thick [gesturing] and you don't see that no more! No more that kind of shape of caribou. Boy, sometime a family takes fifteen to twenty caribou and dries them. The big families will take maybe more than that but . . .

And where would you go for them?

About fifty miles from here, the Big Hill. Anywhere from the Big Hill all the way to Long Cabin. That's another fifteen miles from Big Hill. Anyway, why we all move up there in August when the caribou start moving back to Canada. Anyway they are in really good shape and we pick up twenty to twenty-five caribou maybe for the big family. Well, they do as much as they can anyway, and at the same time while they are drying meat they can pick berries there too. And that's what we put up.

Years ago, when I was a kid, we were making a living off this country really good. People were so healthy, I would say. We never were sick. Nobody ever got a cold. My Mom and them never say that we got a backache, a headache, or, "I can't do this because of my back," and, "Oh, my leg." You don't wear [eye]glasses like this every day. We don't do that kind of stuff. I seen an old grandma a hundred years old [who] can see better than I do today with what I have, and I'm only seventy-some years old. I see they pack wood; today we have snow machine, trucks. Good God, we just bring them in by the truck; we don't even pack it. Then we use a chainsaw. I come from a time when there was hardly any axe in the country. I don't remember what they use for axe. I remember what they use for knife: caribou bone knife.

What do they call that caribou corral in your language?

Tsek, they call it. I was still in the country when they were still using it. There was muzzle-loader shotgun when I was in the country. My Dad always talks about "Save shells as much as you can." So what they do when they get all the caribou in the corral—today they call it corral, I guess—all the caribou come in like this and they just keep going around like that [gestures].

In a circle?

In a circle. Nowhere to go. So they just stand on the fence and they shoot it with a bow and arrow. They could shoot it with a muzzle loader but to save the shell they use bow and arrow. That's how they get the whole damn thing.

How would they get them in the corral?

Just leave it wide open and the caribou comes in.

It gets narrow?

Yeah, it gets narrowed down. It goes way in the hell up over the hill. They know that caribou always migrated through there, and that's how some of them just walk right in there. Sometime they have to chase them in. There's a bunch of people up there.

They have a way of closing it off?

Oh, yes. That's easiest way to kill the caribou. Today we have gun that can [shoot] a quarter-mile, easy. In them days, you gotta hit them with a bow and arrow.

I remember a Tsek from Seventeen Mile—Seven-Mile Turn—from there all the way into Tanana River. Long time ago. That Tsek went right through Tok somewhere, then it hit the river. That's why people that live somewhere right into the Tsek, where the moose or caribou hit that fence, every once and a while they leave it open. That's how their snares would be and they catch moose or something. That's why the end of the Tsek is where people used to live. Every once and a while somebody—they take turns—[would] just check it.

I didn't see that one. That was before me. The last one I seen was [with] my grandpa, Sam Thomas. He was a leader to the people a long time ago. He was a leader to a lot of people from different areas, like

Tetlin. He was a leader to the people here [Tanacross], leader to the people in Kechumstuk. He had Tsek from a couple miles below here, from that river to Mansfield Creek.

When we were kids, my Dad would always say, "Go check your grandpa's fence." We only had little bows and arrows. We killed rabbit with it, too. It's a homemade thing, just a little thing. We killed spruce hen with it. That's all we packed. Geez, not like today. When I was a kid it was hard to get anything. Not even a *gun*. What they had was muzzle-loader shotgun. That's the best there was.

I always tell stories to kids in the school today about how it was when I was a kid. A lot of people would think, "Kenny Thomas, it can't be all that bad." But that's the way it was. I don't have any kind of pictures to show you that's the way it was. *This* is the way it was when I was a kid. What we got here today is really changed from the time when I was a kid until now. I come from a time when there was nothing in the country.

We talk about muzzle-loader shotgun, that's one of the things that come from the white people. They show to the Native people what they can do, how much power they have. They put an inch board [up] and they hit the board with the bullet. It go through *that*. So Native people know that it will kill a moose. That's the reason why they traded white people for the fur, how they buy powder, and stuff like that. I remember my Dad used to get them by the can, maybe that big [gestures] and they pour it into that sheep horn. That sheep horn hangs on the side. I seen that when I was a kid.

DALL SHEEP

Speaking of sheep horn, where you guys hunt sheep?

Up here on the mountain. We got sheep up here right now today. But there's a law for that. We can't do that no more. We got place down here they call Sheep Place. People used to go there all the time. In my Dad's days, they kill it with a bow and arrow. Anywhere from thirty to forty sheep come through that place where they lick salt. They call it, Ch'entaaga. Ch'entaaga is a place where all the animals go for the salt. When a whole bunch of sheep come there, then the people get behind it, get over the hill.

Up above?

Yeah, up above. They waited for them back there. Other people will go up right against it. Then they run up the hill and that's where they get them with the bow and arrow. Sometimes they clean them all out.

You got to go with a whole group, though, to get them. It can't just be one hunter.

Oh, yes. A whole bunch. That's how they get it. Gee, easy place down here where Ch'entaaga is. There's no one or two sheep that goes there, [it's] thirty or forty at a time, forty or fifty at a time.

Them days, is a *lot* of sheep in the country, all kinds of sheep. There was enough food in Alaska for Native people, then. You can see the changes. Anywhere from [19]50 on, the white people start coming in. Some of the white people, they can see that we're making a living off the country, and this is the thing they've got to do, too. Then the game is getting less and less and less and less. Pretty soon you have to go by the law, the permits, and all that good stuff. Today, there's no more. Nothing, for us.

FISH

And then after we finish up for the caribou, we always come back down to Mansfield, and Mansfield is known for a lot of fish that runs during the summertime. My Mom and them would dry fish most of the summer.

You have fish traps up there too right?

We have fish trap and we have a dip net trap thing too. We have dip net that people use to dip the fish out. The fish comes in there. It's about a five-foot rim on it with a twine. They make it with twine, that dip net, with a handle with a five-foot rim on it, with a handle on it. And they put that twine net on it and sometimes you pick up over one hundred fish in one dip. And that's how we do it and everybody is equal. Everybody helps everybody at that time. They were good people; people were really good. What my grandpa and the people whoever were head of the people, they watch whoever is getting all the fish down there [at the creek], and if this person gets enough fish, why they'll tell the next person to go down and fish. And [when] he gets enough then the next person will go down and fish. That's how my grandpa and them—Annie Denny's Dad is my grandpa. They called him, Old Sam, old Moses Thomas's Dad. Well them boys I guess were the head of people. My grandpa was the head of everybody. He is the head of all the people.

You put up a lot of dry fish, too?

Dry fish. They make a grease from fish guts. The fish is so packed that they boil it and they take all that grease and put it in a birch-bark thing. In the wintertime, when that freezes, we eat dry fish with it or dry meat with it. Them's the kind of stuff that I was raised on. That's why today that I have to have some of that food. I can't live with the food that we have today. Can't get used to it that much. I can *live* on it, but I gotta have some of my food in some places. Native food. My food. Like dry fish, some of us still make dry fish. Some of us are still picking berries. Some of us are making a living off this country yet, but not as much as we used to because of the law. There is a good sign that someday there will be hardly anything [left] in the country.

I meant to ask you, do you ever use that fish oil?

Yes, we use fish oil for a lot of things. What we do is, sometimes they fry it or boil it. Put some water in and boil it. You do it either way. Like you can fry it and get oil from the guts, fish guts. And fish guts is good thing to eat. We eat a lot of that, even right today we use that oil a lot. Some of the people can boil it, put water in and boil it. Some people can fry it and still get the grease from it.

They skim it off the top?

Yeah. Take a spoon and take the good oil off from the top [of the pot]. And the oil is used for, time when I was a kid, it was used for many things. Like mix it with the roots from the ground, like Indian call it roots. They boil that in the fish grease. Yeah, Tath [roots] they call it.

Mansfield Village boat landing with remnants of fish trap and dip net station in right center, August 1, 1988. Photograph by Craig Mishler.

And then they can put that fish grease in blueberries or cranberries or any other berries you can use that fish oil in. You can eat the dry fish with the fish oil too. And lot of people I see eat dry meat with *fish* oil. I seen them bake *bannock* with it. Use that for tallow, like. Use that like you do Crisco today. It was using for a lot of things.

RESPECTING NATURE

We respect the nature a lot. Today they say biologists will count caribou, moose, and all that. And nature is how God puts it. I mean game commissioner or biologist can't control anything. Nature is what does it, you know? This Tanana River that flows down, how can you make it go the other way? If it wasn't for nature. Can biologists do that? Them kind of things is what you call really nature. You know how they increase the moose, nature does that. Doesn't matter whether you count caribou or what. That don't mean anything. Nature.

We respect the trees. We respect everything. We respect this country. We don't mistreat all the game. All the animals in this world that we respect. We don't mistreat anything that's a living thing in this world. We're not to play with it. God put it into this world for us to live on it. We don't play with it. Don't take anything that you're not going to use. Don't shoot rabbits for fun. You know you can't do that. If you're going to use it, doesn't matter how you use it. If you're going to use it, shoot it. If you don't need it, don't shoot it. That's the way Native people are. And we have to respect that animal that we live on. If it wasn't for that animal, we're not going to live. That's why we have to respect and take what we can use only.

Don't try to clean out everything. We're going to live here, and our kids are going to live here. We have to leave something for these kids. We have to leave something for the next day. Don't take everything for one day and forget about these other days. That's where I'm coming from. You know, sometimes I can't get this to the kids. You know, there's a few people that traps here in this village. They go out and get ten or fifteen lynx every year. You take that many off of one [trap]line. Gee, that's a lot. And how many you leave for next year? And you take another twenty over here, gee whiz it's hard on the whole country.

Long time ago when I was a kid, my Dad and them, I would say if you get ten lynx, that's a lot. Anywhere under ten where my Dad and them are, just that fur and that lynx. They don't try to kill everything off. They're thinking about next day, next year. They go a long ways ahead, they think about ahead. Us today we don't do that. Lot of these young people don't do that. I seen depression like I told you once before, and my Dad and them it didn't even bother them at all. It didn't bother us at all. I seen a lot of white people that went through the country around here that I seen them with my own eyes that they didn't have place to buy what they need. I seen white people with money, but what the hell can you do? You can't eat money. You can't buy anything. What is there to buy? Nothing. Depression, you got nothing. And a lot of people are hungry because they don't know how to make a living off the country right here. That's the way my people are today. That's why I'm having a culture camp.

First to start with, these people here in this village, I take them up there, and I show them about how we can make a living off this country. Maybe a few of them pick that up. What you learn to take out of this country that can save your life, like roots. What kind of roots can you eat? Part of our food is there in the ground. And berries is there. And

Kenny Thomas Sr. and Ellen Thomas at home in Tanacross, December 1999. Photograph by Craig Mishler.

even the leaves that you can eat. What kind of leaves can you eat if you're way in the hell out there with airplane that fall down with you, about seven days, eight days to walk back? You got to eat something. You got to catch fish. You see that fish down there [in the creek]. You can't run down there and grab it. You got to learn how to catch it. You can take willows and make a loop and fish coming up like this, you just leave it like that, just not moving it, it'll go right in there and get right in the middle of it, and you pull him out. You don't need no fish wheel or fish rod.

Anyway, them kind of thing it's good to learn because we live up here, and many times we fly to different places, and if airplane comes down with us [crashes], nothing to eat, them are good things in case you get lost. Good things to learn is what you can eat out of this country. That's the kind of thing, like survival is a different kind of way of living, *our* way of living.

I don't like to see anything wasted, really. We're going to have to live here in this country, and we don't use no game for any target at all. We're trying to teach the young people here today *not* to do that. You can't shoot a damn bird if you don't need the damn thing. Don't shoot it, okay? That's the way it is. That's the way we're trying to teach our young ones today. Because we're going to have to live here. And you going to have to depend on this game. I don't care what the hell the game warden was saying down there, but we're going to have to do it *our* way. You got to live here, and you got to take care of this damn game because you *don't know* when you going to need this. Like I say, I don't like to see anything shoot in the spring because everything got a young one.

And that's what we're trying to teach. In case that [Great] Depression comes back. If that Depression comes back, lot of white people wouldn't make it because they don't know how. Not only you. Some of my people is going to go with you. Don't feel bad. That's what I'm trying to avoid today. To help these people get through this Depression. But many of my people here in Tanacross, I tell you the truth about it, they wouldn't survive. They don't know how. Me and my wife can survive. We *can* survive.

NO FREEDOM FOR ME

Today I always say that I don't feel freedom like I was a long time ago when I was a kid. The freedom—I lost that. They took it away from me. I feel really bad sometimes because I can't do things I want to do any more. And the white people talks about subsistence. What the hell is subsistence today? Subsistence, that was taken away from me. I can't do any more subsistence because of lot of things that I want to do but there is a law. White people come in with the law. Today, the way it is for me is I was forced to live the way I live today, like the white people. I just [was] forced into the way I live today. I'm learning from these young people. I'm learning from the people today to live like white people because I lost all my subsistence way of living.

What it is for me today is I can't go out and do what I want to with the game. I can't go shoot moose because of the law today. The law is here. The game is over there, and I'm over here. And I can't get to that game because of the law today for us. Long time ago, before the white people settles here, we didn't have no law. We can go out and get the game. We'll make a living off the country! We make a living right off the country out here. And that's what the white people took away from us. And today we got nothing.

We can't get to the game over there, and if you do go over there to shoot one out of the season, you're going to have to go to the jail or pay a fine for it. Today I feel like I'm really in a cage or something. If I want to go out and cut wood or something like that, I got to go see somebody and get wood permit before I can cut down trees. If I want to build a fire, I got to go see somebody to get permit to build a fire. And if I'm hungry [and] I want to go fish, I got to go see somebody because before I can set my net I got to get permit. And if I'm hungry and I want to go hunting, I got to wait until the season is open.

We go by the season just like everyone else, and we have to pay for our license just like anybody else. There is nothing free for us. We can't get the game like we want to out of season. We go by the season like anybody else. So you can see that we are really forced into a different world right now, the way I live right now. And we can't make a living off the country like we used to anymore. Maybe one day, they're going to have a permit to pick berries too. But today I guess that's the only free thing we can get without permit, is picking berries.

Otherwise, any birds or any other game we have to have a permit to take them, just like anybody else. So there I am, whatever. This is a big change for me.

Today, I feel so funny like I, the way I am now that I feel so bad, that I always feel that people [are] looking down at me all the time. There is no freedom for me. That was taken away from me a long time ago. No freedom for me. I feel like people is looking down at me everyday. No freedom here for me, because of all this good stuff I have to do, even if I have to build a fire, I have to get permit. To cut wood, I got to get permit. I got to get permit for everything I do today.

That forced me to change my way here, the way I am now. They forced me to live like the white people. There is some things we do today yet, some things—that we catch few fish, subsistence way, we catch few fish. We catch moose in the fall time, and we pick berries, and we take the birds and ducks and things like that for the kids, and we dry some fish. Just a few things we do for our subsistence, not very much.

Them days when I was a kid there was hardly any law. You shoot a moose whenever you want it. You dry the moose wherever you get him. And today is just one season, only twenty-day season. And we goes out there all summer long. Just dry meat and what not. The more you kill the better you are. That's the way it was.

I feel really bad sometimes. I feel like I don't have freedom to my country any more out here. Lot of times that I wanted to go to the places to tell the people how I feel about this country. I don't feel freedom no more for one thing, no more freedom for me. Today, we can't go to get sheep because of the law. We can't chase caribou into the pen like we used to. We can't catch whole bunch of fish with a dip net anymore, because they allow maybe ten or twelve fish a *day*. The law is taking over the whole thing. Today, for me, the law is here and the game is on the other side and I'm over here, and I can't get to the game because of the law.

It's a really hungry thing. Today, we can't make a living off the country anymore like we used to. Some of us bend some of them laws, get some fish that we're not supposed to, and that's how we make a living off this country. I can't change that. There's nobody that can change me by doing that. Right now, today, the way they got things set up out here, I got to have permit to build a fire out here on this land, I got to have permit to cut the wood, I got to have permit to set my fishnet out, I got to let *you* know how many fish that I got from Tanana River or Mansfield or where. Then I got to have license like anybody else, I got to *buy* my license like anybody else, and I have to go by the law like anybody else. I got to go by the season. And I have to have harvest tag. Gosh, I don't know what else.

Ball and chain, huh? Prisoner.

Yeah, just like a little monkey in a cage, you would say, where people would look up and down at me all the time.

Like today, they're going after Native people more and more because they're not educated. If we're educated like you are, we can get away with lot of things. But we're too soft-hearted, and we just [plead] guilty to most of the things that we shouldn't be.

Like I say, I want to be honest to everything. I want to be that way. The Good Book say, "Thou shalt not lie." That's the way I want to be. I know the law today. I know what the law is. I don't want to break that. I've got to be very, very careful.

CHAPTER 9

Traditional Stories
Yaníidą́'ą Naxułdek

In addition to his talents as a singer, drummer, and dance leader, Kenny is also a splendid storyteller. "Yaamaagh Telcheegh" is a popular story known to many in Tanacross, but it is also related to the widespread northern Dene tale cycle known as the Traveler. The Traveler's name changes from area to area, but there are many overlapping episodes, and the central theme is that the Traveler wanders around the world making hostile animals and monsters friendly to humans or, in some cases, destroys them altogether, and in so doing makes the world a safer place in which to live. In this way he is a friend of humanity. One of the things that makes this telling special is the commentary and discussion that follow the story, something rarely found in the annals of American Indian folklore. Kenny not only tells the story, but helps to interpret it. This occurs again with the local legend of K'eetł'aa Ta' and Sts'ay Nitłe'. The chapter concludes with a bilingual text of "The Crippled Boy Who Saved Mansfield," one of the few stories ever to be published in the Tanacross language.

YAAMAAGH TELCHEEGH

Well, today we're going to talk about Yaamaagh Telcheegh.[1] Yaamaagh Telcheegh, he was a [speaks in Tanacross]. He is blind, really blind. He's a blind man [Tanacross]. And this is the first wife that he had, that took him around all over, while the other one is working around the house. Anyway, why, at that time they was using bow and arrow. And this is the start. He heard the moose coming. In fall time you hear moose when he's walking. He's talking. And you can hear the horn[s] when he hits the trees and stuff like that.

Anyway, why that woman she took her husband to where the moose is coming to, and she told her husband to be ready, and this woman got behind this bow and arrow and pointed right to the moose, and she told him, "Go ahead and shoot." And he shot. "Hey, hey, hey!" [Tanacross.] That means "You missed it."

You know when you hit the animal, us when we hit the animal, we know. We can hear that we hit the body. It got a different noise. When you hit the body you can tell. But this blind old man, he *diythek*. He know [Tanacross].

He hears this long ways. He [the bull moose] fell. By the horn. He hear by the horn. Anyway, he knows that he killed that moose. And this first woman [first wife] she go way out there and build a camp right there and put up all that meat and stuff like that. And she give a little soup to that old man [her husband]. "This was given to me by somebody," she told that old man. And all this time that old man knows that he *did* kill that moose, you know [Tanacross].

"You shot too high," she say.

So every day that woman go out to that meat, and she dries that meat and all that, and this is what she ate, and she don't give anything to this old man. So one day this woman took her old man way out, way out to the trail, somewhere way out. Not trail, but way out [in the bush]. And she told this old man, she say, "You wait [for] me right here. I going to get water for you. You wait [for] me right here," she say. And that old man waited there, waited there, and gee, all day long he wait [Tanacross]. Nothing [Tanacross]. Nothing. So that's where he got left, way out there. And all this time [Tanacross]. She don't want that old man to come back. So she left him way out. Anyway, why close to evening time. It was still good bright light yet.

Anyway, towards evening, afternoon, something like that, he hear *long ways*, he hear Loon, way out [in the distance], long ways. So he hear that Loon.[2] So that's where he go. He walk out to there, just slow. And he listen again [Tanacross]. He drink the water. [Speaks in Tanacross. Makes sound of loon calling.] He was wearing necklace, loon necklace that we call Ching kon. Ching kon they call it, that [dentalium] bone necklace [Tanacross]. That's all he had, that old man [Tanacross]. He told them people [Tanacross].

Loon, they coming, and then they say, "What's the matter?" [Tanacross].

"I can't see nothing. I'm blind [Tanacross]. No way that I can help myself, and I got nobody around me, nor anything. I want you guys to help me," he say [Tanacross]. "I can't see" [Tanacross].

So, he go into the lake with them. At that time, them animal [the two loons] were talking, and they told him, "What happened? What's wrong?" He's already in that lake up to his waist, and they just stand by.

"We want to help you, but you got to tell us. When we come out [up], let us know [Tanacross]. We're going down [diving under the water]. [Tanacross.] Let us know. If you can't see good, we're going down again."

So they took him down [Tanacross]. So they went back in [down]. They're going to go a little farther. Pretty soon, [Tanacross]. Little bit more they put him in [Tanacross].

"Not too much," he say. So there was the third time they went down [Tanacross]. Not too far [Tanacross] they come out [Tanacross].

"It's all right. Everything I can see good," he say. So there they took him back to where they found him [Tanacross], and he took that necklace out, and he give it to that Loon. Today you see Loon still wearing it. The Loon got pattern to it around his neck [Tanacross].

Then old man [Tanacross], he go back to where him and his wife camp. He told his wife, "Oh duu. I want a drink of water" [Tanacross]. That old lady she get water in the birch-bark [container]. She get water where there's lots of bugs in the water [Tanacross]. She give it to that old man. Before he drink it he look [Tanacross]. Lots of bugs in there, you know. So he just spilled it while that old lady is right in front of him. And he was working on that bone. And he just put that bone right alongside of her. And she did see that bone alongside of her. And he knows how this woman treat him [Tanacross]. He find out that woman don't like him.

So what happened is that he just spilled that [water] and didn't drink it. And he sees that bone right alongside, right close to her. And he just got up and not making too much noise, he grab that bone and he just kill that woman. And he drag that woman by the hair, and he took her out there where she got that water, and he stuffed that woman's head in there and stepped on it.

That's why he call himself Yaamaagh Telcheegh. Telcheegh is "he was mad" because she didn't treat him right. That's why he left. That's why they call [him] Yaamaagh Telcheegh. So he goes around this world, they say. Around the world.

[Tanacross.] He got to Wolverine [den]. Wolverine have place in the wintertime. He have place where he slide down [Tanacross]. Way down there, you can fly down the hill. They put good water and everything down there, so you can just slide down easy. Good, nice, good place. And he got to there and he try to figure out, what the heck is this? A lot of people what they do is go through there, they slide down, and they go into this really sharp thing [like a trap]. And they get killed.

And that's the first thing he got to, [Wolverine,] the first animal [he] got to. He don't like, he want to kill them. And Yaamaagh Telcheegh, some bad things he gets rid of. He keeps the good ones. He keeps moose. He keeps anything that's good. He don't kill.

He want to get rid of Wolverine, but he can't. So anyway he see what happened. After he got way down there and he see them [sharp] sticks like that. When somebody slides down, why he goes right into that stick, and he [Wolverine] kills them.

Ho ho, he [Yaamaagh Telcheegh] went down there, and he act like he pick his nose, and his nose bleeding. He make it look like there's blood there [Tanacross]. That's what he say. What he say is, "You should have been smarter than that." That means that Wolverine think he outsmart that Yaamaagh Telcheegh. So they took his stick out, and they didn't know that they didn't kill that. He's got a lot of power too, that old man. Make it look like he was *dead*.

And they pack him back, heavy pack. Back to his family. And he go across a little creek. When he [Wolverine] step over, he [Yaamaagh Telcheegh] farted. Whoops! [laughs]. Wolverine, he look at him, he look at him. He take him down, and when he fart, that Yaamaagh Telcheegh laugh a little bit. And that Wolverine knows that there's a little tightness got into that body. So he take him down and look at him and nothing. He's dead. He play dead.

That Wolverine he thought to himself, "Well I hope that knife and stuff like that will just get lost. Wouldn't be there when I got there." Gee, when they bring him in, they bring him back to camp, Wolverine's camp [Tanacross]. Stay all that knife [Tanacross]. No knife, no axe.

Just little axe—*little* bitty old-time axe—what you call hatchet, little hatchet, like. And they got that out, but they can't find that knife. Finally they took all that rope back off of him, and then, "Gee, I hope they take all the rope off of me," he [Yaamaagh Telcheegh] thought. And that's what they did right away. He's a powerful man and he make people do that. And pretty soon they unloose him, and everybody in that whole family was there. And what he did is he kill everybody in there.

At that time, young girl become a woman. And at that time we call it Injih [taboo], when I was a kid. Young girl become a woman, then they have to take them out away from us. Way out there somewhere. Not too far. But they put her someplace where she'll be by herself. He kill everybody but her out there. And she knows what happened, so she went up a tree. There's a thing that he does. He's trying to knock that tree down, and some kind of water coming down. She go to bathroom, water coming down. Make that thing freeze.

Urine?

Yeah. Can't cut that tree down, no way.

This is the Girl Wolverine?

Yeah. And she told him, well there's nothing he can do. She have more power, that woman, than that man. So he let her go, and he didn't kill her. That's why there's [still] a Wolverine [today]. Then all the time he went long ways to find that Wolverine.

Then he went from there, and he went to the lake, big lake. And lot of people around in that village, and lot of animals at that time. And he says, "Everybody say, [Tanacross]. Everybody say that. And finally he got into this fox, red fox. Cross Fox, I would say. He go home with this Cross Fox. Then he come long ways, so he tell stories about what happened.

Just before he got to that lake—I'm going back again—just before he got to that lake, his wife caught up with him. That second wife. He killed one [his first wife], and that's the last one caught up with him. And he built a big tower like, and he put her way in the hell up there, so nobody wouldn't kill her. He's going into the people he don't know.

That's why he did that. And he tell lots of stories about what he did and all that, and to that Fox.

Old Ch'et'en, Ch'et'en they call her. She's laying right close to the fire. And he listened. He trying to listen to what's going on. And evening time he told his friend, "I left my wife over across the lake." And that Ch'et'en she hear that. Toe shake like that. You know how that fire going that way right over her, and all that smoke and soot and stuff like that's on top of her, and she just shake that off. And she [Ch'et'en] go out. He [Yaamaagh Telcheegh] thought she [was] going to the bathroom or something like that, but she took off, and she heard that woman over there. So she took off. She went long ways. Then she holler. She holler back to her people, "[Speaks in Tanacross in loud voice]," she say. "Somebody coming. Someone coming in, different person coming in." Then everybody really running back over there. He [Yaamaagh Telcheegh] didn't catch up with her. She [Ch'et'en] did kill that woman. She kill that Yaamaagh Telcheegh's [Tanacross].

His wife.

She [Ch'et'en] kill that woman. So Yaamaagh Telcheegh he kill that Ch'et'en.

I don't know that word.

Ch'et'en. At that time there was nothing in this country. Ch'et'en is a big person like a seal. And maybe it's a seal. I don't know. It's a bad thing, anyway, what it is.

Some kind of monster?

Yeah. Something like that. Anyway, she ate that woman. And that Ch'et'en she got killed. And no way that they can kill her! And after he killed her, he put snow over her with water and stuff like that and let the water freeze. But in the morning time, that Ch'et'en's kids over there say, "Ho oh [Tanacross]. My Mom will come back. My Dad will come back," they say. And he can't kill her, no way. So she [Ch'et'en] came back [to life] again.

And this time he [Yaamaagh Telcheegh] took her out there and he cut her [up]. He cut that Ch'et'en, cut her all up. He just chop her into little pieces, right down to the tail. When he get to the tail end, then Whoom! Something. Something goes out. And that means she didn't get killed. And she come back next morning. So the third time, he killed that Ch'et'en [for good]. This time he went to sleep, and he dream about it, and he went the other way, from tail first into the head. Back into the head he cut it [up]. Then he didn't hear Whoom! or anything. He didn't hear that. So then he knows. He put a lot of snow on her, and then put water on her. When he start on the tail end to the head, he didn't hear that [spirit] going out, so next morning that thing didn't come back.

But it's a female, huh?

Yeah. So no more Ch'et'en from there on. That was a bad thing for this people in this country. And he [Yaamaagh Telcheegh] goes to Moose, and he let them go. He goes to Caribou; he let them go. Just the bad things.

The bad animals.

Yes, animal he gets rid of. You know, like trapping things, like Lynx and Wolf, and different things that he just let go. And he got to this bird. They were man at that time. They were people at the time. And he got to these two people who lives on the trail. He got there, and he said, "Well, [Tanacross]." Each one of them say that. They want him to be a partner. So they got mad at each other, this Camp Robber and Woodpecker. They were together.

You know Woodpecker [makes rapping noise on table], you hear that for his food. The woodpecker [repeats rapping noise] you hear him do that to get food. And they start arguing with each other. That Camp Robber over here, he's stealing your food. He's stealing the fat from somebody [rapping noise]. And Woodpecker goes like this [still rapping]. That's how he gets the food.

And they start arguing. They say, "[speaks Tanacross] [resumes rapping]. You get that fine food." And then they argue about it, and then he told that Camp Robber, "[Tanacross]." He give him fat and stuff like that, to this man. And that's what they're arguing about it. And that's why they start fighting with each other. You see the Woodpecker got a small tail? If you watch the Woodpecker really close, the tail is kind of short, shorter than any kind of animal. You notice that?

I never see it.

Well, you watch the Woodpecker sometime. If you see it, his tail will be short. That's when he wrestle. He put his tail in the fire in the burned out part of it. That's why his tail is short. Then they were wrestling, and you know Camp Robber kind of white up in here [pointing to his head]?

Yeah.

Right up in here [gestures toward the crown of his head with both hands]. Right in the middle. That Woodpecker put his face in the fire. That's why he's so white up there [laughs]. [Tanacross,] they call it. And finally he let them go. He stay with both of them. After the fight they shake hands.

COMMENTARY ON YAAMAAGH TELCHEEGH

And right now today, to me, I heard it for long, long time when I was a little boy. The old ladies talk about it. And today you hear from white people about the Bible. Creator. To me, I think that's what it is. That's what Yaamaagh Telcheegh is.

Kind of like Indian Bible?

Yes. He separate bad and leave the good. And that's what he's doing, all this time. And he goes to different good people, like good Moose. He stays overnight with them. He goes to Caribou. He just let them go. Whatever is going to be good for our people, he just let that go [Tanacross]. Anything. All the animals he stopped overnight with. He left the good and he took the bad ones. It was a world populated with bad ones [animals]. And he took the bad ones out and left the good ones. And from the time when I was a kid until now I think about it, and it was something like Creator. God's the only one who can do that, you know. And that's probably what it is.

Yaamaagh Telcheegh's story reflects some of the things that you heard in the church, at the school. What you should do is learn to listen to the stories told in these places, the church and the school. Listen to them and get what you can out of everything that you hear. We should think, "How can these [white] people that we don't know come and teach us about the Christian way?" We don't know who they are, yet they care enough to come and spend time and teach us the ways of their church.

But even before we knew there was a church and there was God, we knew way, way back that there is God. We knew that. That knowledge didn't come with the church. The knowledge was there already. My grandparents, my grandmothers, my Mom, all of them prayed and lifted up their hands to God, even back then. How do them people then know that there's the Lord? That there's Christianity? How do they know that? Today we should make a practice of going to church. Sit there and listen and ask yourself, "What are they saying and why?"

And you heard this when you were a kid?

I was little boy. That story is one long week long. Long story.

They tell it every night.

Mmm hmm, every night. From there on, I tell you. This old man, this man he left the country. He left the place when he was young, as a blind man.

That name Yaamaagh.

"Yaamaagh" that means "the whole world." He went around—Yaamaagh, Yaamaagh. He went around the whole world to get rid of the bad things, and he left the good things.

And that Telcheegh, "He's mad"?

Yeah. He's mad. Telcheegh. He was mad when he left, for how they treated him. And that's why he left the country.

The whole thing would be, "He went around the whole world after he got mad?"

Uh-huh, yeah. He was mad when he left. Telcheegh. But after he started out, he's doing good things for us, all the way. And that's why I say, today you hear Creator, about God makes all this stuff or us. And that's what they're probably talking about, the Native people.

He went all the way around the world. We didn't realize way back then that the world is round. We thought it was flat. Today, that's how we learn it. And we thought it was just flat country everywhere. The whole world was flat country. We thought the world was flat. So he went around the world.

Yaamaagh Telcheegh went around the world and he killed or got rid of all the evil and harmful things in our world. No-good things, he get rid of them.

And he left behind all the things we are going to use and depend on. That's all he left for us. He left all the animals as we see [them] today. He left all those because these are the things we depend on.

I didn't realize it, but prior to this particular part of this story, Yaamaagh Telcheegh made a journey before this. This is his second journey that is so famous. When he left, he was just a young man, but when he was done with his journey, he was old. He had grey hair. He must have really traveled around the world, because when he came back to this country, his hair was all grey. He was no longer a young man.

When we were small, this story was never told just any time. Just in the wintertime. This story isn't told during the summer or throughout the winter. It's only told from October through December. Those are the only times that it can be told. It used to take my grandmother and them seven days to tell this story completely. One week, they say, and that's how long it lasts.

They don't tell this story—it's not a story you can just talk about, like the fairy tales you can tell now. This is a very serious story. You don't tell it lightly. You don't tell it for nothing. It comes from your heart. The only people who can tell this story are the ones who know about life. They're the only ones who are smart enough to tell this story.

In order to tell this story you should really listen and get all your facts right. People who tell this story have to know how the story goes. You can't just tell it without knowing the full meaning of the story.

My grandmother and them told each other this story and it was handed down to them.

My grandfathers and my grandmothers, [it's] just like they made this world—my world—according to this story. My grandparents, my parents, they knew their clans, they knew where we came from, how we came to be here, and why. That's the way my grandparents were. That's the way they were educated.

My grandpa and my grandma, they got a high education in our Native way. Just like today, people would say, you graduated from college, master's degree or something like that. That's the kind of people where I'm coming from. But I didn't spend too much time with my grandpa and with my Dad because I was in the army, spent four or five years in the army, and that's why I miss quite a bit of it. I try to hang on to what little is left.

Even so I don't know how to teach the young people today. The young people who are with me in this village. I don't know how to teach them. I don't feel capable of the knowledge that this story has taught. I don't know that much about Yaamaagh Telcheegh. I missed a lot of it. I know the part of it when he start, and when he come back. I don't want to teach the young people things that I don't know about. That's why I'm reluctant to teach anything.

I really can't teach anything that was told to me by my father and them because I didn't experience what they were talking about.

There aren't very many of us any more, and these young people should hold each other's hand and guide each other and learn the truth. Don't tell each other any lies, don't make up stories and say that [they are] true. Don't make up any stories that aren't true when I'm gone. I don't like it that way. I got to see with my own eyes. Then I know it's coming from my heart. I want to be honest to the people today, with the young people.

Even Yaamaagh Telcheegh did not fabricate the story he told. That's a great story. He told things as they are, as he saw them, as he experienced them. This is the way the people right now should leave their stories behind.

The Loon you hear out there on the water, they put Yaamaagh Telcheegh underwater to fix his eyes. He repaid the loon with the dentalium [shells], and that's what you see on the Loon right now around his neck, the dentalium necklace. That dentalium on the Loon, even that gesture is what we were told as part of the lesson.

DISCUSSION OF THE BLIND MAN AND THE LOON

I've got a question for you about that Yaamaagh Telcheegh and the Loon. Just one loon?

No, two. Man and wife. They hanging on him like this [gesturing], one on one side, and the other on the other side. He's a really medicine man. You don't fool around with it today.

The Loon?

Yes. We don't shoot him, we don't do nothing. Same thing with the Raven.

That Blind Man and the Loon [first part of Yamaagh Telheegh] is well known all over, that story? Everywhere you go in Alaska people know that story, and I wonder what's in that story that made it so well known.[3]

[Aside to Ellen.] Well, it's a true story.

It's about healing too.

Yeah. That's what it is. You see he healed this old man? Blind old man? He fixed that.

It's about the handicapped in a way. How about when he gets back at his wife? That's kind of a sad ending, huh?

No, gee. There's no more wife. He had two wives. He killed that one because he was mistreated. His wife mistreated him.

Did he have a right to kill her?

Oh yes. You see she lie to this old man. This old man shot that moose. He hit him. When you hit animal, you hear it, different noise.

With arrow?

Yeah. And he heard that he hit that moose, and then she listened for it, and pretty soon when he fell like this, he heard that horn that he fell and no more after that. He didn't hear nothing. So he know damn well he got that moose.

So he had a right to get even with her?

Yeah. So that's when he didn't feel right, after he kill that woman. But she was guilty. About killing this woman, his wife, his own wife. But he want to even up on how he was treated.

Kind of like eye for eye and tooth for tooth.

Yeah. So that's why he got rid of her. It's not going to change.

INTRODUCTION TO RAVEN STORY: THE CLAN ANIMALS

I want to talk a little bit about the Raven. I want to say a little bit in my language, a little bit in the white man's way because I'll explain better that way. A long time ago in this country, in this world, I would say, Raven is the one who put the moon up there. He's the one who put the sun up there. And our way, he's the one who put the sun up there. He's the one who put the moon up there, and he did lots of good for the people. That's why we respect the Raven so much. We don't shoot at him. And he happened to be on my clan, so . . .

He's Ałts'įį dendeey?

No, no, no. He's Naltsiin. You see, I'm Naltsiin too, and I call myself Ałts'įį dendeey. So, we don't shoot at that [Raven]. And that Seagull, that Ch'aadh. All the animals belong to the clan.

Oh, I didn't know that. Each clan has one animal?

Like Tsûug—Marten, that's our clan. It's in our clan.

Dik'aagyu?

Dik'aagyu is Silver Fox. That's a high-priced people, these people. They're high, and we're the highest. They're next highest. My clan was. They're pretty near just as much as us, but we're a little bit more farther than they are. Anyway, why we together all the way, in our clan, together.

Well, let me ask you about other clans. Niiṣaas?

Niisaas, that's Walter Northway's clan.

What kind of animal do they have?

Tiikaan—Wolf. They're from Canada.

And Naltsiin is Raven.

Ah-hah [confirming]. I mean they're in our clan too.

And Ch'aadh? Do they have animal or bird?

That's fish tail, Fish.

I thought that Ch'echeelyu was Fish tail.

Ch'echeelyu and Ch'aadh are just brothers and sisters.

I see.

And that other one too that goes along with it is Taandîidz altsiil. Ch'aadh, Taandîidz altsiil, Ch'echeelyu. Three different things. They're all in one boat.

And how about that Wudzisyu?

Wudzisyu. That's Peter John's tribe. That's the one, that Wudzisyu, Ch'echeelyu, Tsesyu, and them are all down there. Taandîidz altsiil. Four different clans they have. Tsesyu—the name of that paint thing I talked about a little while ago. That's them people. Then that's the clan of that Tsesyu.

They don't have an animal, just a paint?

Paint. So he have a power, this Raven. He have a lot of power. Trick, I would say. Today they call it trick. He have a lot of that. He can trick you any way he can. He get anything easy.

RAVEN TRIES TO MARRY

Long time ago, the story say, lots of people want to marry big chief's daughter. That chief's daughter is just good, with all the beads, big chief's daughter. And everybody wants to marry that girl. And he going to make meeting with them. See who's going to marry that girl. Man, he got himself into this trick. He's tricking people, you know? He just dress himself with one of the best [suits of clothes] there is in the world. Man, he looked so sharp! With all these beads and all this.

And that man he said, before he had meeting, he seen the tracks on the new snow. They took his old dog that died of old age. They took him out on the drift pile on the river. They took him out there. And somebody's out there hunting and coming back. He seen track from there. Three tracks like this [gestures with fingers]. What track? It's not like our track. He got track like three-pronged, you know? And he's the one that eat that eye, off that dog. That old dog. He eat that eye. And all this time it was the Raven doing that. And they know that. They don't know that for sure. They don't know who's doing it, but that night everyone want to marry that woman, so he had meeting with them, and everybody, gee, they put on good moccasins, beaded moccasins.

The old man said, "Well [chuckles], everybody take your shoes off! [Laughs]. Take your moccasins off! Everybody took their moccasins off, and when he come to this old Raven, "Caw!" He say he took off.

And that's when they find out that he's the one that's doing it. Like, right now, that's what the old Crow, ravens are doing. But way before us, people really respect that Raven.

Even today, me, I always talk to the birds about my grandkids. Yes, right now today I do that when I goes out in the brush. I talk to the Raven. I talk to different things. Like different birds. You hear them singing in the summertime. It's a certain kind of birds that I talk to.

Do you think they understand you?

Oh yes! They were people before us. They were people a long time ago. They understand us a long time ago.

Your language?

Yes. Not English, *my* language. Even that Camp Robber, I respect that. I give him food once in a while. 'Cause they tell me when or if I'm going to get a moose or what. They'll tell me. Yeah. If moose [is] around, they'll tell me. Raven will tell me.

Really?

Caw! Caw! Coo! Coo! Coo! Coo! He going to go sideways to me, and I got to talk to him. Why am I there? Then, which way that moose is, that's the way he fly too.

I'll be darned.

I'm not supposed to say that, but just [to] you. My Dad and them taught me that [for] years and years. Sometimes it's close, I can really feel it.

K'EETŁ'AA TA' AND STS'AY NITLE'

I am originally from Mansfield.[4] My father, my grandfather, and my grandmother are all from Mansfield. My Mom was from a different place.[5] There were a lot of old men in the group at Mansfield. One of them was their leader or chief, and this story is about that person.

K'eetł'aa Ta' (center) with his son (right) and Deshyen Gaay ("The Little Shaman" aka Deshaddy, left), ca. 1885. Photo from the Henry Allen Expedition, apparently taken at Eagle Village on the Yukon River. James Wickersham Collection PCA 277-17-20, Alaska State Historical Library, Juneau.

K'eetł'aa Ta' is the name of this old man. *In other words, in the white man's way he was the leader for the people at Mansfield at the time.*

K'eetł'aa Ta' and his friend were the leaders of the group. K'eetł'aa Ta' was the main leader, but Sts'ay Nitle' was his close friend.[6]

Sts'ay Nitle' was also known as Ch'aadh Ch'et'ąandiidz, which means he was the main person in the Ch'aadh clan. He was related to Maggie Isaac and Jimmy Walter *and that side.* When he was alive and here on earth at that time, Sts'ay Nitle' was known to be a bad medicine man. *He's a really bad man.* Na'eetę̃. *In white man's way* Na'eetę̃ *is a medicine man.*[7]

These two men were paired up in everything they did. K'eetł'aa Ta' and Sts'ay Nitle' really worked closely in everything. *They go places and they travel around the country, and they partners together for many, many, many years. They like each other and they travel together.* They're the ones who found whitefish at Dihthâad, that old village there on Fish Creek [actually Mansfield Creek].[8]

My grandpa always tells me, a very, very long time ago, people did not stay just in Mansfield. They spread out *all the time*. Back where Ellen and I have a cabin upriver from Tanacross is a place called Táxélts'íh Keyh.[9] That was the name for the site our cabin is built on, and there used to be a village there. That's what my Dad told me. *That's as far back as I remember.*

When they left Táxélts'íh Keyh they traveled to Ch'aghadh Menn'. And Łuug Menn' (Fish Lake), which is bigger than Ch'aghadh Menn'. And from there when they found Uljaadh Menn' [Northern Pike Lake]. Anyway, they went down to those places, and that's when they started Dihthâad. These two men, K'eetł'aa Ta' and Sts'ay Nitle', were traveling around these areas. They found northern pike in the creek joining the lakes. There's a hill by Dihthâad, and they refer to this hill as Mesiin Tsiits'iig. The present-day Mansfield Village was formed much, much later than Dihthâad.[10]

So some people stayed at Dihthâad, and some later on settled at the new Mansfield Village, *two different places*, and there were more people also at Fish Creek, that came from [a place] called Táxélts'íh Keyh. Long ago, way before my time, all of the stories that I'm telling come from my grandfather and them. I don't really want to make a mistake and make up any stories, so it's really hard for me to tell any kind of story, because there aren't very many young people in the village of Tanacross right now, and I want these stories to be authentic. I do not want to make a mistake and tell a story that is not true. I'm passing on what I learned from my elders and my grandparents.

K'eetł'aa Ta' and Sts'ay Nitle' were the people who lived well on this earth. They were the descendants of my great-grandfather and them. Sts'ay Nitle' was the one that didn't grow up to be the way his grandfathers wanted him to be. He was always known to be doing things that were not right and not according to his elders' teaching. He didn't live right inside the village. He always lived just outside the circle of the village. He lived in Ni Maal house.

One time the people were doing a sad dance, and there was a boy who kept looking at them laughing at them. He was mocking them, saying, "This one dances like this, and that one dances like that." He was just ridiculing them.

But Sts'ay Nitle' got really angry because this boy was making fun of all these people who were doing the sad dance, and so he sneaked up behind him with a small axe and killed him for making fun of the people. *He killed that boy!* The story goes way back that Sts'ay Nitle' was a murderer. Sts'ay Nitle' was the grandfather of Maggie Isaac and Jimmy Walter and that side. My grandfather and the whole family really did not like what the old man Sts'ay Nitle' did. They all came out of their houses and started making speeches.

They told each other not to touch the murdered child. That Sts'ay Nitle' will have to dispose of him as best as he can, probably by cremation. At the old village of Dihthâad there's a big rock by the trail, and there's a rusty red spot on there. Sts'ay Nitle' took that boy he murdered and carried him up to that big rock and draped him over there, and his blood soaked into that rock, and that's why that rusty red stain is there on the rock today. Throughout my entire life I've seen it there, and I think it's still there. *Right now I think it's still showing, if I'm not mistaken.*

He packed that boy into where the lake is, Łii Menn', Dog Lake. Right behind there, and that's where he cremated him. After he cremated that boy that he murdered, he never came back to the village again. He was not really not a person at all. He was an exceptionally bad man, that Sts'ay Nitle'.

But as he was growing old, towards the end of his days, he finally did come back to the village, and the day that he was going to die, he told his family, "I want all the elders and all the people, all my relatives here in the village to come here before I die." Even though he couldn't speak very loudly, and his voice was really weak, he took that opportunity to speak to his people who had gathered there.

And he said to his people, "Whatever kind of man I became here on earth, don't follow my footsteps. From now on, make sure that you follow the steps of the good people, the straight people. Don't follow my steps," he told them. "Where you have heard of God and how that trail is, that's the one to follow."

"Don't be like me," he always say. "I want to leave that with you people. It's not a good way, the way I did. And I want to leave you with a good way." Like in white man's way, he said, "I don't want you guys to be the way I used to been when I lived here with you people. I was a bad man. I don't want you people to be like me. I did lots of bad things in my life. I don't want that for you people. So from now on, today, try to go straight." That way. That's a good word that he left with his people.

He was buried on top of the hill—not Mansfield Hill but the next one over. They're the ones that are buried up there. Sts'ay Nitle' and K'eetł'aa Ta' are the ones that's buried on that particular hill—all the medicine people.[11] That's why we couldn't go up there.

We respect everything. My Mom and Dad tell us to respect that. They don't want to let kids go there [up by that graveyard]. I don't think we've ever been there. What I say here, I wish you could have been here to hear me. This is what we hear.

COMMENTARY ON K'EETŁ'AA TA' AND STS'AY NITLE'

If you want to make sure what I'm telling you is true, Isabel John is one of the people you can ask for the authenticity of my story.[12] Isabel's Dad and them were my uncles, and I was like their child. They have told me from the beginning of their teaching that this is the way to be as a person. Many times they put these words in my ears. My uncles thought of me as their own child as I was growing up.

In white man way, I don't want to make up a story. And I really think it's a very true story because my grandpa always tells me about it.

My grandfather's name was Gah Xąą' Ta' (literally "father of an arctic hare's front leg"). He was the leader of all the people. His other name was Sts'ay Uudaagh Kol (literally "one who is blind"), but they are one and the same man. After K'eetł'aata', he was the last great leader back in those times. *In white man way he's the head of everybody, like all the people here, Mansfield, Kechumstuk.*

As we were growing up, all of the stories that we heard went back to Gah Xąą' Ta' or Sts'ay Uudaagh Kol. In the Native way, he was our teacher. The teachers back then really knew our old way of life. "Nee'adeetnii" is a great word because it means "learning and doing."

Since I was a child, I have gone throughout this area, and I was taught how to hunt by my Dad. So it was easy for me to be successful at hunting. It was easy for me to kill moose. *Always I kill moose when I'm home.* It was just like going out to kill snowshoe hares because I was taught so well by my Dad. Now that I'm older and can't get around so well, I wish for the old ways. I'd like to be able to hunt all over again and to be successful in getting meat.

There aren't very many young people in Tanacross any more. I am the only elder left behind to be with them. How I was taught by my elders, and what I remember is what I'm passing on to the kids when I take them to Mansfield each summer. During these culture camps we have in Mansfield, there's only me, my older sister, Emma Northway, and my wife, Ellen, are the only ones who teach up there.

All at once I found out that we are the elders, and we're the only ones who teach the young people of Tanacross up at Mansfield each summer. What little we know up to now is what we're passing on to our younger people right now during the culture camp. How well we put food up, how we handled the food, how we kept and preserved our food, that's the teaching we're handing to our young people each summer.

When I was small, the white people converged onto this land, and the Native people were known to be very generous and kindhearted. They have always been that. The white people came up here to our country not knowing how to survive. So the Natives shared with them what they had, which was dry meat and food like that. *Always they get little dry meat and give it to them, little dry fish.* We did not distinguish the very differences between whites and Natives. They just didn't know the difference. So they shared what they had with the white man, as they've always been known to do. *They always have to help.*

Each evening I would hear my grandparents, my parents, all of them in prayer. Wut'aagh dįt'eey refers to God as we know him.[13] And I always hear them pray each evening, talking to Him. *I hear my Mom yet.* My grandparents and my parents, when they receive a gift of food or whatever from someone, they would pray for them right there instead of saying "Thank you." Their good way of saying "Thank you" for these presents was to pray for those people. We don't realize until now how valuable that lesson was. That was the most valuable lesson they taught us. If we had continued to practice this lesson right now, this world would be a lot better place to live in.

THE CRIPPLED BOY WHO SAVED MANSFIELD: TANACROSS LANGUAGE VERSION

Mansfield xt'een iin,[14]
sheg dąą łąą nalt'ee—
when I was really young boy,
shtá' iin,
nakedaltth'ii łaa dąą,

Elder Emma Northway with model birch bark canoe she made at the
Mansfield Culture Camp, July 1999. Photograph by Craig Mishler.

nah'og ts'atk'aats xetk'aadh.
we're trained for the weather,
we're trained for everything.
ts'intsudl dą'ą neetleh,
nee*shirt*, nee*coat*, neekentsįįth,
xut'êey k'á xú' ts'į́',
ts'éhłêg ts'į́',
ndée *one place.*
Everything.
While we go to sleep we put everything in one place
where we could
xen t'êey tthuu ghandek ts'į́',
xen t'êey gha nats'ahtl'uh ey keh dahtsaadlaa.
This is the way . . . xwnu'enéltenh.
Just like in the white man way,
you ready.
You ready for the war.
You ready to go in case enemy coming.
êy gha jah xwnu'eneltąą.

Mansfield gha,
k'ahdú' yaadąą Dihthâad dihnii dé'.
xandég ch'ejiil keey xughinłęę.
more people xandég.
xandég êy shég dąą,
k'ahdú' jah—
long time ago shtá' iin shnąą éł xandég shtá'.
dąą,
tá' xi'éł nee'éł naxalndiig.
nah'og nak'etl'eh xatxąą ts'į́'.
k'ahdú' nondlêd iin *war* xudinii.
êy keh naan dendeey iin xunitháat ts'į́'
Mansfield xt'een iin *many times* wa-naxatmaax.
xuk'etl'aa haa dehtseyh.
he really good at that in Mansfield.

K'ahdú' êy shég dąą *last time* xandóg.
dench'eduug naxetmaak *Mansfield.*

only place xexeldéyh *I guess*
êy shég naxetdeetł, *I think.*
or somebody see them.
somebody saw kéxdéníndlah,
lé'e jah.
shég naa xitmaagh éł dendeey t'êey kôl.

Anyway now,
dąą xatdąą êy shég Dihthâad gha ts'isdę́'
dii s͟hę́ę' di'eedah ts'į́'
êy shég dąą êy tses k'ee
łuug gha eedah.
wuchaay dú',
k'á nach'ehdaag dé' natetdes.
wutsųų dú' gha shég shax eedah.
xahshog niimaal t'aagh eedah.
yandog *some kind* k'aaz tsets ka'eltiiyh
natetdes dé'.
k'aaz tsets ka'eltiiyh.
yandiidz k'aaz tsets deljeh
nts'é txunt'eh chíh náhdeg?
tsintsiy tthiig tthiit'aag
wux͟ú' ch'iigod, ch'iigod
wus͟hųų xedinii
ch'igod xedinii
êy yaat'aa ee'aa

êy da'its͟hah ts'į́' êy ntih.
"Tsųų nahdeg nts'éxunt'eh,
k'ęy ndée dąą k'ęy nehshąą dé'
nahdeg nts'exunt'eh."

"Ndée nah'og díi t'êey k'á nees͟héen!
Nts'é jah dinęy?"
wuchaay éł

She want to go outdoors and she's—
just like she's doing something out there,

and she looks up there every once and a while,
you know.
"Nenaxdindeetl,"
she say.
That kid . . . crippled kid,
he goes up to get wood,
êy éł t'êey,
dâ'it<u>sh</u>ah dé'
She tells her grandkid,
"Nahdée tsets,
tsets kanaghindaał ts'į'
êy âaz nidenįhtíiyh tl'áan
êy âaz nidenįhtąą dú'
you go back again
êy shég t'êey ye'én dé' yandég.
Mansfield shég dendeey deltth'ii iin,
xałt'êey dé' xu'edinii."
êy dú' nii dé' ye.

Ts'enh xu' tsets *one* de-detąą
tl'áan *last time* tsets k'aaz nik'etąą dé',
ts'į' k'ôd ndaay tetdes.
ts'į' aandeg *Mansfield* gha.
nahdaa tsintsiy tthiig éł *people* iin êy nadindeetl.
xdąąda' dewu<u>sh</u>ųų
all dé' naxundaak
sheth ts'į' xuuts'ehtę́ę' xú' dąą
ts'ehtę́ę' éł taxunghinłé'.
k'aath éł ndohk'e na'én ndeeth ts'į'
xú' ch'e *all ready.*
díi k'á' naxughinłęę ha'
êy shég dąą
xuuts'ehtę́ę' éł
xu' ch'e *all* ts'idenaax dé' ts'į'
naxehsheł ts'į'

Êy sheg . . . jah dú' xudinii.
"*Too many times,*

people iin ts'inxą́ą́'ą
this time naxuts'etnu<u>sh</u>uud.
just kind of chase them back.
We don't want to kill anybody."
That's what the leaders say.
"We don't want to kill nobody no more," he said.
That's what he did, you know.
xuunaxdindeetl
dąą stsę̖ęy xuunaxdindeetl

And they all come around to them,
but in the meantime,
when that kid went up to Mansfield,
that old lady,
she go out,
"Eeey,
ntíh yanahdog dóo iin ts'etden?
aan!
jah shaa nenahdeetl."
xu'éł.
And she'd say that three or four times.
They kind of hesitate to come down.
In English you'd say,
"Nobody here with me.
and come down and eat some dry fish,"
she said.
"Jah ndâadz dąą,
dé' tth'ih maa shég łuug,
má' na'e'aał,
áan.
shí' gęy jah dhihdaay nts'étxunt'eh,"
she said.

So finally they all come down.
They say it's big place she stay.
They all come in and they give them dry fish,
they all eating dry fish,
they put their swords,

you know them swords that out there,
you know them . . . what you call spear?
they all hang it out there,
they didn't have no—
the people that came,
they didn't have no bow and arrow.
That sword's the only thing they had.
Anyway when they all went in there,
they all come down,
the Mansfield people.
xunaxdendeetł,
they come in.
Each time when she goes around,
she takes that bridge out,
you know,
that pole,
you know,
she take that out.
No bridge to run across,
so they all surround the place.
ts'enh tuu ts'į' xu'éł nindeetł.

Êy shég ts'į',
one guy he start hollering
"eeey nuhtah ts'enindeetł"
they all took off . . . out to the doorway.
they got no way to go,
they all surround them like this.
"Nuhtah ts'enindeetł" xenii.
ey *everybody* naniłaxnetdek
k'ôd éł <u>sh</u>íi dé' taniłaxnedek ts'į'
you just swim across.
êy shég ts'į' k'ôd *last time* naxetmaak dinii Dihthâad.
êy shég dú'.
nandîidz sheg *Mansfield* xt'een iin k'á t'êey . . .
xutthuu<u>x</u>a̱a̱ ch'e k'á xú' xudinéy dé',
xa'andeddh ndée xnindeetl xuhninmaak dé'
xuh dé' naxuhne<u>sh</u>uut

êy shég dú' txuhnaa *Tanana River*,
xuta' xį̖įth chox xehtsii.
êy ét xiyk'et diniłatnetdeetl
naxį̖įthxnii'aa ts'į́'
aadaa,
what today they call it Yerrick Creek,
us,
in our Indian way of saying Yerrick Creek is . . .
Dach'indeedl Ndiig.
xu'én Dach'indeedl Ndiig xedinii.
xu'én dé',
naxuxnatdeł ts'į́'.

Somehow,
just for fun
they hit one of them,
with a bow and arrow, you know,
that have a . . . some kind of pointer in it,
really sharp,
They hit one of them just for fun.
and that guy,
it's hanging on his butt,
and it fall off he put it back in again.
He want to show it to the people.
"T'ogh tah,
people iin
wux̱ú' dełyaan."[15]
Just like he say that it's really sharp.

Êy shég ch'e k'ôd,
last time naxetmaak xu'exdinii.
Êy shég ch'e ch'ek'ôd tthiixdetkeyh
yehts'eyh dą̖ą,
dendeey iin jah nak'edaltth'ii
any place stay,
naxemaak
yitsį́' naxetmaak dadą̖ą ts'į́'

all over,
people iin niłxatx̲ą̄.

K'ahdú',
not too long ago,
ch'ek'od xexdindiig éł dexughindeetth.
Êy shég teey k'a dé' ts'enîin,
wugheek'ą̄ dihnii,
t'êey êy shég ch'ek'od *last time* náxetmáak dé',
êy ts'eniin gheex̲ę̄ êy shég.
Êy shég *long time ago,*
chih t'êey k'ahdú',
not too long ago dextsenh ch'ek'od
people iin niłettsayh ch'e nuhxwdelnii.
Neex̲ón nettseyh dą̄,
êy shég nakedeltth'ii dą̄ ts'į́' dú'
people iin niłalk'ę́'.
k'á dé' ts'į́' niłxettsayh dé',
niłxalk'ę́'.
not too long ago,
gįįhii iin ch'e naketetdeetł dé',
ey sheg ch'ek'od *people* iin niłettsah.
chih nuhdelnii
ey stsę̄ey dą̄ dú',
all of people niłxalk'ę́'.
jah k'ahdú' tth'én'
k'á dé' nii *not many*
ts'į́' łeey ts'į́',
de ch'e,
I like this way.

THE CRIPPLED BOY WHO SAVED MANSFIELD: ENGLISH LANGUAGE VERSION

When I was really young boy,[16]
a long, long time ago,
even before me,
young people at Mansfield Village were trained to be physically strong.

We're trained for the weather.
We're trained for everything.
Physical strength meant more to people than mental strength
because everything depended on your physical abilities.
We were taught too when we went to sleep
that all our clothing was to be left in one place,
that nothing was to be left scattered around.
Stay one place.
Everything.
While we go to sleep we put everything in one place where we could.
We kept it all in a pile so we could grab it in case of emergency.
Just like in the white man way, you ready.
You ready for the war.
You ready to go in case enemy coming.

The new Mansfield as we know it now
had more people than the old village of Dihthâad did.
Long time ago the story goes
that there has always been a war in this part of the country.
People from far, far away used to come to this part of the country
and make war upon our people,
the people of Mansfield and the surrounding area.
Mansfield people were known to kill off all the warriors
because they were really good at that.
Someone had already seen this type of war going on prior to this last war
I'm going to tell you about.
When the enemy warriors from this other country came to Dihthâad,
there was nobody there.
They came to an empty village.

Anyway now, there was an old woman who still lived at Dihthâad.
She was by herself down there
at the fish trap when they all came there.
Her grandchild lived with her.
Her grandchild couldn't walk.
He could only crawl or hop along on his knuckles.
The grandchild was gathering wood and bringing it to her
because she was staying home.

Even though he was crippled,
he was gathering dry wood for her.
As he was coming back from getting dry wood,
he noticed something that looked like pitchforks on top of that Mans-
    field Hill.
He saw all of that up there.

He came into the house and told his grandmother,
"Grandma,
how come there is a bunch of brushy willow-like trees on top of that
    hill?
It's never been like that before.
I've never seen anything up there before," he said.

"There's nothing growing up there!
What are you talking about?" his grandma said to him.

She want to go outdoors,
and just like she's doing something out there,
and she looks up there every once in a while.
Then she realized they were surrounded by warriors with spears.
"They have us surrounded," she said.

That crippled kid he goes up to get wood.
So she came back into the house and told her grandchild:
"Go back up that way for more dry wood.
Just keep bringing the wood in as you would normally do," she told
    him.
"You go back again.
As you are doing this,
tell those people staying over at Mansfield what's going on here.
Tell them we're surrounded by enemy warriors."

So he acted just like it was normal when he brought the wood in.
He went back out to get more,
but then he just went clear on up to the other village and told the people
    there
that they were surrounded by warriors.

As soon as he said that,
the people around there went for their bows and arrows.
That was their main weapon,
and they always had them where they could grab them and run
because they were used to war.
Along with the bow and arrow,
they also had alder poles that they sharpened to a point and used as
  weapons.

They told each other then,
before they went to rescue the old lady,
"Too many times we have always killed all of the enemy warriors.
This time let's not do that.
Let's just kind of chase them back.
We won't kill anybody."
That's what the leader says.
"What we want to do is just chase them back to where they come from.
I don't want to kill nobody no more," he said.
That's what he did, you know.
They said this to each other before they left.
And they all came around to them,
but in the meantime when that kid went up to Mansfield,
that old lady she go out:
"Hey, What's going on up there?
Come here! Come here! Come here to me!
Have some dry fish with me.
I'm by myself here," she told the enemy warriors.
She say that three or four times.
They kind of hesitate to come down.
In English we would say,
"There's nobody with me.
Come down and eat some dry fish!" she said.

So finally they all come down.
They say it was a big place.
They all come in and they give them dry fish.
They're all eating dry fish,
and they put their spears outside.
They all hang them out there.

The people that came they didn't have no bow and arrow.
That spear is the only thing they had.
Anyway, when they [the enemy warriors] went in there
[to the old lady's house],
they all came down,
the Mansfield people.
Each time when they go round,
that old lady she take that bridge out—
that pole [bridge across the creek]—she take that out.
No bridge to run across on.
So they all surround the place.

One [Mansfield] guy he start hollering:
"Hey, hey! You are surrounded!" [Claps his hands]
They all took off out through the doorway.
They got no way to go.
They all surround them like this [gesturing].
"Hey, you are all surrounded!" they say.
Everybody jump in the water.
Right away they just jump in the water.
You just swim across [the creek].
The Mansfield people from upriver did not want to kill them,
so they just chased them back to where they came from.
They say that was the last time they had war in Dihthâad.

They chased them downriver
from Dihthâad all the way down to the Tanana River,
where they made a big raft.
They jumped on it and went across.
Down below,
they chased them all the way down the Tanana River to the mouth of
    Yerrick Creek
and then they continued chasing them up Yerrick Creek.
What today they call Yerrick Creek.
Us, in our Indian way of saying Yerrick Creek is Dach'indeedl Ndiig ("Get-
    away Creek").

Somehow, just for fun I guess,
they hit one of them with a bow and arrow that have some kind of a pointer in it?

Old cache at Mansfield Village, in midnight fog, July 1999. Photograph by Craig Mishler.

Really sharp thing, [arrow]head of bow and arrow.
And that guy, it's hanging on his butt.
And it fall off [but] he put it back in again, you know?
He want to show it to the people.
"Ooh, these arrowhead barbs are really sharp," he said.
He say the teeth are really sharp, he would say.

During those times, there was a lot of war going on, they say,
upriver, downriver, towards the Copper River.
All over they used to have war.
It wasn't too long ago when they quit all this warfare.
Way back then, during those times, there were no burials.
People were always cremated.
It's just recently, during my time, that people started practicing burials.
Not too long ago,
the practice of burials began when the missionaries first came here.
They're the ones who initiated burials.
Prior to that, everybody practiced the cremation of the dead.
I like this way.

CHAPTER 10

Some Final Words

Living by the Straight Board

In his book So They Understand: Cultural Issues in Oral History, *William Schneider makes the point that Athabaskan elders presenting their life stories are not just telling what they did but are passing on "their code of life" to future generations. What follows here may be called Kenny's "code of life," his ethical philosophy told through an extended metaphor. Sections in serif-italics have been translated from the Tanacross original.*

I want to talk about my language a little bit, and I want to explain about what I'm going to say. Long time ago, my Dad and my uncle, my grandpa, my auntie, and everybody knows everybody in Northway, Tetlin, and all the people are related. People are related all together up that way. We're all relation. We know how we are related and there is different clan. We have a different clan; all of us have different clan: I'm Ałts'ii̜ dendeey, my wife is a Dik'aagyu. And there are different [other] clans. A lot of people are Ch'aadh, Ch'echeelyu, Tsesyu, Wudzisyu, Tandîidz altsiil. Tandîidz altsiil means "The Middle People" that related to both sides of the clan [both moieties]. So we all have a different clan.

What it's all about, what I'm going to say in my language is, my Dad and Chief Peter and all those people, like my uncle and grandpa, place I used to live up that way where my Dad and them is friends and we all related to each other. My Dad and all those friends up that way, they put one long, straight board or pole up this Tanana [River]

237

between those villages. They put a straight board, like. We call it Dechę t'ii dee'aii. That's the board that we have to obey in our clan, in our culture. This board mean we have to be straight.

We don't want to talk about somebody else, we don't gossip about somebody else, we don't want to talk about somebody in [behind] their back. If you're mad at somebody or talk about somebody else, they're going to stop you right now, and they going to straighten you out. This mean you've fallen down, fallen off this board when you do something like talk about somebody else. Mad to the people. That's not what they want. They going to talk to you and they going to bring you back on that board, and you have to go around straight. That's the way they are.

Now, my language: *My father, and my ancestors and them, they were the characters that did no wrong. They were straight people, as straight as they can be. I grew up after these people who were good, straight people. I grew up in their footsteps. My grandfather, my grandmother, my uncles, my aunts, they all helped to teach me the right way: "Don't even talk bad about each other. Don't tell lies about each other. Don't talk about each other."* [1]

Just like [if] one guy fall down, we all have to go there and bring him back on the board. That's what this means.

All of us people who lived along this river [the Tanana], it's just like we were brought up hanging onto this pole, as straight as that pole, and we were all connected like that. If we're not that kind of people, we will be discredited. We'll hurt people's feelings. They won't like what we're saying.

The people want us to be straight, that's why they put that lumber, like—I don't know how to explain but the only thing nearest I can get to it is, "the lumber." That's straight, you got to be straight at the time. If you're a straight man or woman, they going to like you. That's what they want you to be, a straight person. Not to fall off this board.

My Dad and my uncles and all of them, they were like friends and they shared this straight pole with each other. That's how they were connected. "Be that kind of people," they used to tell each other. "Don't say mean things about each other. Hold each other's hand and keep each other on this straight pole. That's the kind of people you should be."

My grandfather and them taught us all the right way to live. They didn't tell us anything out of the ordinary. They only told us how to live the right way.

What I'm remembering now was told to me by my aunts, my mother, my father, my grandfather. Whatever they used to teach me when I was young, all of that is coming back to me now as I'm getting older. Some things that I forgot is coming back to me today, when I am getting old.

What grandpa told me a long time ago, you can't learn whatever you need to know in a day or two. It takes a long time. It all comes back, all the things that you were taught, all the things that you've heard as a young person, they come back as you get older. I don't remember very much of what I was taught. I really don't. That's why I'm reluctant to speak because I don't want to tell anything that's not true. I want to be right with people. I want to be honest.

We are supposed to know by now the place names of where we live. So I named what I remembered [for the U.S. Air Force Backscatter Radar research project in 1988]. I named the hills and stuff like that. The hills, the lakes, the river, all of these have names. We know the name of all these little hills, all the trails, all the waterways. If someone told us a story about a moose crossing this trail, we would automatically know which part of the country he's talking about just from knowing these names.

We go to Dog Lake and all that. In their language it's Dog Lake. Us, [we call it] Łii Menn'. Why don't we use that [name] today? Don't try to be somebody else. Sometime, step back and try to think about who you are. It's good to learn little things. Get what you can. It's good to ask questions. Ask people older than you are about things that they know.

I [heard] somebody else make a speech and say, "Oh, this young generation don't know nothing." Whose fault is it? I *blame* myself for that. I blame myself for that when somebody say that. Why didn't they teach these kids like I did, to *their* family? Where were they? Why didn't they teach their kids, instead of saying, "The young generation don't know nothing."

It's *our fault* they don't know nothing. I'm ashamed to say that.

Young people really hungry to learn our ways, but there's no teacher; nobody leads them. I don't call myself teacher because I'm just trying to lead my people the right way, that's all I'm doing. Today, my kids teach a lot of this. Lot of time they come back to me [to ask] if they're doing right or what, but I correct them, and that's what we should do in different villages. I think that's the only way it will help our younger people.

Way back, my Dad and all of them, what kind of people they were I have heard from them. What they meant by leaving and hanging onto the straight pole, what they were trying to say, now, at my age I'm beginning to figure out what it is that they were trying to teach me. "This is the kind of people I want you to be," they told us. That's the symbol of that pole. The symbol of that pole that they put here for us, just by that gesture they're telling us to be good, to be straight people.

Our grandfathers and them used to tell us all these people that live in Tetlin, Northway, all these villages, live like they did—good, straight people. They didn't want us to talk about each other or hurt each other. That's why the symbol of that straight pole, the legend of it, was left with us. That's the kind of people they want us to be. Something wrong, they go there. They put us back on that board.

That's the kind of people they wanted us to be, that's why they taught us by that. We're only here for a few days. We shouldn't gossip about each other. Don't gossip about each other. Try and get along.

The young people today are struggling to survive. I feel so sorry for them. I just wonder how else I can help them. I don't know. I need help but I don't know where else we could go to get help. But I'll do my best, the best I can to pass on what little I know to these people. That means, *I'm teaching them the way my father and them old people have taught me, that's what I'm passing on to them.*

If you want to know something, always ask people who are older than you. They're all around you. If you don't know how to answer that, go to somebody else.

Since the old, old time, people used to make public speeches to each other. Now, in the present time, there are certain people who want to make speeches to each other. But the practice of making public speeches is no longer practiced. If I were to get up and make a speech in my grandfather and them's way today, nobody would understand what I'm talking about. They used to use the speech to keep us straight. Whatever is going wrong around us was always straightened out during these speeches and we were all turned back to do things right again. That was the use of the speeches.[2]

Kenny Thomas Sr. in beaded moose-hide potlatch vest, Tanacross, August 2001. Photograph by Craig Mishler.

The tetł is gone, the speech is gone. I can say lots of things in my speech, but I don't want it to say that because I don't think nobody can understand it [Tanacross]. All the old people are gone [Tanacross]. Every day, during the day, I think of all these things that my father and them taught me. Today, it seems like very short days that I'm here with my young people. What very little I know and remember is what I want to leave on this earth for them.

All those people that I spoke of, my uncles, my grandfather, all of them, they're through walking this straight pole. They're gone, they're done with, and they left these words behind.

Thomas Family Tree

The number to the left of each name indicates the generation, starting with Laura and Old Jim as the first. Six generations are represented. Sp. represents "Spouse." Birth and death dates, where known, are in parentheses, along with nicknames. Current to December 10, 2002.

A. Kenny's Mother's Side

1. Laura
   Sp: James (Old Jim)
   2. Charlie James (b. 1889 in Batzulnetas)
      Sp: Eliza (daughter of Old Saul, b. 1905 in Kechumstuk)
         3. Frances
            Sp: Unknown
         3. Arthur
         3. Harvey
         3. Myra
         3. Elsie
         3. Elmer
   2. Annie James (b. 1885, d. 1918)
      Sp: Peter Solomon (b. 1883)
         3. Silas Solomon (b. 1904)
         3. Archie Solomon (b. 1906)
         3. Mary Solomon (b. 1908)
         3. Elsie (b. 1909)

       Sp. David Tega (b. 1881)
          4. Edbert Tega (b. 1934)
          4. Ada Marie Tega (b. 1937)
          4. Charlie Tega (b. 1942)
2. Sarah James (b. 1887 or 1890)
  Sp: Peter Thomas ("Peter Onion") (b. 1875)
    3. Silas Peter Thomas (b. 1909, d. 1950)
      Sp: Eva Northway
        4. Danny Thomas
        4. Bertland Thomas
        4. Bentley Thomas
        4. Sherman Thomas
        4. Gary Thomas
        4. Bobby Thomas
    3. Lena Thomas (b. 1917; d. 1938)
    3. Kenneth Thomas Sr. (b. 1922)
      Sp: Ellen Joseph (b. 1930)
        4. Mildred Thomas (b. 1947)
           5. Sharon Lee Thomas (b. 1965)
             Sp: Lee Henry
               6. Doran Henry
               6. Preston Henry
               6. Sharrisa Henry
                 Sp: Alfred Jonathon
           5. Richard James Jonathon (b. 1964)
           5. Tashina Jonathon
           5. Karen Jonathon
             Sp: Alfred Grant
               6. Kashana Grant
           5. Gabriel Jonathon (adopted)
        4. Betty Thomas (b. 1950)
          Sp: Roy Glen Denny (b. 1943)
           5. Colleen Denny
           5. Chris Denny
           5. Sarah Denny
        4. Kenneth Thomas Jr. (b. 1951)
          Sp: Anna Northway
           5. Sarina Northway

      6. Lakota Northway
      6. Shoshanna Northway
      6. William Parks [?]
    5. Charo Thomas
   4. Raymond Thomas (b. 1952)
     5. Alicia Thomas
   4. Diane Mabel Thomas (b. 1955)
     Sp: Ray Titus
      5. Delbert Titus
      5. Derick (Devon) Titus [?]
      5. Marshiann Titus
       6. Kayleana Titus-Demit
      5. Dalen Titus
   4. Kirby Willard Thomas (b. 1957)
     Sp: Michelle Emerson
      5. Kerchelle Thomas
   4. Nancy Thomas (b. 1959)
     Sp: Kenny Moe
      5. Stephanie Moe
     Sp: Brian Allen
      5. Kyle Allen
   4. Debbie Thomas (b. 1964)
      5. Michael Thomas
  3. Lucy Thomas (d. 1936)
  3. Lula Thomas (b. 1927)
  3. Minnie Nannie Thomas (d. 1946)
  3. Calvin Thomas (b. 1931)

B. Kenny's Father's Side (only the first three generations are shown)
1. Thomas
  Sp: Old Gert (?)
   2. Sam Thomas (b. 1869)
    Sp: Bessie
   3. Albert Thomas (b. 1894)
   3. Moses Thomas (b. 1899)
   3. Walter Thomas (b. 1901)
   3. Annie Thomas (b. 1904)
    Sp: Thomas Denny

      3. Joseph (Alfred?) Thomas (b. 1905)
2. Peter Thomas ("Peter Onion") (b. 1875)
   Sp: Sarah James (b. 1887 or 1890)
      3. Silas (b. 1909, d. 1950)
      3. Lena (b. 1917; d. 1938)
      3. Kenneth Thomas Sr. (b. 1922)
      3. Lucy Thomas (d. 1936)
      3. Lula Thomas (b. 1927)
      3. Minnie Nannie Thomas (d. 1946)
      3. Calvin Thomas (b. 1931)
2. Jennie Thomas
   Sp: Henry Luke
      3. Elsie Luke
      3. Richard Luke
      3. Moses Luke
      3. Paddy Herbert Luke
2. Julia Thomas
   Sp: Old Paul Stuu'ta'
      3. David Paul
      3. Julius Paul
      3. Saline Paul

Notes

The notes are by Craig Mishler, unless otherwise identified by initials: IA (Irene Arnold), GH (Gary Holton), ET (Ellen Thomas), and KT (Kenny Thomas Sr.).

INTRODUCTION

1. Frederick Blount Drane, "A Circuit Rider on the Yukon—Life among the Sourdoughs and Indians of Sub-Arctic Alaska; A Narrative of Ten Years Experience and Travel [1915–1925]." Unpublished mss., Rasmuson Library Archives, University of Alaska, Fairbanks, box 7, folder 15, p. 189.

2. Robert A. McKennan, *The Upper Tanana Indians* (New Haven: Yale University Publications in Anthropology, 1959). Although this classic ethnography is long out of print, McKennan's overview essay simply entitled, "Tanana," appears in June Helm, ed., *Handbook of North American Indians: Subarctic* (Washington, D.C.: Smithsonian Institution, 1981), 562–76. McKennan's forthcoming field journals of the Upper Tanana and the Chandalar are currently being edited by Craig Mishler and William Simeone.

3. Walter Goldschmidt, *Delimitation of Possessory Rights of the Villages of Northway, Tanacross, and Tetlin in the Interior of Alaska* (N.p.: U.S. Office of Indian Affairs, 1946). Copies of the 2003 revision are on file at the ARLIS Library, Anchorage, Alaska.

4. *Transcript of Proceedings, Village Meetings*, volume 8, *Tanacross* (Anchorage: Alaska Native Review Commission, 1984–1985).

5. Marie-Françoise Guédon, *People of Tetlin, Why Are You Singing?* (Ottawa: National Museums of Canada, 1974). See also Guédon's essay "Upper Tanana River Potlatch," in Helm, *Handbook*, 577–81.

6. Libby Halpin, *Living off the Land: Contemporary Subsistence in Tetlin, Alaska.* Technical Paper No. 149 (Fairbanks: Alaska Department of Fish and Game, Division of Subsistence, 1987); William Simeone, *Rifles, Blankets, and Beads: Identity, History, and the Northern Athapaskan Potlatch* (Norman: University of Oklahoma Press, 1995); Curt Madison, *Hitting Sticks, Healing Hearts: A Minto Memorial Potlatch,* video, 58 mins. (Manley Hot Springs, AK: River Tracks Productions, 1992).

7. Lt. Henry T. Allen, *An Expedition to the Copper, Tanana, and Koyukuk Rivers in 1885,* ed. Terrence Cole (1887; Anchorage: Alaska Northwest, 1985); E. H. Wells, "Exploring the Tanana River Region," *Alaska Journal* 5.1 (1975): 41–48; Alfred H. Brooks, "A Reconnaissance of the Tanana and White River Basins, Alaska, in 1898," *Twentieth Annual Report, U.S. Geological Survey,* part 7, pp. 431–94; C. Michael Brown, *Indians, Traders, and Bureaucrats in the Upper Tanana District: A History of the Tetlin Reserve* (Anchorage: U.S. Bureau of Land Management, State Office, 1984); Geoffrey Bleakley, *A History of Chisana Mining District, Alaska, 1890–1990* (Anchorage: National Park Service, Alaska System Support Office, Division of Cultural Resources, 1996). Tanacross web page: http://www.nativevillageoftanacross.com/nvhistory.html

8. Howard Luke, *My Own Trail,* ed. Jan Steinbright Jackson (Fairbanks: Alaska Native Knowledge Network, 1998); Yvonne Yarber and Curt Madison, eds., *Walter Northway* (Fairbanks: Alaska Native Language Center, 1987), and *Andrew Isaac* (Fairbanks: Central Alaska Curriculum Consortium, 1988); 12. Alice Brean, *Athabascan Stories* (Anchorage: AMU Press, 1975); Gaither Paul, *Stories for My Grandchildren,* transcribed and edited by Ron Scollon (Fairbanks: Alaska Native Language Center, 1980).

9. A recently published guide to learning the language is Irene Solomon Arnold, *Dihthâad Xt'een Iin Aandĕeg'—The Mansfield People's Language: Tanacross Athabascan Phrases and Conversations* (Fairbanks: Alaska Native Language Center, 2003), a booklet and CD with Gary Holton and Rick Thoman.

10. For an in-depth reflexive look at the way collaboration works, see Theodore Rios and Kathleen Mullen Sands, *Telling a Good One: The Process of a Native American Collaborative Biography* (Lincoln: University of Nebraska Press, 2000). The theoretical basis of this appproach to texts is articulated in Dennis Tedlock and Bruce Mannheim, eds., *The Dialogic Emergence of Culture* (Urbana: University of Illinois Press, 1995).

11. Andra Cole and J. Gary Knowles, *Lives in Context: the Art of Life History Research* (Walnut Creek, CA: AltaMira Press, 2001), 89; Julie Cruikshank, "The Social Life of Texts: Editing on the Page and in Performance," in Laura Murray and Keren Rice, eds., *Talking on the Page: Editing Aboriginal Texts* (Toronto: University of Toronto Press, 1999), 108, 114.

12. One of the first to recognize this paradigm shift was Julie Cruikshank. See her "Telling about Culture: Changing Traditions in Subarctic Anthropology," *The Northern Review* 1 (Summer 1988); 27–39. William Schneider, in his book *So They Understand: Cultural Issues in Oral History* (Logan: Utah State University Press, 2002), 114, argues persuasively that the greatest challenge for scholars working on life histories is to provide context and understanding "without usurping the voice of the teller." In this volume, the Introduction and notes provide an important part of this context.

CHAPTER 1

1. KT: My name, Wu eł nahts'aa xughin xeed, means "He was given to us as a replacement." In other words, I replaced my brother who died. IA: Kenny's Indian name literally means "We paid for it with this." In Tanacross, when we choose to name a child with a dead person's name, we have to make a potlatch and tell people. [For example] My first grandson's name is Silas, after my father, Silas Solomon, and we had to go buy my father's name for him because he was from the opposite clan. So this is what they were talking about when they gave Kenny his Indian name. Kenny's mother's name Xeh Xulnah, has a hint of "dependable, reliable."

2. The Spanish flu pandemic of 1918–1919, which took the lives of many Alaska Natives, arrived just a few years before Kenny Thomas was born, but there were undoubtedly several other flu epidemics during his youth, including one that took the lives of his parents.

3. Dihthâad is an old village site located on Fish Creek, locally known as Mansfield Creek, a short ways downstream from Mansfield Village. Archaeological excavations were undertaken there by Froelich Rainey, Robert McKennan, and John Cook.

4. Chisana was a gold-mining town established on the Chisana River, a tributary of the upper Tanana River during the stampede of 1913.

5. Kenny may actually be referring here to his younger sister, Lula, who was about seven years old in 1934, and his younger brother, Calvin, who was born in 1931.

6. For more information about John Hajdukovich and the early fur trade on the Upper Tanana, see my *Born with the River: An Ethnographic History of Alaska's Goodpaster and Big Delta Indians* (Fairbanks: Alaska Division of Geological and Geophysical Surveys, Report of Investigations No. 86-14, 1986); and C. Michael Brown, "John K. Hajdukovich and the Tetlin Indians, 1924–1941," *Alaska History* 14.1–2 (1999): 1–29.

7. Rika's Roadhouse, located on the south bank where the Richardson Highway crosses the Tanana River, is named after Rika Wallen, a Swedish immigrant

who owned and managed the place. It has now been restored and is part of a state historic park.

8. Located in 1995, this is the Pogo Gold Mine, operated by Teck Cominco, the most lucrative new find in recent Alaskan history. Kenny's oldest daughter, Mildred, has worked there as a cook.

9. Central Creek is a tributary of the Goodpaster River where there was once a telegraph station.

10. A description of this famous potlatch can be found in H. Wendell Endicott's book, *Adventures in Alaska and along the Trail* (New York: Frederick A. Stokes, 1928). Endicott was one of John Hajdukovich's wealthy clients who came to Alaska from Boston to hunt big game as trophies.

11. Located across the river from old Tanacross, on the south bank, the Tanacross airfield was rebuilt, paved, and upgraded to two runways during the early years of World War II and became an important U.S. military post. Planes landed there for refueling as part of the lend-lease project, and a detachment of soldiers was stationed there, including the distinguished anthropologist Robert A. McKennan. Today the airfield, adjacent to the new village, serves as a refueling stop for Bureau of Land Management forest-fire- suppression efforts.

CHAPTER 2

1. In these years Kenny stayed out trapping from November 1 through early March.

2. Mehtseh Taiy' (Flint Hill), is located on the southeast end of Kechumstuk Mountain.

3. The "party" Kenny refers to here is a memorial potlatch.

4. Ladd Army Airfield, known today as Fort Wainwright, is located adjacent to the Interior Alaskan city of Fairbanks. Construction of Ladd Field started in 1938, with the airfield becoming fully operational in 1940. (See Chapter 4).

CHAPTER 3

1. This divination cane for locating game animals is reminiscent of the ceremonial rod used by men such as Nabesna John, Scottie Creek Titus, and Follett Isaac. See McKennan, *Upper Tanana Indians*, 152.

2. Kenny is referring to the Tanacross language place names map we made with the help of several elders for the U.S. Air Force Backscatter Radar project in 1988. This map now resides with the Tanacross Tribal Council.

3. There are numerous stories about Stick Indians or Brush Indians, known in Tanacross as Guu. For others, see Paul, *Stories for My Grandchildren*.

CHAPTER 4

1. By "walk the Cat," Kenny means he slowly drove the Caterpillar tractor overland where there were no roads.

2. Adak, Kiska, and Shemya are islands in the Western Aleutians where Kenny was stationed. Those interested in the history of his outfit may wish to consult John Cloe, *The Aleutian Warriors: A History of the Eleventh Air Force and Fleet Air Wing 4* (Missoula, MT: Pictorial Histories, 1990).

3. When U.S. troops invaded Kiska on August 15, 1943, they found the Japanese had already given up their foothold and left the island two weeks before.

4. The USS *Yukon* was an Alaska Steamship Company passenger liner appropriated as a troopship during World War II. It operated in the Aleutian Islands from Dutch Harbor to Adak and Shemya. After the war it grounded on sharp rocks and broke in two during a severe southeasterly gale southeast of Seward, Alaska, on February 4, 1946. Eleven people died in the wreck, but the rest made it to the beach where they were rescued by a flotilla of seven ships.

5. VJ stands for "Victory in Japan." It was celebrated on September 2, 1945, and marked the formal surrender of the Japanese to the Allied forces.

6. Kenny is probably referring here to Unalaska rather than Shishmaref. Unalaska is directly adjacent to the major port of Dutch Harbor.

7. The Tok VFW is one of the places Kenny and Ellen regularly go to play bingo.

8. Kenny was discharged from the military on March 1, 1946.

CHAPTER 5

1. Gambell is a Siberian Eskimo village on St. Lawrence Island, Alaska. Red Devil is a small Yup'ik Eskimo village on the Kuskokwim River in southwest Alaska.

2. Warbelow Air Service. Warbelow's operates chartered and scheduled flights out of Tok, Fairbanks, and Tanacross.

3. Glenallen is a small community at the junction of the Glenn and Richardson highways, about 150 miles south of Tanacross.

4. Harry John was an Ahtna man from Copper Center, a traditional chief and former pastor of the Copper Center Community Chapel. He died January 31, 2004.

5. New Tanacross was built on the south bank of the Tanana River close to the airfield in 1971, and the old village across the river was gradually abandoned due to repeated flooding and fire.

CHAPTER 6

1. A lot of the things that are Injih or forbidden are related to the fear of contamination by a girl's or woman's menstrual blood. It is believed that if a girl or woman having her period comes into contact with a man's gun, ammunition, clothing, or other hunting gear, he will have very poor luck hunting. For more on the notion of Injih, see my *Born with the River*, 28–29. Additional background data on early Tanacross potlatches may be found in Anonymous, "A Big Feast at Tanana Crossing," *The Alaskan Churchman* 12.2 (1918): 47–49 and W. C. Denny, "A Northern Potlatch," *The Alaskan Churchman* 17.1 (1923): 8–9. An extended description and interpretation of the Tanacross potlatch ceremonial can be found in Simeone, *Rifles, Blankets, and Beads*.

2. KT: "Shtaa'in refers to "my father's family" going way back.

3. KT: Gifts given at the memorial potlatch are called Tiitł. We call those gifts "*really* potlatch." These gifts include rifles, blankets, beadwork, and bolts of calico, as well as cash money.

4. Walti' dun iiyuu ziidii is an unidentified place name.

5. An honorary or get-well potlatch was held for Kenny and several others at the Tanacross community hall August 23–25, 2001. My family and I were invited guests and received gifts from Kenny's children, who are of the Dik'aagyu clan.

CHAPTER 7

1. The Tanacross word for song is "Chiłiig" and the word for dance is "Chadzes." The ganhook is often written as "gunhawk" or "gunho," but Gary Holton (personal communication) insists that its etymology has nothing to do with rifles or guns.

2. It is not known exactly what year the Han songs and ganhook were first introduced, but the residents of Eagle Village and Moosehide were invited to a big potlatch at Tanacross in April 1917 or 1918. See Anonymous, "A Big Feast at Tanana Crossing."

3. The late ethnomusicologist Thomas Johnston observed that Upper Tanana drum rhythm "consists of unvarying quarter-notes in a continuous, even pulse, the melody providing clues as to where the beginning of each measure lies. Measures consist of uneven groupings of these quarter-notes, in additive combinations such as 4 + 4 + 2 + 6, and so on." See his article, "The Social Role of Alaskan Athabaskan Potlatch Dancing," *Dance* 3 (1993): 183–226.

4. To make a potlatch "on" his uncle is the vernacular way of saying he made a potlatch to honor his uncle. In spite of the beatings his uncle gave him, he realized it was for his own good. Sometimes Tanacross people will say they made a potlatch "over" someone, with the same meaning.

5. These are some of the Gwich'in fiddle dances Kenny has seen performed at the Athabaskan Old-Time Fiddlers Festival in Fairbanks. They are described in my book, *The Crooked Stovepipe: Athabaskan Fiddling and Square Dancing in Northeast Alaska and Northwest Canada* (Urbana and Chicago: University of Illinois Press, 1993).

6. "The Twist" was initially recorded by Hank Ballard and the Midnighters in 1958, and Chubby Checker's version hit the top of the charts in both the United States and the United Kingdom in 1960 and 1961 and initiated a national dance craze, with many imitations and variations. In Tanacross this dance, performed with drum accompaniment, has two parts: a slow part, the Two Step, which is speeded up slightly, followed by a fast part, the Twist.

7. This hook game was first described in McKennan, *The Upper Tanana Indians*, 102, as part of a traditional winter festival. In *People of Tetlin*, 201–2, Guédon includes a description of the game and a drawing of the hook apparatus, made like a short fishing rod dangling a wooden hook on a babiche string and surrounded with six little rattling sticks.

CHAPTER 8

1. For more on the Goodpaster River people, see my *Born with the River*.

2. Morris Thompson was an Indian leader from the village of Tanana who rose to prominence as the twelve-year president and CEO of Doyon Limited, a Native corporation he helped create. He was also former Commissioner of the U.S. Bureau of Indian Affairs. Thompson was killed with his wife and daughter in the crash of Alaskan Airlines flight no. 261 near Los Angeles on January 31, 2000.

3. It is part of Indian religious belief that at least one moose be taken to honor the deceased. Alaska state hunting regulations now allow for taking moose for potlatches, but only by special permit from the Department of Fish and Game.

CHAPTER 9

1. The Traveler tale cycle of Yaamaagh Telcheegh is supposed to be told each year only in the month of October. Kenny told this version on October 30, 2000, but the first time I heard him tell it was actually at the Tanacross tribal council office on August 12, 1988. Two kindred Traveler tale cycles are those of Tsa-o-sha (collected in McKennan, *Upper Tanana Indians*, 175–89) and of Tsà'Wëzhaa as told by Han elder Louise Paul (see Craig Mishler and William Simeone, *Han, People of the River* [Fairbanks: University of Alaska Press, 2003], 145–57). The code-switching seen here generally represents Kenny's attempts to translate himself

from English into Tanacross and vice versa. While the tale is essentially based in English, Tanacross is often used, especially where dialogue (quoted speech) is concerned. To avoid redundancy, these self-translations have not been transcribed but are simply indicated by [Tanacross]. IA: "He [Yaamaagh Telcheegh] went around this world and beyond." That's what his name means, literally. ET: Yaamaagh Telcheegh left when he was young and didn't come back from his travels around the world until he was old with gray hair.

2. IA: The loon that Yaamaagh Telcheegh encounters is a common loon, which we call Ah'aala'.

3. CM: I have written a comparative study and interpretation of this widely known folktale in "Diving Down: Ritual Healing in the Tale of the Blind Man and the Loon," a paper given as part of a symposium on Narrative and Healing at the International Association for Arctic Social Sciences meetings (ICASS 4) in Quebec City, May 2001. The paper was published in *Arctic Anthropology* 40.2 (2003): 49–55. A second Tanacross version of this story, "The Loon and the Blind Man," is included in Brean, *Athabaskan Stories*.

4. This historical legend was told mostly in Tanacross and was translated by Irene Arnold. English phrases and sentences are intermixed and, within this story, are indicated by italics.

5. KT: My Mom was part Ahtna and part Russian and came from Batzulnetas.

6. IA: K'eetł'aa Ta' means "the father of someone who has been over that route before." Sts'ay Nitle' means "Really my grandfather" or "Truly my grandfather." K'eetł'aa Ta' was from the Ałts'įį dendeey clan.

7. IA: Ch'etąandiidz literally means "in the middle of." "Na'eetęę," our word for "medicine man," literally means "a dreamer."

8. KT: Before they found whitefish they found northern pike in the small lake between Wolf Lake and Fish Lake.

9. IA: Táxéłts'íh Keyh means "where you toss a stick or club into the water."

10. KT: "Dihthâad" is an old word that means "deep creek." Teetiinthaad means "deep water."

11. CM: "Ehchin" is the Tanacross word for medicine. IA: The cemetery is all overgrown now, but we were never allowed to go up that way. It's Injih. "You don't want to disturb the spirit," they told us, "because of the kind of man he was." He wasn't the only one buried there. There's a lot of medicine men buried up there.

12. Like the story itself, this commentary was told primarily in Tanacross, with some English interspersed, as shown in italics. It was translated by Irene Arnold.

13. IA: "Wut'aagh dįt'eey" literally means "the one whom we depend on."

14. Kenny performed this story in Tanacross on December 10, 1999. It was recorded by Craig Mishler on video, dubbed to audiotape, and transcribed by

Gary Holton in verse form. This legend is told primarily in Tanacross, with fre-
quent code-switching to English. English words and phrases are shown in italics. Craig first heard it told in English by the late Julius Paul on August 24,
1988. Mansfield Lake and Mansfield Village were named in 1890 after Lt.
Commander Henry Buckingham Mansfield of the U.S. Navy. See Wells,
"Exploring the Tanana River Region." However, the ancestors of Kenny
Thomas Sr. and other Tanacross people resided there and at the old village of
Dihthâad long before that. The two communities are located about a half-mile
apart.

15. GH: This "dełyaan" is an Ahtna (Mentasta) word, meaning "really sharp."

16. This is a free translation by Irene Arnold, with assistance from Kenny
Thomas Sr., edited by Craig Mishler. English phrases and sentences are shown
in italics.

CHAPTER 10

1. KT: "Nełgha ts'ax tothil" means "We're gossiping about each other."

2. Kenny is referring here to the great tradition of upper Tanana and Tanacross potlatch oratory.

Bibliography

Alaska Native Review Commission. *Transcript of Proceedings, Village Meetings.* Volume 8. *Tanacross.* Anchorage: Alaska Native Review Commission, 1984–1985.

Allen, Lt. Henry T. *An Expedition to the Copper, Tanana, and Koyukuk Rivers in 1885.* Edited by Terrence Cole. 1887. Anchorage: Alaska Northwest, 1985.

Anonymous. "A Big Feast at Tanana Crossing." *The Alaskan Churchman* 12.2 (1918): 47–49.

Arnold, Irene Solomon. *Dihthâad Xt'een Iin Aandeeg'—The Mansfield People's Language: Tanacross Athabaskan Phrases and Conversations.* Fairbanks: Alaska Native Language Center, 2003. Booklet and CD with Gary Holton and Rick Thoman.

Bleakley, Geoffrey. *A History of Chisana Mining District, Alaska, 1890–1990.* Anchorage: National Park Service, Alaska System Support Office, Division of Cultural Resources, 1996.

Brean, Alice. *Athabaskan Stories.* Anchorage: AMU Press, 1975.

Brooks, Alfred H. "A Reconnaissance of the Tanana and White River Basins, Alaska, in 1898." In *Twentieth Annual Report, U.S. Geological Survey.* Part 7, pp. 431–94.

Brown, C. Michael. *Indians, Traders, and Bureaucrats in the Upper Tanana District: A History of the Tetlin Reserve.* Anchorage: U.S. Bureau of Land Management, State Office, 1984.

———. "John K. Hajdukovich and the Tetlin Indians, 1924–1941." *Alaska History* 14.1–2 (1999): 1–29.

Cloe, John. *The Aleutian Warriors: A History of the Eleventh Air Force and Fleet Air Wing 4.* Missoula, MT: Pictorial Histories, 1990.

Cole, Andra, and J. Gary Knowles. *Lives in Context: The Art of Life History Research*. Walnut Creek, CA: AltaMira Press, 2001.

Cruikshank, Julie. "Telling about Culture: Changing Traditions in Subarctic Anthropology." *The Northern Review* 1 (Summer 1988).

———. "The Social Life of Texts: Editing on the Page and in Performance." In Laura Murray and Keren Rice, eds., *Talking on the Page: Editing Aboriginal Texts*. Toronto: University of Toronto Press, 1999.

Denny, W. C. "A Northern Potlatch." *The Alaskan Churchman* 17.1 (1923): 8–9.

Endicott, H. Wendell. *Adventures in Alaska and along the Trail*. New York: Frederick A. Stokes, 1928.

Goldschmidt, Walter. *Delimitation of Possessory Rights of the Villages of Northway, Tanacross, and Tetlin in the Interior of Alaska*. N.p.: U.S. Office of Indian Affairs, 1946. Copies of the 2003 revision are on file at the ARLIS Library, Anchorage, Alaska.

Guédon, Marie-Françoise. *People of Tetlin, Why Are You Singing?* Ottawa: National Museums of Canada, 1974.

———. "Upper Tanana River Potlatch." In Helm, *Handbook*, 577–81.

Halpin, Libby. *Living off the Land: Contemporary Subsistence in Tetlin, Alaska*. Technical Paper No. 149. Fairbanks: Alaska Department of Fish and Game, Division of Subsistence, 1987.

Helm, June, ed. *Handbook of North American Indians: Subarctic*. Washington, D.C.: Smithsonian Institution, 1981.

Johnston, Thomas. "The Social Role of Alaskan Athabaskan Potlatch Dancing." *Dance* 3 (1993): 183–226.

Luke, Howard. *My Own Trail*. Edited by Jan Steinbright Jackson. Fairbanks: Alaska Native Knowledge Network, 1998.

Madison, Curt. *Hitting Sticks, Healing Hearts: A Minto Memorial Potlatch*. Video, 58 mins. Manley Hot Springs, AK: River Tracks Productions, 1992.

McKennan, Robert A. *The Upper Tanana Indians*. New Haven: Yale University Publications in Anthropology, 1959.

———. "Tanana." In Helm, *Handbook*, 562–76.

Mishler, Craig. *Born with the River: An Ethnographic History of Alaska's Goodpaster and Big Delta Indians*. Fairbanks: Alaska Division of Geological and Geophysical Surveys, Report of Investigations No. 86-14, 1986.

———. *The Crooked Stovepipe: Athabaskan Fiddling and Square Dancing in Northeast Alaska and Northwest Canada*. Urbana and Chicago: University of Illinois Press, 1993.

———. "Diving Down: Ritual Healing in the Tale of the Blind Man and the Loon." *Arctic Anthropology* 40.2 (2003): 49–55.

Mishler, Craig, and William Simeone. *Han, People of the River*. Fairbanks: University of Alaska Press, 2003.

Paul, Gaither. *Stories for My Grandchildren*. Transcribed and edited by Ron Scollon. Fairbanks: Alaska Native Language Center, 1980.

Purdy, Ann. *Tisha: The Story of a Young Teacher in the Alaska Wilderness*. New York: St. Martin's Press, 1976.

Rios, Theodore, and Kathleen Mullen Sands. *Telling a Good One: The Process of a Native American Collaborative Biography*. Lincoln: University of Nebraska Press, 2000.

Schneider, William. *So They Understand: Cultural Issues in Oral History*. Logan: Utah State University Press, 2002.

Simeone, William. *Rifles, Blankets, and Beads: Identity, History, and the Northern Athapaskan Potlatch*. Norman: University of Oklahoma Press, 1995.

Tedlock, Dennis and Bruce Mannheim, eds. *The Dialogic Emergence of Culture*. Urbana: University of Illinois Press, 1995.

Wells, E. H. "Exploring the Tanana River Region." 1891. *Alaska Journal* 5.1 (1975): 41–48.

Yarber, Yvonne, and Curt Madison, eds. *Walter Northway*. Fairbanks: Alaska Native Language Center, 1987.

———. *Andrew Isaac*. Fairbanks: Central Alaska Curriculum Consortium, 1988.

ARCHIVAL SOURCES

Frederick Drane Collection. Alaska and Polar Regions Archives, Rasmuson Library, University of Alaska Fairbanks.

John Hajdukovich Collection. University of Alaska Archives. Rasmuson Library, Fairbanks.

Robert A. McKennan Collection. University of Alaska Archives. Rasmuson Library, Fairbanks.

James Wickersham Collection. Alaska State Historical Library, Juneau.

Index